Alexandra Hachmeister

Informed Traders as Liquidity Providers

WIRTSCHAFTSWISSENSCHAFT

ebs Forschung

Schriftenreihe der

EUROPEAN BUSINESS SCHOOL

International University Schloß Reichartshausen

Herausgegeben von

Univ.-Prof. Dr. Utz Schäffer

Band 66

Die EUROPEAN BUSINESS SCHOOL (ebs) – gegründet im Jahr 1971 – ist Deutschlands älteste private Wissenschaftliche Hochschule für Betriebswirtschaftslehre im Universitätsrang. Dieser Vorreiterrolle fühlen sich ihre Professoren und Doktoranden in Forschung und Lehre verpflichtet. Mit der Schriftenreihe präsentiert die EUROPEAN BUSINESS SCHOOL (ebs) ausgewählte Ergebnisse ihrer betriebs- und volkswirtschaftlichen Forschung.

Alexandra Hachmeister

Informed Traders as Liquidity Providers

Evidence from the German Equity Market

With a foreword by Prof. Dr. Dirk Schiereck

Deutscher Universitäts-Verlag

Bibliografische Information Der Deutschen Nationalbibliothek
Die Deutsche Nationalbibliothek verzeichnet diese Publikation in der Deutschen Nationalbibliografie; detaillierte bibliografische Daten sind im Internet über <http://dnb.d-nb.de> abrufbar.

Dissertation European Business School Oestrich-Winkel, 2007

D 1540

1. Auflage Juli 2007

Lektorat: Frauke Schindler / Britta Göhrisch-Radmacher

Der Deutsche Universitäts-Verlag ist ein Unternehmen von Springer Science+Business Media.
www.duv.de

Umschlaggestaltung: Regine Zimmer, Dipl.-Designerin, Frankfurt/Main
Gedruckt auf säurefreiem und chlorfrei gebleichtem Papier
Printed in Germany

ISBN 978-3-8350-0755-0

Foreword

Today, the majority of large international stock exchanges operates electronic trading systems and abandons more and more floor trading which relies upon specialists and market makers. The preferred trading mechanism is the so-called open limit order book, which induces continuous double auction trading without any market participants designated to facilitate trading through their own trading activity. Trading in these market structures is considered the more attractive the smaller the spread between the highest buy and the lowest sell limit order, i.e. the more liquid a market is. This leads to the question which market participants are willing to enter buy and sell limit orders in the open limit order book to enable liquid trading. Traditional theoretical literature concludes that exclusively uninformed traders enter limit orders and provide liquidity while impatient informed traders enter liquidity-consuming market orders. Recent, primarily experimental studies question this rigid distinction.

This is the starting point for Ms Hachmeister's thesis, when she analyzes – based upon an individually compiled extensive set of transaction data – informed traders' order type choice. To my knowledge there exists no comparable analysis of order selection strategy by informed market participants in equity markets in Germany. Thus, this thesis (surprisingly) enters unknown scientific territory. In several, also explorative analyses she documents a detailed picture of order type choice of institutional investors in the German equity market. The findings result in an objective state of knowledge which forms the basis for substantiated recommendations for the design of exchanges, which in turn should result in further efficiency gains in German exchange trading.

Ms. Hachmeister fully achieves the objectives of her dissertation. The analysis contains many intriguing results and is written in a way that the reader will be pleased to read from the start to the end. I wish for the dissertation to gain the wide dissemination it deserves.

Professor Dr. Dirk Schiereck

Acknowledgements

This thesis is the result of my external doctoral studies at the Endowed Chair of Banking and Finance at the European Business School (ebs) in Oestrich-Winkel, while working at Deutsche Börse AG.

Many people have contributed to the success of this thesis. I'm especially grateful to Prof. Dr. Dirk Schiereck for his supervision, enthusiasm and guidance. During the entire process he just knew, when it was time to ask questions, to provide answers and to challenge my results ensuring that I stayed on track. I am grateful to Prof. Dr. Lutz Johanning for kindly acting as co-evaluator for my study. I also thank Deutsche Börse AG for providing the data and for creating a flexible environment that allowed me to realize my thesis.

For the inspiring discussions, constructive feedback and data support I thank my colleagues at the Endowed Chair of Banking and Finance and at Deutsche Börse AG – Jürgen Cremer, Dr. Kai-Oliver Maurer, Matthias Menke, Carl-Frederik Scharffenorth, Uwe Schweickert and Christian Voigt.

For their spare time invested I would particularly like to thank Sigurd Pollmann for his assistance with handling the vast amount of data and introducing me to the world of sql databases, Nicola Schaefer for proofreading the entire thesis and Dr. Sabine Sauermann for supporting and motivating me in many ways from the initial decision to start my studies until the preparation of the disputation.

I am very much indebted to my family and friends. Without their support and enthusiasm finalizing this project would not have been possible. I would like to thank my parents for their continued support and love, my friends for keeping my spirits; and finally my husband above all for his patience throughout my ups and downs. To him I dedicate this thesis.

Alexandra Hachmeister

Table of Contents

List of Exhibits

List of Abbreviations

AG	Aktiengesellschaft
am, AM	ante meridiem
APM	adverse price movement
approx.	approximately
ASX	Australian Stock Exchange
BaFIN	Bundesanstalt für Finanzdienstleistungsaufsicht (Federal Financial Supervisory Authority)
BA	best ask
BB	best bid
BBA	best bid ask
bn	billion
bp, BP	basis points (1 bp = 0.01 %)
CAC40	Cotation Assistée en Continue 40 (French blue chip index)
CESR	Committee of European Securities Regulators
DAX30	Deutscher Aktienindex 30 (German blue chip index)
DBAG	Deutsche Boerse AG
ECN	electronic communication network
e.g.	exempli gratia
ES	effective spread
€	Euro
f.	following (one page following)
ff.	following (several pages following)
FSE	Frankfurt Stock Exchange
HÜSt	Handelsüberwachungsstelle (German exchange supervisory body)
IBIS	Integriertes Börsenhandels- und Informations-System (fully automated open limit order book system introduced in April 1991, predecessor of the Xetra trading system)
ID	identification
i.e.	id est
KGaA	Kommanditgesellschaft auf Aktien
KSE	Korea Stock Exchange
LP	liquidity premium
LSE	London Stock Exchange
m	million

MDAX	German equity index: 50 mid-cap issues from the traditional sectors that rank below the DAX30
MI	market impact
MIB30	Milano Italia Borsa Index 30 (Italian blue chip index)
MiFID	Markets in Financial Instruments Directive
MP	midpoint
NASDAQ	National Association of Securities Dealers Automated Quotation System
NC	not classified
NEMAX50	German equity index: 50 largest issues from the technology sector, calculated until March 2003 and predecessor of the TecDAX
ns	not significant
NYSE	New York Stock Exchange
OLS	ordinary least squares
OTC	over the counter
p.	page
PE	partial execution
PI	price impact
PINF	probability of informed trading
pm, PM	post meridiem
pp.	pages
RS	realized spread
SDAX	German equity index: 50 small-cap issues from the traditional sectors that rank below the MDAX
SEC	Securities Exchange Commission
SEHK	Stock Exchange of Hong Kong
TecDAX	German equity index: 30 largest issues from the technology sector, successor of the NEMAX50
TSE	Tokyo Stock Exchange
US, U.S.	United States
VAR	vector autoregression
vol.	volume
Xetra	fully automated electronic trading system of Deutsche Boerse AG introduced in November 1997
XLM	Exchange Liquidity Measure
WpHG	Wertpapierhandelsgesetz (Securities Trade Act)

1 Introduction

1.1 Problem Definition

A well functioning capital market is a determinant for economic growth and the development of the economy. Exchanges have a central role for the capital market, as they organize primary and secondary markets. Primary markets enable the public offering of newly listed shares while secondary markets allow investors to exchange listed shares in accordance with the defined set of rules of the exchange.

The main function of an exchange lies in minimizing transaction costs by pooling investors' supply and demand, defined as the liquidity concentration function.[1] Then, liquidity can be defined as the ability to buy or sell large amounts of shares quickly at low costs, i.e. without adversely affecting the price.[2]

Consequently, from the perspective of the investor, liquidity determines his transaction costs when trying to achieve a desired portfolio. The gains and losses of any security portfolio are determined by two factors: the success of the underlying strategy of the portfolio and the costs incurred when achieving the desired portfolio structure. The value of liquidity is in the circumvented price impact of executing an order. Hence, professional investors incorporate liquidity costs as decision criterion in their trading strategies. They require a higher rate of return for instruments with a lower liquidity.[3]

From the perspective of the exchange, liquidity is a competitive factor in the fight for investors' order flow, as investors prefer market places with higher liquidity.[4] However, it is not the exchange itself that provides liquidity but its trading members, while the underlying market structure determines how liquidity is provided.

---

1 Usually four functions are distinguished: the market organization function, which means standardization of processes and products in the secondary market, the liquidity concentration function, i.e. the pooling of supply and demand in a time and location dimension, the price discovery function which reflects the relation of supply and demand, and the information function which includes the publication and dissemination of price information. For a detailed discussion see Book (2001), pp. 38-56.

2 For a detailed description of the term liquidity and its measurement, see Chapter 3.

3 This proposition was first made by Amihud/Mendelson (1986), p. 224. Jacoby/Fowler/Gottesman (2000), p. 69 present a capital asset pricing model that incorporates liquidity. Amihud/Mendelson/ Lauterbach (1997) test the relation for liquidity improving measures in the trading mechanism of the Tel Aviv Stock Exchange. Amihud (2002), p. 52 proves that this relation does not only hold across stocks but also over time.

4 Schiereck (1995) empirically analyzes institutional investors' decision behavior when choosing among international trading venues and finds that liquidity is the most important quality criterion. Schmidt (1977) also finds that transaction costs are the most important cost component of a market's organizational costs. However, he bases his results on the theoretical concept of operating efficiency. Both authors, although coming from different angles, define liquidity as the most important quality criterion. See Schmidt (1977), p. 21, Schiereck (1995), p. 136, (1996a), p. 1065f., (1996b), p. 189, and Bikker/Spierdijk/van der Sluis (2004), p. 1.

In line with the initial prediction of Glosten's (1994) celebrated paper, the number of electronic limit order books (order-driven market structures) has grown rapidly following developments in information technology and financial market deregulation.[5]

In these markets, without any market participants designated as liquidity providers, liquidity is provided by limit orders standing in the order book while it is demanded by those orders that are immediately executable, i.e. market orders or marketable limit orders.[6] That means traders that enter limit orders are liquidity providers while traders that enter market orders are liquidity demanders. As open limit order books are viable and self-sustaining even without designated liquidity providers, the central question for an exchange provider is: Who are these traders that provide liquidity on a voluntary basis?

Following the information paradigm that assumes information asymmetry in financial markets, traders can be categorized according to their level of information as uninformed traders that trade for liquidity purposes only or informed traders that try to profit from their information.[7] On the one hand, informed traders make prices more informative when trading (increasing information efficiency), while on the other hand, they redistribute wealth to the disadvantage of uninformed traders. The initial literature followed the assumption that informed traders only implement liquidity demanding market orders as they are impatient traders. As their information is short-lived, they have to profit immediately. In contrast, uninformed traders implement both order types, i.e. they also provide liquidity through limit orders. However, as they fear loss when trading with informed traders, they will offer less favorable prices, in turn reducing liquidity as all traders (informed and uninformed traders) have to buy or sell, incurring higher costs. Thus, the general theoretical notion from this literature is that uninformed traders are the sole providers of liquidity, while informed trading and liquidity are negatively related.

A potential liquidity providing role of informed traders has long been neglected in the literature. Only recently, a new branch has evolved that relaxes the restrictive assumption that informed traders only enter market orders and models endogenous order type choice between market orders and limit orders for informed traders. Theoretical, experimental, and empirical results conclude that informed traders do provide liquidity questioning the existing negative relation to liquidity. However, a review of this literature reveals a two-fold research gap: Although open limit order books are a considerably important market structure by now, there is no empirical analysis of the liquidity providing behavior of informed traders in a pure order-driven market structure without any designated liquidity providers. So far, empirical results are only provided for the New York Stock Exchange (NYSE), which relies upon a

---

[5] Jain (2003), p. 40 shows that almost half of the equity markets worldwide are organized as pure limit order books. Clayton/Jorgensen/Kavajecz (2006), p. 34 find for developed countries that more than half of the exchanges implement trading mechanisms where market participants provide liquidity instead of market makers. This follows Glosten (1994), who predicts that the open limit order book is inevitable.

[6] For a description of market and limit orders, see Chapter 2.3.

[7] For a detailed discussion of the information paradigm and corresponding trader types and motives, see Chapter 4.

hybrid market structure, i.e. liquidity is provided through the specialist and limit orders standing in the order book.[8]

The second major shortcoming of the existing research concerns the identification of informed traders. As informed traders do anything to disguise themselves, the existing empirical analyses do not directly identify them but found their analyses on assumptions. These assumptions are drawn from the type of trading institution, account types, and order sizes that are expected to be implemented by informed traders and can only provide indications, as none of the criteria allows a clear distinction of informed and uninformed traders. However, the need to work with assumptions is caused by the lack of suitable data.

This study aims at closing both presented research gaps based upon the analysis of the electronic open limit order book operated for the German equity market (Xetra trading system). First, it implements a unique data set that includes the trader ID at the transaction level, enabling the identification of the different traders behind each transaction. It presents a new approach for the identification and classification of traders according to their level of information. Second, derived from this trader classification, it provides insight into the liquidity demand and supply behavior of informed traders based on separate analysis of market orders (liquidity demand) and limit orders (liquidity supply) in an open limit order book.

The empirical results provide strong evidence for liquidity provision by informed traders in an electronic limit order book. As this trading mechanism is common among exchanges, the transferability of results from the empirical analysis of the Xetra trading system to other electronic limit order books in Europe, the US, or Asia is discussed in the résumé.

1.2 Purpose of Study

The purpose of this study is to provide evidence on the liquidity providing behavior of informed traders in electronic open limit order books. This purpose can be broken down into several research objectives that are formulated as questions. These questions will be reflected in the research approach underlying the empirical analysis.

(i) Does the anonymous electronic open limit order book Xetra behave fairly normally?

Theoretical and empirical results for open limit order books predict certain patterns for liquidity and informed trading. Based on this framework, the answer to this question fulfills a twofold intention: First, the results provide a descriptive basis and as such function as the point of reference for the interpretation of the results of the different trader categories. Second, the transferability of this study's results is directly related to the usualness of this market. The purpose is to determine whether the results for the trading of highly liquid instruments in Xetra are comparable to other electronic limit orders books. If this question is positively answered, the research results on the behavior of informed traders can be transferred to other markets.

---

8 A classification of market mechanisms is provided in Chapter 2.4.

(ii) How can informed traders be identified?

This study aims at overcoming existing deficits in the identification and consecutive analysis of informed traders. The objective is to define a methodological approach that can be implemented to identify the level of information on the trader level. To achieve this goal, the individual transactions and underlying orders of each trader have to be identified. The choice of method follows two dimensions: (i) the ability to determine the level of information of an individual transaction and (ii) restrictions by the available data.

(iii) Do informed traders provide liquidity in the anonymous electronic open limit order book Xetra?

Once the individual traders are classified regarding their level of information, their transactions and underlying orders are flagged accordingly. Therefore, for each individual order it is indicated whether it is entered by an uninformed or an informed trader, enabling the analysis of these trader categories. To determine informed traders' choice of order type and consequently the choice between liquidity provision (limit orders) and liquidity demand (market orders), their orders are analyzed first separately for each order type and then in comparison resulting in the net role, either liquidity provider or liquidity demander, of this trader category. These analyses will provide evidence against the general theoretical notion that informed traders do not provide liquidity.

1.3 Layout of Study

The thesis consists of two parts: part I includes the institutional setting and academic framework. It provides the foundation for part II, the empirical analysis.

Part I, starting with Chapter 2, describes the institutional setting defining the research object as high liquid instruments in the electronic open limit order book Xetra. It follows a top down approach describing the German equity market in general, the Frankfurt Stock Exchange in particular, and the Xetra market model applied for instruments with high liquidity (DAX30 instruments).

Chapter 3 develops a definition of liquidity as a multi-dimensional concept. It describes and categorizes liquidity measures according to their dimensionality and their calculation base (ex-ante or ex-post). Furthermore, it provides the rationale for choosing the Exchange Liquidity Measure (XLM) for the empirical analysis in this study.

Chapter 4 applies a similar outline, starting with the underlying information paradigm and the definition of trader types and motives, followed by a description of measurement methods. The selection of the adequate measures is based on the purpose of the study, which determines the need to identify the level of information on a transaction level and the data availability. The model-free ad hoc method is chosen for implementation in the empirical analysis. Therefore, Chapters 3 and 4 provide the terminology and determine the methods applied in the empirical part of this study.

Within Chapter 5, the theoretical, experimental, and empirical research on open limit order books is presented. The literature review is distinguished into two parts. The first part includes the literature where informed traders implement market orders only, developing the general theoretical notion that liquidity and informed trading are negatively related. It derives hypotheses sets for liquidity and informed trading in general. The second part covers the literature where informed traders are allowed to implement both market orders and limit orders. The hypotheses sets derived cover informed traders' trading behavior, i.e. their choice between market orders and limit orders. Chapter 5 develops the different sets of hypotheses that are tested in the empirical analyses. It concludes part I.

Part II comprises the empirical analyses: Chapter 6 includes the research approach, the data implemented in the analysis and a first set of descriptive statistics for the DAX30 instruments. The research approach is subdivided into three steps based upon the above defined research objectives and corresponding questions.

The first step (Chapter 7) provides a detailed market description by analyzing standard trading parameters, liquidity, and informed trading in general as well as the relation among these parameters. The outcome determines if the Xetra open limit order book is comparable to other limit order books, i.e. if results can be transferred to other markets - objective (i). It integrates the market model description (Chapter 2) with the general hypotheses derived for limit order books (Chapter 5), providing the point of reference for interpreting the results of the different trader categories.

The second step (Chapter 8) proposes a trader classification along their relative importance in terms of trading volume and their level of information calculated as the average price impact per trader ID. As a consequence, trader IDs are categorized either as uninformed, partially informed or informed traders - objective (ii).

Based upon this classification, the third step (Chapter 9) analyzes the liquidity demand and supply behavior of the different trader categories, specifically comparing the results for informed traders to the other trader categories. This chapter yields at confirming recent evidence that informed traders implement limit orders as part of their trading strategies, thus taking on the role of liquidity providers - objective (iii).

Chapter 10 consists of a résumé and critical discussion of the insights of this thesis. It concludes with a discussion of the transferability of results to other equity markets and an outlook into possible future areas of research.

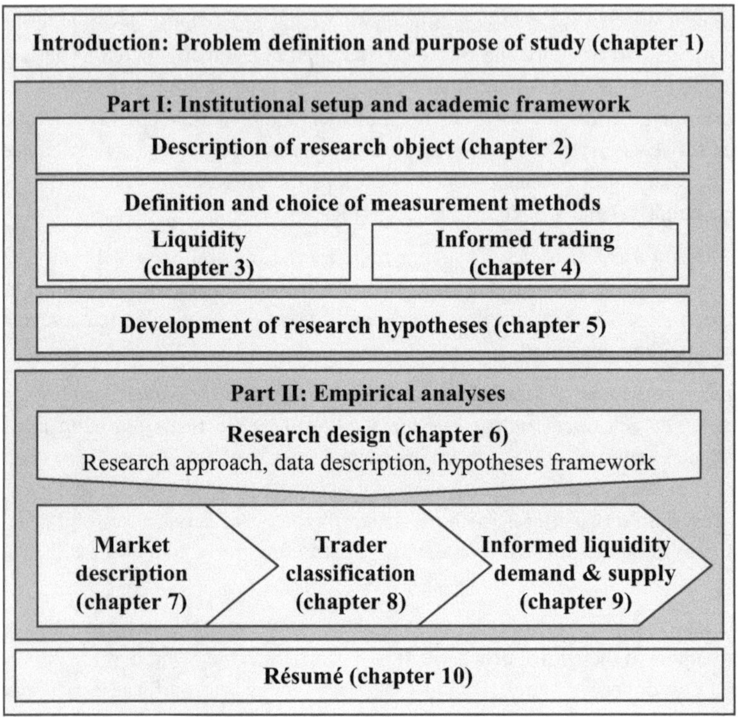

Exhibit 1-1: Layout of study

Part I: Institutional Set-up and Academic Framework

Following the purpose of this study, i.e. the question, if informed traders do provide liquidity in an electronic open limit order book, part I of this study lays the basis for the empirical analysis: It describes the underlying research object (Chapter 2), the methods to be implemented in the empirical part (Chapters 3 and 4), and the theoretical, experimental, and empirical results on open limit order book markets (Chapter 5) that provide the academic framework for the hypotheses tested in part II of this study.

2 Institutional Setting

The objective of this chapter is to describe and classify the underlying research object for the empirical analysis. Therefore, it provides an introduction to the German equity market in general and to the Frankfurt Stock Exchange (FSE) with its primary trading platform Xetra. It also includes a detailed description of the market model for equities. As the choice of market structure has important implications for the microstructure results, a classification of trading mechanisms is provided and the Xetra trading models are categorized accordingly.

The detailed description of the market model and its corresponding categorization are particularly important to understand the trading environment in which market participants (informed and uninformed traders) implement their trading strategies, choosing whether to demand or supply liquidity.

2.1 German Equity Market

The German financial system is historically seen as bank-dominated. Recent developments such as the increase in market capitalization and share ownership show a conversion to a more market oriented system.[9] At the same time, its operational efficiency measured through transaction costs is comparably high.[10] As a consequence, the role of the capital market for the allocation of capital increases constantly. Germany's capital market is fragmented horizontally between seven German Stock Exchanges.[11] FSE, which operates the fully electronic trading system Xetra[12] in addition to its traditional trading floor, is by far the largest.

Exhibit 2-1 shows the total order book turnover in million € individually for all asset classes traded on German exchanges during 2005 as well as corresponding market shares. It provides data for both trading platforms of the FSE and summarizes the remaining six regional exchanges as 'Other exchanges'. In equities, the FSE plays a dominant role, with Xetra being responsible for a market share of 90.1% and an additional 5.6% coming from its trading floor. In DAX30 (DAX) instruments, the dominance is even stronger, with a market share of 97.4%

---

9 Market capitalization as a percentage of GDP increased from 23.9% in 1995 to 43.7% in 2005 while share ownership almost doubled between 1997 and 2005, reaching a level of 16.6%. See Deutsches Aktieninstitut (2005), p. 05-3 and p. 08-3. It has to be noted that compared to the US capital market -a completely market oriented system - the German capital market has a large potential for development. Theissen (2003a) describes the development level of the German capital market based upon the dimensions volume and operational efficiency.

10 Pagano/Padilla (2005), p. 32 present an analysis comparing explicit and implicit transactions costs for the major European exchanges, concluding that Germany is at the higher end. In contrast to these results, Jain (2003), p. 49f. finds that Germany's transaction costs are lower than in the UK. Domowitz/Glen/Madhavan (2001), p. 224ff. compare explicit and implicit transaction costs across 42 exchanges worldwide from 1996 to 1998. They find that European exchanges reveal a stronger decrease in implicit transaction costs compared to the US and ascribe this development to technological developments.

11 The stock exchanges in alphabetical order are Berlin-Bremen, Dusseldorf, Frankfurt, Hamburg, Hanover, Munich, and Stuttgart.

12 The first fully electronic trading system at FSE was introduced in April 1991. The system called IBIS was designed for institutional investors to facilitate their trading. The Xetra trading system replaced IBIS in 1997.

for the Xetra trading system.[13] DAX instruments account for 75% of the total order book turnover in equities.

	Frankfurt Stock Exchange				Other exchanges		All German exchanges
	Xetra		FSE floor				
Asset class	**Total order book turn-over (m €)**	**Market share**	**Total order book turn-over (m €)**	**Market share**	**Total order book turn-over (m €)**	**Market share**	**Total order book turn-over (m €)**
Equities	1,125,486	90.1%	70,049	5.6%	53,749	4.3%	**1,249,284**
- thereof DAX	921,657	97.4%	14,276	1.5%	10,737	1.1%	946,670
Warrants	21	0.1%	2,477	14.4%	14,731	85.5%	**17,229**
Bonds	16	0.0%	43,371	37.7%	71,599	62.3%	**114,986**
Total	**1,125,522**	**81.5%**	**115,893**	**8.4%**	**140,084**	**10.1%**	**1,381,499**

Exhibit 2-1: Total order book turnover 2005[14]

For warrants (structured products) and bonds, the picture is different, showing that the market is split between FSE and 'Other exchanges'. The Stuttgart Stock Exchange which operates EUWAX[15] (a market for warrant trading and other structured products) is the market leader in this asset class and accounts for the high market share of 'Other exchanges'. The same holds true for bonds.

Trading on the FSE floor and the regional exchanges is organized similarly to the trading protocol of the NYSE. The 'Skontroführer' in Germany is responsible for order matching and fulfills the same functions as the specialist at NYSE, having partially exclusive access to the information of the limit order book. The level of anonymity in the trading process is the main difference between floor trading and electronic trading and has been at the heart of the debate of floor versus automated trading systems.[16] Due to the dominance of the electronic trading platform Xetra, in equities the following description is restricted to the FSE and particularly the Xetra market model.[17]

---

[13] DAX30 is the German blue chip index which includes the thirty largest German companies listed at the FSE. It is comparable to the French CAC40 or the Italian MIB30. For a description of Deutsche Boerse AG's indices, see Deutsche Boerse AG (2006b).

[14] See Deutsche Boerse AG (2006a), p. 11 and p. 15ff.

[15] The Stuttgart Stock Exchange has specialized in trading of structured products. EUWAX stands for European Warrant Exchange, which is a trading segment of the Stuttgart exchange.

[16] Theissen (2002), Theissen (2003b) and Grammig/Schiereck/Theissen (2001) have compared the floor trading mechanism and electronic trading systems (IBIS or Xetra depending on the time period of their samples) in Germany. They find that non-anonymity in floor trading allows the 'Skontroführer' to identify informed traders and to price discriminate accordingly. This leads to a reduced probability of informed trading in the floor trading system. Details on informed trading are given in Chapter 4.2.

[17] Freihube/Theissen (2001), p. 297 and pp. 302-307 find that Xetra is dominant in the contribution to price discovery for DAX instruments, while the reverse is true for the midcap index MDAX based on data for the first quarter in 1999. Deutsche Boerse AG (2006c), pp. 16-22 shows that since their analysis the Xetra market share in DAX instruments increased further from 89% in March 1999 to 97.4% in 2005. The same holds true for the MDAX segment were the Xetra market share almost tripled from 39% in March 1999 to 92% in 2005. Due to the strong increase in market share in MDAX instruments by now Xetra also plays the major role in price discovery in the MDAX.

2.2 Frankfurt Stock Exchange

FSE is an entity under public law with partial legal capacity[18] operated by Deutsche Boerse AG.[19] The executive management of the FSE runs the exchange in line with the rules set by the Stock Exchange Act (Börsengesetz). It is controlled by the exchange council which is responsible for the appointment, withdrawal, and supervision of the executive management. In that function, the exchange council discusses and decides upon important issues at FSE and issues rules and regulations (exchange rules, fee regulations, and conditions for transactions on the exchange).[20]

Additional supervisory bodies are the market supervision responsible for ensuring fair and orderly trading, the trading surveillance office (HÜSt) as an independent exchange body, the Hessian Ministry as the exchange supervisory body, and the Federal Financial Supervisory Authority (BaFin) for the investigation of insider trading.[21]

Access to the capital market through listing is provided for three segments:[22] Prime Standard, General Standard, and Entry Standard. These segments vary in relation to their listing requirements and cater different listing objectives. The General Standard is subject to statutory legal requirements for the regulated market (Geregelter Markt) and official market (Amtlicher Handel). It is oriented towards companies which target national investors and opt for a cost-effective listing. The Prime Standard is a sub-category of the General Standard, which requires the companies to fulfill additional internationally accepted transparency principles, e.g. quarterly reports, ad hoc disclosures in English, and analyst conferences. It is oriented towards international investors. In contrast, the Entry Standard[23] is regulated by the FSE itself, i.e. it is a regulated unofficial market. It is particularly attractive for young and established small-cap and mid-cap firms.

A Prime Standard listing is required to be included in one of the selection indices provided by Deutsche Boerse AG. The index family[24] is constituted of the DAX, the German blue chip segment comprising the thirty largest and most actively traded companies that are listed at the FSE, the MDAX, consisting of the following fifty mid-cap issues which, in terms of size and turnover, rank below the DAX, and the SDAX comprising the next fifty issues that are ranked

---

18 This means it is a public authority under administrative law, thus it may issue administrative acts.

19 Deutsche Boerse AG has been a publicly listed company since 5 February 2001 and a constituent of the DAX index since 23 December 2003. The composition of its shareholders has changed considerably from approx. 80% German banks before the initial public offering to over 80% international investors at the end of 2005.

20 The acting exchange council was elected for the term of three years on 11 November 2004 and constitutes 24 members. Regular meetings are scheduled three times a year, allowing for extraordinary meetings when necessary. A permanent guest is the Exchange Supervisory Body (Hessian Ministry for Economic Affairs, Transport and Regional Development).

21 This reflects that rules and regulations are enforced on two levels, i.e. by enforcement organizations of the exchange and by a national or federal agency.

22 A detailed description of the three segments and their requirements is given in Deutsche Boerse AG's listing brochures; see Deutsche Boerse AG (2003), p. 7 and Deutsche Boerse AG (2006d), pp. 4-8.

23 The Entry Standard was introduced on 25 October 2005 as a segment within the open market (Freiverkehr).

24 To be included in one of the indices, a company has to have its operating headquarters in Germany or the major part of its stock exchange turnover at FSE. A detailed description of the indices' composition and calculation methodologies is provided in Deutsche Boerse AG (2006b), pp. 16-39.

below the MDAX. Both MDAX and SDAX combine companies from the traditional sectors. In addition, the TecDAX[25] tracks the thirty largest and most liquid issues from the various technology sectors.

2.3 Xetra Market Model[26]

Xetra is a fully electronic trading system introduced by Deutsche Boerse AG in 1997 for cash market trading in equities and a variety of other instruments; these are exchange traded funds, bonds, warrants, structured products, and subscription rights.[27] Since this study focuses only on the trading of equities, any specialties or market models related to other asset classes are excluded from the following description.[28]

A market model describes the fundamental rules of order matching and price determination as reflected in precedence rules which determine the sequence of execution.[29] It defines market participants, order types and prioritization thereof, available trading models[30], and transparency regimes defined through the type and the extent of information available to market participants during trading hours.[31]

The market model for equities is order-driven. However, for certain specified equities, market participants acting as liquidity providers are allowed to enter quotes.[32] It foresees extensive pre-trade and post-trade transparency as all orders and prices in the limit order book (pre-trade) and all transactions with volume and price (post-trade) are immediately distributed to the trading members. However, trading is anonymous, as the identities of traders for both orders and trades are concealed.[33]

In accordance with the rules and regulations of the FSE, market participants are admitted entities with traders (individuals) equally accredited to Xetra. Xetra provides dual capacity trading, i.e. trading on behalf of customers (so-called agency trading) and principal trading

---

25 The TecDAX was launched on 24 March 2003. It was introduced as the smaller-sized successor index to the NEMAX50. The historical index data of the NEMAX50 is continued seamlessly.

26 This chapter is based on Deutsche Boerse AG (2004a) and (2004b).

27 The Xetra trading system is implemented by further equity markets, the Vienna Stock Exchange and the Irish Stock Exchange. In addition, Xetra is also operated at the European Energy Exchange, where the underlying of an instrument is not a company or financial product but an energy contract.

28 Different market models cater the differing needs of asset classes. In addition to the initially implemented market model for equities, a market model for bond trading was introduced, followed by a market model for warrant trading (so-called continuous auctions), a market model for block crossing (trading of large transaction sizes in a completely closed order book) and the market model Xetra Best, which foresees a possibility for internalization of order flow.

29 Usually price, display and time precedence are implemented in trading; volume precedence is sometimes implemented in block markets (markets for large orders), see Harris (1990), pp. 17-21.

30 The different trading models are described in Exhibit 2-3.

31 Exchange Rules (Börsenordnung) and the Terms and Conditions for Transactions (Geschäftsbedingungen) determine the legally binding terms for trading at the FSE, with the market model forming their basis. A description of the governance structure of the FSE is given in Chapter 2.2.

32 There is no obligation for market participants to enter quotes. For those market participants that take on the role of designated liquidity providers, Deutsche Börse AG (DBAG) has implemented a performance measurement and publishes a quarterly rating to ensure minimum quality standards.

33 While pre-trade anonymity was implemented with the initial set-up of the trading system in 1997, post-trade anonymity was introduced in a two-step approach on 27 March 2003 and 10 April 2003. This change in market structure led to a significant increase in liquidity, as documented in Hachmeister/Schiereck (2006), p. 12.

(proprietary trading).[34] In addition, in certain instruments traders can act as liquidity provider (so-called "designated sponsor"). The type of trading is reflected through the account type that is provided for each order number: (i) account type A for agent trading, (ii) account type P for proprietary trading, and (iii) account type D for liquidity provision.[35]

Three basic order types are foreseen for price determination: market orders, limit orders and market-to-limit orders. While market orders are unlimited bid or ask orders that execute (immediately) at the next price established, limit orders are bid or ask orders that execute either at their defined limit or at a better price. Market-to-limit orders are initially treated as market orders when entering the book. Any remaining part of the order enters the order book with the limit equal to the execution price of the executed part.

These basic types can be detailed further through execution conditions, validity constraints, and trading restrictions[36] as described in Exhibit 2-2.

	Name	**Description**
Execution conditions	Immediate-or-cancel	Execution is immediate and full or as full as possible with non-executed part of the order being deleted.
	Fill-or-kill	Execution is immediate and full or not at all. If execution is not possible, the order is deleted.
Validity constraints	Good-for-day	Validity is given for the current exchange trading day.
	Good-till-date	Validity is given until a specified date (up to a maximum of 90 days, including the current exchange trading day).
	Good-till-cancelled	Validity is given until the order is either executed or deleted by the originator or the maximum validity of 90 days is reached.
Trading restrictions	Opening auction only	Validity is given only during opening auctions.
	Closing auction only	Validity is given only during closing auctions.
	Auction only	Validity is given only during auctions.

Exhibit 2-2: Additional order specifications[37]

---

[34] In December 2005, Xetra had 268 participants from 18 different countries. Non-German participants had a share of 49%. See Deutsche Boerse AG (2006a), p. 3.

[35] In addition to traders, other users may also have access to the trading system. These are administrators which are not admitted for trading and include also personnel in settlement, operations, and compliance.

[36] Trading restrictions are only provided concerning the trading form 'auction', which is introduced in the following paragraphs of this chapter. The functionality of auctions is explained in detail in Chapter 2.4.

[37] Exhibit 2-2 consolidates information provided in Deutsche Boerse AG (2004b), p. 11f.

Xetra allows additional order types. Stop orders enter the order book for execution once a specified price is reached. They are available as stop market and stop limit order and enter the order book as market or as limit order when triggered by the stop limit. Iceberg orders are from a market design perspective designed to enable traders to provide liquidity when they do not want to reveal the full size of their orders. The hidden quantity of an iceberg order loses its priority to visible quantities at the same limit.

Order amendment rules foresee that when modifying orders their time priorities change if either the limit is modified or the amendment has a negative impact on other orders already standing in the book, e.g. volume increase. In the case of a new time priority, a new order number is assigned. Orders entering the order book can be executed fully, partially, or not at all, generating one, several, or no trade at all. For equities traded in Xetra, the current round lot size is defined as one; thus, all orders submitted to the system are composed of round lots.[38] The instrument tick size, the minimum increment by which prices can move and thus the smallest possible variation for price setting of limit orders, is defined as € 0.01.[39]

Trading phases define the flow of trading. Trading starts with the pre-trading phase followed by the trading phase and ends with the post-trading phase. Between the post-trading and pre-trading phase, the system does not provide operational availability for trading. The pre-trading phase and the post-trading phase are identical for all instruments, whereas the process of the trading phase is determined individually; this includes several trading models and different trading hours. The trading phase starts at 9.00 a.m. and ends at 5.30 p.m. and is identical to the trading hours for all instruments traded continuously.[40]

Exhibit 2-3 describes the general flow of trading on Xetra. Based on the available trading forms 'auction' and 'continuous trading' for on-exchange trading, different trading models are defined. For equity trading, two trading models are supported: (i) continuous trading with periodic calls (opening auction, intraday auction, and closing auction)[41] and (ii) auction only with one or several auctions per day at predetermined points in time.

---

[38] A round lot consists of one or multiple round lot parts. Odd lots are smaller than the round lot size and consist of odd lot parts and possible additional round lot parts. The distinction between round lots and odd lots is only relevant for the case where the round lot size is larger than one. In this case, the distinction between trading forms is relevant for the order. Odd lot orders can only be traded during auctions, while round lots are also allowed for continuous trading. As both are the same and defined as one (round lot one) for all equities traded in Xetra, no further distinction will be made.
As an example, consider that the round lot size is defined as 100: Then an order for 500 shares would be a round lot consisting of five round lot parts tradable during continuous trading and auctions. In contrast, an order for 150 shares would be an odd lot consisting of one round lot (100) and an odd lot (50), thus not tradable during continuous trading but only during auctions.

[39] In contrast to other exchanges (e.g. Euronext), the tick size for equities traded in Xetra is not a function of the stock price level, but a function of the smallest unit of the currency. However, for structured products an additional tick size is foreseen: When the instrument's price is below € 0.25, the tick size is reduced to € 0.001.

[40] Trading hours were reduced on 1 November 2003, when the close of trading changed from 8:00 pm to 5:30 pm. However, the FSE trading floor remains open until 8:00 pm.

[41] The London Stock Exchange (LSE) and Euronext also apply continuous trading with auctions for their most liquid instruments. They start and end the trading day with auctions, but do not provide an intraday auction as Xetra does.

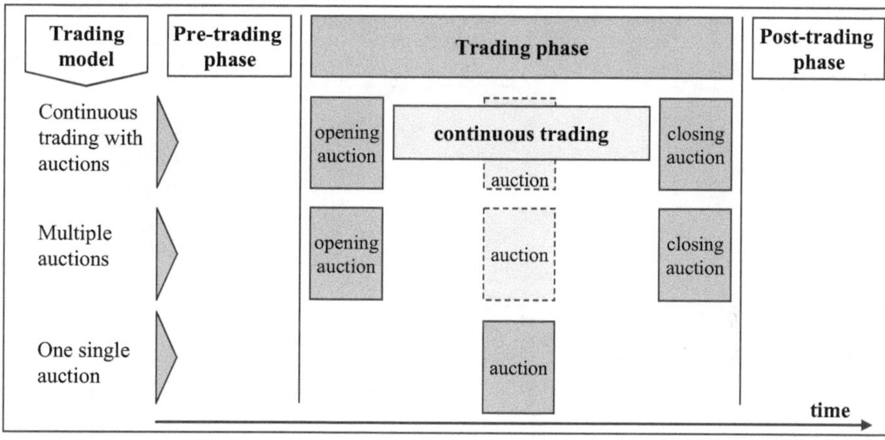

Exhibit 2-3: Flow of trading and basic trading models[42]

Price determination in the different trading forms follows pre-determined rules that define the matching algorithm applied. In auctions, price determination is conducted in accordance with the principle of most executable volume and follows price-time priority.[43] The order book remains partially closed as market participants receive either an indicative price or the best bid-ask limit. During continuous trading, each order entering the order book is checked for immediate execution against orders on the other side of the book, while price determination is based on price-time priority. The order book is open, thus market participants are able to see the full order book, i.e. the limits, the accumulated volume, and the number of orders at the limits.

Based on two characteristics - the average liquidity[44] of an instrument and the order book turnover (average daily trading volume) - the executive management of the FSE decides upon the trading model in which an instrument is traded. Exhibit 2-4 provides an overview of these rules. To be traded in the trading model, continuous trading with periodic auctions, a minimum liquidity, and trading volume are required. For those instruments that do not fulfill the requirements, one or more designated sponsors are required. Otherwise, the instrument will be assigned to the trading model auction only.[45]

---

42 Exhibit 2-3 is adapted from Deutsche Boerse AG (2004b), p. 14.

43 Price priority determines that orders are executed in sequence of their price, i.e. the best limit first. In addition, if there is more than one order at a specific limit, orders are executed in accordance with their time priority; i.e. the order that was entered into the system first executes first.

44 The average liquidity of an instrument is measured by the Exchange Liquidity Measure (XLM) with a reference order size of 25,000 €. A detailed description of this measure is given in Chapter 3.2.2.

45 Schwartz/Francioni (2004), p. 28f. describe a similar approach for market segmentation and choice of trading model.

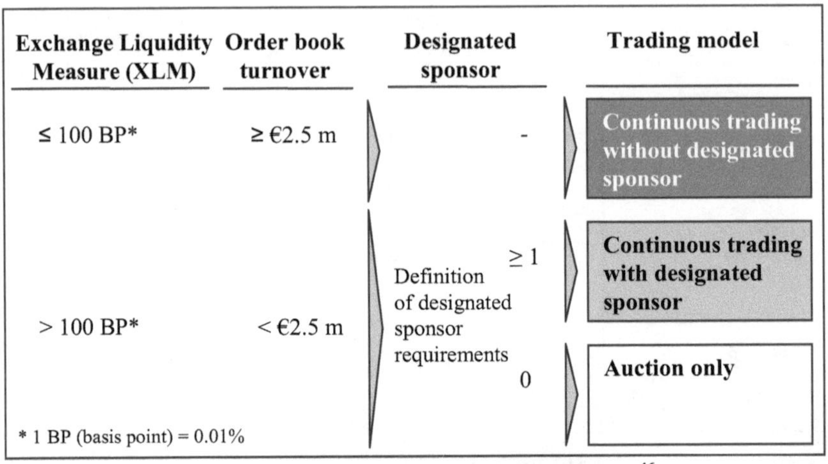

Exhibit 2-4: Choice of trading model based on liquidity and trading volume[46]

The Xetra system has also implemented trading safeguards in auctions and during continuous trading to enhance price continuity and raise the execution probability of market orders. These are volatility interruptions and market order interruptions. Volatility interruptions are triggered if the potential execution price lies outside a defined static or dynamic price corridor around a reference price (e.g. the last traded price).[47] Market order interruptions do not play a role in DAX instruments.[48]

2.4 Classification of Trading Mechanisms

Trading mechanisms transform through price discovery (finding a market clearing price) underlying demands of market participants into transactions. They differ considerably concerning order types, transparency regimes[49], times at which trading can occur, and types of liquidity providers. Implications of market structure for measures of market quality, such as spreads, liquidity, and volatility, influence the ongoing debate about floor versus electronic markets and auction versus dealer markets.

---

[46] Exhibit 2-4 is adapted from Deutsche Boerse AG (2003), p. 10.

[47] The dynamic price range is based on the last traded price and is adjusted continuously throughout the trading day. The static price range is based on the last price determined in an auction during the trading day and remains mostly unchanged during the course of the trading day.

[48] Market order interruptions are only implemented for auctions. If at the end of an auction market orders or market-to-limit orders are not or only partially executable, then the auction is extended and the market is informed accordingly. Due to the high liquidity in DAX instruments, no market order interruption has been triggered until today.

[49] In the microstructure literature, there is an arm that analyses the different transparency and anonymity levels following the notion that the degree of trader anonymity is important for market participants' behavior. Institutional traders prefer anonymous set-ups, as they do not want to disclose their trading needs. At the same time, anonymous trading, which can increase the adverse-selection problem, is preferred by informed traders. In non-anonymous markets, specialists have the possibility to price discriminate. See also Footnote 16 and Chapter 5.1.2.

When categorizing these mechanisms, two dimensions, (i) the degree of continuity and (ii) the reliance on market makers[50], have to be taken into account:[51]

The first distinction, the degree of continuity, describes whether trading is foreseen with a continuous or a periodic mechanism. In a continuous market, orders are executed upon submission enabling sequences of bilateral transactions at (possibly) different prices. In contrast, periodic systems (so-called call auctions or batch markets) execute multilateral transactions at one price as orders and quotes are accumulated for simultaneous execution at a pre-determined time. Periodic auction markets organize liquidity at a certain point in time; however, they do not provide liquidity at any other time. Thus only a continuous market can provide liquidity for immediacy demanding traders that intend to trade at other times than the periodic call.

As described in the previous chapter, Xetra foresees two trading forms (auction and continuous trading) which form the basis for the different Xetra trading models. These trading forms reflect the two characteristics of the degree of continuity as the first dimension of trading mechanisms.

The second distinction is between quote-driven and order-driven markets, i.e. the reliance on market makers. In quote-driven markets, market makers provide firm bid-ask prices to traders prior to order submission. Traders have the choice of trading at the posted prices immediately. In order-driven markets, the orders of all traders are accumulated and matched in accordance with order precedence rules. Order-driven systems are either periodic auctions or continuous auction systems:

In periodic auctions[52], orders are stored for execution at a single clearing price; i.e. the auction mechanism follows a uniform pricing rule. As order-driven markets use order precedence rules to arrange their trades, traders do not have a choice for their counterparty.[53] In continuous auctions, investors submit orders for immediate execution against existing limit orders submitted by liquidity providers; the formal term is continuous double auction - double

---

50 The term *market maker* reflects an obligation to ensure a fair and orderly market based on a contractual commitment. In contrast, dealers as intermediaries also supply liquidity to the market but they are not obliged to do so.

51 Madhavan (1992), p. 608ff. provides a classification among two dimensions, while Madhavan (2000), pp. 225-228 includes a third dimension: the "degree of automation". As this study focuses on the fully electronic trading system Xetra and not on a comparison floor versus screen based trading there is no need for a further distinction. Domowitz (1993), p. 621 provides a classification of automated trading venues; according to his classification, continuous trading in IBIS classifies as hit-and-take market. Xetra would be classified accordingly.

52 Auctions enable information concentration, suggesting call auctions are especially valuable when uncertainty over fundamentals is large and market failure is possible. Many continuous markets use single price auction mechanisms when uncertainty is large, i.e. at the opening and closing and as security mechanisms (e.g. volatility interruptions as implemented in the Xetra trading system; see trading safeguards in Chapter 2.3). Madhavan (1992), p. 627 compares an order-driven and a quote-driven setting with a rational expectations model and concludes that if a continuous market fails a trading halt might exacerbate the problem and proposes to switch to auctions.

53 To prevent settlement failures, as there is no individual credit relationship between the counterparties of a trade, sophisticated mechanisms to ensure creditworthiness of traders are implemented. See Harris (2003), p. 95 and pp. 139-144.

as buyers and sellers can simultaneously attempt to arrange their trades.[54] There is no intermediary determining the market clearing price, but order precedence and trade price rules determine the price for a trade. Following a discriminatory pricing rule, market orders are executed at successive prices by the limit orders on the order book. The latter rule protects liquidity providers less. A large market order will prefer the discriminatory price rule, leading to a better average price for the market order. Thus liquidity providers prefer the uniform pricing rule as implemented in periodic auctions, while liquidity demanders prefer the discriminatory pricing rule. In continuous markets it is almost impossible to implement a uniform pricing rule, as liquidity demanders could split their order to ensure discriminatory pricing.

In pure order-driven markets, market makers trade on an equal basis with all other traders. There is no obligation for any market participant to submit limit orders, thus no liquidity supplier of last resort. In contrast to quote-driven markets, order-driven mechanisms provide a free-entry and a free-exit option.[55] Most markets are hybrid markets that mix characteristics of both quote-driven and order-driven markets.[56]

Exhibit 2-5 shows the classification of Xetra trading models in accordance with the outlined classification. As presented in Chapter 2.3, the Xetra trading system provides different trading models depending on the liquidity of instruments.

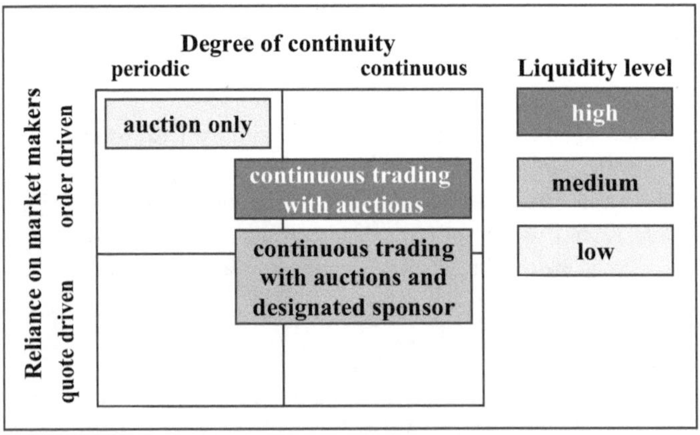

Exhibit 2-5: Classification of trading mechanisms and Xetra trading models

---

[54] Domowitz (1992), p. 311 provides a description of automated continuous double auction markets: "In automated double auction systems, bids and offers are submitted continuously over time. Transactions occur when the orders cross, i.e. when the price of the best offer to buy is equal to or greater than that of the best offer to sell. Price is determined endogenously in the system, based on order flow and a set of priority rules. These priority rules determine the place of an incoming bid or offer in the queue of orders. Priority can be set in terms of price, time, quantity, order type, and trade classification, among others."

[55] Brockman/Chung (2002), p. 522 explain that traders in order-driven markets are free to enter and exit the market whenever they want. In contrast, the market maker in a quote-driven market is obliged to provide bid-ask quotes during trading, thus he does not have a free-entry and free-exit possibility.

[56] Examples for hybrid markets are the NYSE, which is essentially an order-driven market with a specialist who adds the quote-driven element. NASDAQ is basically a quote-driven market, but dealers' requirements to display and execute public limit orders add an order-driven element.

For instruments with a low liquidity, one or multiple auctions are conducted. For medium and high liquid instruments, continuous trading with opening, intraday, and closing auctions is implemented. It should be noted that the Xetra denomination continuous trading is a synonym for a continuous double auction mechanism. For medium liquid instruments, trading is supported by so-called designated sponsors, which are obliged but not forced to provide a minimum liquidity determined through a minimum volume, maximum bid-ask spread and a minimum percentage of quoting in auctions and continuous trading[57] by simultaneously providing limit buy and sell orders, defined as quotes.

2.5 Synopsis

This chapter started with a description of the German equity market in general. Trading in Germany is fragmented between seven exchanges, with the FSE playing a dominant role. FSE provides two separate trading platforms: the traditional floor trading and the fully electronic trading platform Xetra. Xetra has a central position in equities trading in general and especially in DAX instruments with a market share of 97.4% in terms of order book volume.

The Xetra trading system allows for different trading models depending on the liquidity of an instrument. An instrument is either traded in auctions only (low liquidity), continuous trading with auctions and liquidity providers (medium liquidity), or in continuous trading with auctions without any additional liquidity provision (high liquidity). These models can be classified according to two dimensions, the degree of continuity and the reliance on market makers.

The empirical analysis of this study (Part II) will be based on a sample including the DAX instruments. Based on their classification as highly liquid instruments, they are traded in the trading model continuous trading with periodic auctions. As there are no designated liquidity providers or other incentives, such as a fee and pricing schedule that would differentiate between order types, the DAX instruments are particularly suitable to analyze informed liquidity provision. The fact that there are no incentives given by the exchange operator to provide liquidity ensures that any liquidity providing behavior is part of the trading strategies and not the outcome of stimulated order flow.[58]

The next two chapters will present common measures of liquidity and informed trading as well as the selection of those methods that fit the underlying research object (Xetra) and the purpose of this study best. As the DAX instruments are traded in a pure order-driven continuous double auction market (with periodic calls) it follows that the theoretical and empirical literature on open limit order books applies directly to this study.

---

57 These parameters constitute the quality requirements for designated sponsors. They receive certain privileges for meeting the defined requirements. Currently exchange fees for trades that a designated sponsor executes in the instruments he is responsible for are waived depending on his performance. The results of the performance measurement are published quarterly in a rating report.

58 In contrast, the LSE does not charge any fee for so-called passive executions during continuous trading, i.e. limit orders standing in the order book. This pricing schedule privileges liquidity providing orders. See London Stock Exchange (2006), p. 2.

3 Liquidity

This chapter starts with a definition of the term *liquidity* and its description as a multi-dimensional concept. Only the most frequently implemented liquidity measures are presented and categorized according to their dimensionality (one- or multi-dimensional) and their calculation base (order book data or transaction data). The result of this chapter is the choice of a multi-dimensional liquidity measure implemented in the empirical part of this study.

3.1 Definition

Modern finance theory assumes that markets are frictionless and efficient. Thus an asset can be traded any time, for both buy and sell sides at the same price for any given volume. In this view, only risk and return determine investors' decisions to buy or sell an asset.[59]

In contrast, market microstructure theory assumes frictions.[60] Stoll (2000) distinguishes frictions into two categories: Real frictions, i.e. deficits in market organization, consume real resources and affect all market participants alike, while informational frictions reallocate wealth between market participants.[61] Kempf (1999) uses perfect liquidity in a frictionless market as a reference point when determining liquidity. Thus liquidity becomes an additional decision criterion for investors.[62]

Although the term liquidity is common in research and practice there is still no agreement on its measurement.[63] In this study, liquidity is defined as follows:

"Liquidity (is) the ability to buy or sell significant quantities of a security quickly, anonymously, and with relatively little price impact."[64]

This definition includes three elements: Volume ("significant quantities"), price continuity ("relatively little price impact"), and time ("quickly"). These definition elements can be operationalized through liquidity dimensions.[65]

---

59 Markowitz's (1952) seminal work on portfolio theory and the development of the Capital Asset Pricing Model by Sharpe (1964) are both based on the assumption of frictionless capital markets.

60 The central research object of microstructure theory is the trading process. See Cohen/Maier/Schwartz/Whitcomb (1986), p. 1. O'Hara (1997) provides a comprehensive literature overview on microstructure theory, Coughenour/Shastri (1999) provide a review of empirical research, Madhavan (2000) reviews theoretical, experimental, and empirical results relating to trading and markets, and Biais/Glosten/Spatt (2005) offer a synthesis of theoretical and empirical results concerning the consequences of market structure for price formation.

61 See Stoll (2000), p. 1481ff. He states: "Friction in financial markets measures the difficulty with which an asset is traded." See Stoll (2000), p. 1479.

62 See Kempf (1999), p. 13.

63 See Oesterhelweg/Schiereck (1993), p. 390.

64 Campell/Lo/MacKinlay (1997), p. 99f. Closely related definitions are "a market is liquid if traders can quickly buy or sell large numbers of shares when they want and at low transaction costs", Harris (1990) p. 3. A similar definition is provided by Bernstein (1987), p. 54 stating that an asset is liquid, if it can be bought or sold immediately and without adversely affecting the price. Schwartz (1988), p. 532 describes liquid assets as "traded quickly at reasonable prices".

65 See Oesterhelweg/Schiereck (1993), p. 390f.

Following Harris (1990), four dimensions of liquidity can be identified: Width, depth, immediacy, and resilience.[66]

The first dimension, *width*, is defined as the available bid-ask spread, i.e. the difference between an immediate buy and sell at the spread without change of the order book. For transaction volumes that do not exceed the volumes given at the bid and ask prices, the difference is exactly the bid-ask spread. This is based on the assumption that the median between the highest bid price and the lowest ask price reflects the current true value of the asset. Then the difference between the true value of the asset and the bid or ask price for an immediate execution is exactly the half spread.

The corresponding volumes of the different bid and ask prices define the *depth* of the order book of an asset, as the second dimension. The following relationship holds: the more units of an asset can be bought or sold at a defined bid-ask spread the deeper the limit order book is. The two dimensions are reflected in the above definition by "*significant quantities*".[67] However, quoted bid-ask spreads only represent execution costs during normal market conditions and for small volumes available at the bid-ask spread.

The third dimension, *immediacy*, refers to the time needed to accomplish a trade of a given size at a given cost. It is often argued that immediacy is implicitly assumed in trading systems that offer continuous trading. As described in the previous chapter, Xetra also offers trading models that allow only for discrete trading, i.e. during auctions at predefined time periods. These trading models do not provide immediacy. Immediacy is reflected in the above definition by the *"... ability to buy or sell [...] quickly"*.

Resilience refers to the speed with which prices recover to former levels after a large transaction has taken place. This follows the assumption that when a large order causes a price change without affecting the underlying value of the asset, the asset price should move back to its equilibrium level.[68] In contrast to the other dimensions that are determined for a certain point in time, resilience can only be determined through time. It is reflected in the above definition by *"... relatively little price impact"*.

The various liquidity dimensions are interdependent. Width and depth are determined together, as for a given point in time width defined through the bid-ask spread is an increasing function of order size. An increase in liquidity is reflected either in the fact that for a given

---

66 See Harris (1990), p. 3. Earlier works of Garbade (1982), p. 420, Kyle (1985), p. 1316 and Bernstein (1987), p. 57 define liquidity in terms of three dimensions: tightness, depth, and resilience. These dimensions cover three of the four dimensions of Harris. However, they implicitly assume that immediacy is not a dimension but given in automated markets as Schwartz (1988), p. 524 states "because transactions in highly organized markets can be obtained almost instantaneously".

67 Kempf (1999) p. 17f. describes the combination of both dimensions as the price dimension which exists in addition to the time dimension of liquidity.

68 Hasbrouck (1988), p. 235 distinguishes between transitory and permanent price changes. While the former are randomly introduced through large orders or order imbalances the latter are caused by information driving the price to its new equilibrium level. The above liquidity definition only excludes transitory price changes. Thus, liquidity and (information) efficiency are compatible. For a description of the potential conflict between liquidity and information efficiency, see Bernstein (1987), p. 62 and Oesterhelweg/ Schiereck (1993), p. 391.

volume the respective spread is smaller or for a given spread a larger volume is provided.[69] Both dimensions depend on immediacy, as patient traders could possibly realize a different price for a given volume when deciding to delay their transactions. Resilience and immediacy also show a strong interrelation, as immediacy is directly determined through resilience. Immediacy is only given if a market is resilient; otherwise, the possibility to trade instantaneously without or only with a minimum market impact is not given. The four dimensions allow, due to the congruence with the elements of the definition, a complete mapping of market liquidity.[70]

3.2 Measurement Methods

In open limit order books, liquidity is supplied through the limit orders standing in the book and demanded by those orders that initiate a trade by entering the order book as market orders or marketable limit orders.[71]

It is the order type (market or limit order), not the direction of the order (buy or sell order) that determines liquidity. Thus, a categorization into liquidity demander and provider is done by the aggressiveness of orders, immediately executable orders (market order or marketable limit order), and orders remaining in the order book (limit order). Orders that remain in the order book can be further distinguished into orders that entered the order book at or better than the current best bid ask (BBA)[72] and orders that entered behind the current BBA.[73]

Market and limit orders are distinguished concerning the probability of execution and the price. While limit orders determine the price at which they are executed, they face the risk of not being executed (execution risk). In addition, limit orders face adverse selection risk, when new information arrives at the market and these limit orders are mispriced when executed - often referred to as picking off risk. In contrast, market orders are executed with certainty but face price risk as they are executed against the available orders in the order book. Thus traders are confronted with the trade-off between execution, price, and adverse selection risk when choosing whether to supply or demand liquidity.[74]

---

69 See Lee/Mucklow/Ready (1993), p. 349ff. The authors describe this relation in detail and note that any study of liquidity has to take the changes in both prices and depth into account, requiring a multi-dimensional view.

70 See Schiereck (1995), p. 25, Oesterhelweg/Schiereck (1993), p. 392 and Brunner (1996), p. 6ff.

71 See Harris (1990), p. 5 and Handa/Schwartz (1996a), p. 45. An exception is a market order that enters a limit order book with an empty opposite side. These orders remain in the order book as unlimited orders. Instruments with an empty order book side would be classified as illiquid and traded in auction only. See Exhibit 2-5.

72 The best bid (BB) is the highest buy limit order and the best ask (BA) is the lowest sell limit order in the order book. Together they form the best bid ask (BBA), often referred to as available spread.

73 A similar classification is implemented by Anand/Chakravarty/Martell (2005), p. 295. Oesterhelweg (1998), p. 18f. proposes a distinction into four categories, additionally distinguishing orders entered at or better than the current BBA into two categories.

74 See Bae/Jang/Park (2003), p. 517f. Cohen/Maier/Schwartz/Whitcomb (1981), p. 298 explain the existing spread due to gravitational pull effects: As limit orders face execution risk, it becomes relatively more attractive to execute a market order with certainty than to place a limit order and narrow the spread when the spread is already small, and vice versa.

Liquidity is a dynamic concept, as traders' decisions to implement market or limit orders have an impact on subsequent liquidity supply and demand.[75] Liquidity measures determine liquidity from the viewpoint of liquidity demand, thus the available liquidity for an impatient trader (ex-ante) or the liquidity consumed by an impatient trader (ex-post). These measures do not provide any information on the type of trader that provides the liquidity and the motives for providing liquidity.

A distinction of liquidity measures[76] can follow

(i) the number of dimensions they cover and

(ii) their calculation base being either order book or transaction data.

While the first distinction classifies liquidity measures as single- or multi-dimensional, the second distinction categorizes them as ex-ante or ex-post measures. Additionally, liquidity indicators that do not directly measure any liquidity dimension belong to the group of ex-post measures.[77] Due to the strong interaction of the different dimensions of liquidity, the dimensions should be measured jointly to provide a complete picture of the liquidity in an instrument, an index, or a market. Thus multi-dimensional measures are preferred over one-dimensional measures, as they are able to capture several aspects of liquidity in one figure.[78]

Admati/Pfleiderer (1988) introduce the distinction between discretionary (strategic) and non-discretionary traders. In contrast to non-discretionary traders, discretionary traders have the choice of when to trade. The underlying assumption is that ex-ante liquidity affects trading strategies of traders who have the choice; i.e. discretionary traders will trade when liquidity is high, in turn reinforcing the concentration of volume and liquidity.[79] Monitoring possibilities as provided through an open limit order book allow for discretionary timing of trades. Thus traders can add value through strategic trading behavior. Transaction based (ex-post) measures ignore the fact that trades might only have taken place because of the provided level of ex-ante liquidity. They do not take into account the available average liquidity but only the liquidity when investors are ready to trade. As a consequence, transaction based measures might overestimate the liquidity in an instrument.[80]

This study follows the argumentation of strategic trading behavior and prefers order book based measures over transaction based liquidity measures as Gomber/Schweickert/Theissen

---

75 Order submission strategies include the choice of market versus limit order placement, limit order prices, and trade size. Daníelsson/Payne (2001) analyze the dynamic behavior of liquidity supply and demand in the foreign exchange market on Reuters. Biais/Hillion/Spatt (1995) examine the dynamics for Paris Bourse. Foucault (1999) and Parlour (1998) provide theoretical models for order submission strategies.

76 Although commonly labeled as liquidity measures, most of them are in fact measures of illiquidity. That means when interpreting the results it follows that higher results indicate a lower liquidity.

77 See Aitken/Comerton-Forde (2003), p. 47. Kindermann (2005), p. 109 also provides a classification methodology for liquidity measures along the calculation base.

78 Fernandez (1999), p. 1 points out the need to compute several liquidity measures to capture the different dimensions. Amihud (2002), p. 33 doubts that one single measure will be able to capture all dimensions of liquidity, while one-dimensional measures can provide insight to certain questions of a market's liquidity. Von Wyss (2004), p. 9 distinguishes between single and multi-dimensional measures, concluding that "for a global liquidity measure, certainly one of the multi-dimensional liquidity measures has to be used".

79 See Admati/Pfleiderer (1988), p. 33ff.

80 See Kempf (1999), p. 35 and Aitken/Comerton-Forde (2003), p. 58.

(2005) provided evidence for discretionary trading in the underling research object Xetra. They find that large transactions are timed; i.e. they take place when liquidity is unusually high.[81] Consequently, ex-ante measures based on order book data are preferred over ex-post measures, as transaction based measures only capture liquidity in the case of a transaction taking place.

The description of commonly used liquidity measures in the next two sections follows the classification in one-dimensional and multi-dimensional liquidity measures. Following the above argumentation, the preferred choice for a liquidity measure is a multi-dimensional measure based on order book data (ex-ante).

3.2.1 One-dimensional Measures

In this chapter, liquidity measures for the individual liquidity dimensions width and depth are described. Immediacy is directly defined by the trading model implemented and does not require a separate assessment. For the fourth dimension, resilience, the literature does not provide a direct measure, but foresees dynamic analyses.

The dimension width is measured through the bid-ask spread.[82] However, there are several possibilities to measure bid-ask spreads that incur a different economic meaning. The quoted spread is measured as the difference between the best bid (BB) (buy order with the highest limit price) and best ask (BA) limit (sell order with the lowest limit price) in the order book and is observed before a transaction takes place. As such, it is a hypothetical ex-ante measure. In contrast, the effective spread is the difference between the execution price and the midpoint of the prevailing bid-ask spread. Thus it is an ex-post liquidity measure determining the liquidity of an individual transaction.

In open limit order books, in contrast to specialist or dealer markets, the effective spread can per definition not be smaller than the quoted spread. This is due to the fact that orders cannot receive any price improvement but are executed at the specified price. It follows that the results of liquidity measures depend on the underlying market's structure. However, the effective spread can be larger than the quoted spread if orders due to their large size are executed against several limits in the order book. In that case, the results also reflect the dimension depth becoming a multi-dimensional ex-post liquidity measure.[83]

Although the spread only captures one dimension of liquidity, it has been applied widely to measure and compare liquidity across exchanges. The reasons are that often order book data

---

81 See Gomber/Schweickert/Theissen (2005), pp. 13-19. Coppejans/Domowitz/Madhavan (2004), p. 8f. find evidence for strategic order placement behavior in the Swedish futures market.

82 Spreads are often measured in relative terms (divided by the midpoint) eliminating differences in stock price levels allowing comparing results across instruments.

83 For quote-driven and specialist markets, effective spreads have been reported to be significantly smaller than quoted spreads due to price improvement granted by the market maker or specialist e.g. Chordia/Roll/Subrahmanyam (2001), p. 506 find supporting results for within-quote trading in their long term study for securities traded at NYSE (1988 to 1998). See Glosten/Harris (1988), p. 128, Lee/Ready (1991), p. 739f. and Huang/Stoll (1996b), p. 28ff., as well as a series of articles by Bessembinder, (1997) with Kaufman, p. 296f., (1999), p. 393f. and (2003a), p. 388.

beyond the best bid and ask were not available[84], and that the theoretical literature on spread decomposition (see Chapter 4.3.1) gives clear predictions regarding the determinants of the spread while estimators of spread components were successfully developed and implemented.[85] To capture the second dimension, depth, the average quoted depth (in terms of units) at the bid and ask limits can be calculated. When multiplying the number of units with the respective limit prices, this results in the quoted € depth. Liquidity measures related to depth include the number of orders and their respective volume on each side of the book.[86]

In addition to these liquidity measures, so-called liquidity indicators are often implemented. The main advantage of indicators is that they are readily observable and do not require extensive data analysis.[87] The most common are number and volume of trades, trade frequency (number of transactions executed during a certain time span), and turnover ratio, defined as the ratio of trading volume and outstanding volume (free float).[88]

Additional ex-post liquidity measures are calculated based on transaction prices: The 'Amivest Liquidity Ratio' developed by Cooper/Groth/Avera (1985) is quite common. It is determined as the ratio of average traded volume and average relative price change during a defined time interval. The result provides the average trading volume needed to induce a one percent price change. It follows that the higher the ratio the higher the liquidity. Liquidity ratios do not directly operationalize any liquidity dimension and are at the same time transaction based ex-post measures.[89, 90]

The described liquidity measures only take into account one liquidity dimension at a time. Although width and depth are measured separately, they should be interpreted in a context.

---

84 Starting with Demsetz (1968), seminal work bid-ask spreads were widely implemented: Schmidt/Iversen (1991), Lee/Mucklow/Ready (1993), Iversen (1994), Booth/Iversen/Sarkar/Schmidt/Young (1995), Lin/ Sanger/Booth (1995), Treske (1996), Brockman/Chung (1998), Chordia/Roll/Subrahmanyam (2001), Chung/Van Ness (2001), and Wolff (2003).

85 The two described spread measures (quoted and effective spread) are based on the assumption that bid-ask spreads are readily observable. Additional measures were developed that estimate effective spreads from time series data of transactions alone, so-called implicit spreads (Roll (1984) and Hasbrouck/Schwartz (1988)). The main difference to spread measures lies in their elimination of the effects of changes to the underlying value on the transaction prices; i.e. the size of bid-ask spread does not react to changes in the underlying value consequently precluding asymmetric information.

86 Demsetz (1968), in his attempt to define market depth, focuses on the marginal increase of the bid-ask spread if the defined trading volume increases. Engle/Lange (1997), p. 9f. propose a statistic for the measurement of the depth of liquidity based on the one-sided volume sustained before a subsequent price move. It is calculated as the sum of the number of shares traded over all transactions within a given price duration. Aitken/Comerton-Forde (2003), p. 50f. compute the relative depth, which is defined as the total volume in the order book divided by the total number of shares in the issue.

87 Kempf (1999), p. 13 and p. 45ff. distinguishes between liquidity measures that are founded theoretically and heuristic liquidity measures, so-called liquidity indicators. Empirical implementation of the measurement methods was often a problem leading to the implementation of liquidity indicators.

88 Examples are Chordia/Roll/Subrahmanyam (2001), Hasbrouck/Saar (2002), Hasbrouck/Seppi (2001), Hautsch/Pohlmeier (2002), Lee/Mucklow/Ready (1993), and Lin/Sanger/Booth (1995).

89 See Cooper/Groth/Avera (1985), p. 25, Grossman/Miller (1988), p. 630, Marsh/Rock (1986), p. 5 and Oesterhelweg/Schiereck (1993), p. 392.

90 To overcome conceptual problems of the Amivest Liquidity Ratio (the proportional relation of trading volume and price changes, which potentially overestimates liquidity in frequently traded instruments), Marsh/Rock (1986) develop a liquidity ratio computed as the sum of percentage price changes divided by the number of transactions during a defined time interval. However, the same criticism applies as to the Amivest Liquidity Ratio.

This can be done by implementing just one liquidity measure that captures several dimensions or computing several measures to cover the different dimensions.

The following example shows why it is necessary to analyze liquidity from a multi-dimensional perspective: The reduction in tick size on the NYSE in June 1997 is a market structure change that allows analyzing liquidity before and after its implementation. Goldstein/Kavajecz (2000) demonstrate that while NYSE spreads declined, cumulated order book depth also declined, meaning the outcome of the structural change depends on transaction size: While execution costs for small orders decreased as the spread decreased, large orders in the best case did not see a benefit but saw an increase in costs due to the decrease in order book depth. Concluding, the structural change did not lead to an unambiguous welfare change. If the analysis had only taken spreads into account, it would have assessed the outcome differently.[91]

3.2.2 Multi-dimensional Measures

To overcome the deficits of one-dimensional liquidity measures, the information provided through the limit order book can be relied upon: A limit order book allows one to understand the available liquidity beyond the quoted spread and respective volume. As Kempf (1999) demonstrates, the price dimension (depth and width) of liquidity is determined through the slope of the demand and supply curve of liquidity.[92] Order book information enables calculation of the liquidity supply function. This function is non-linear, leading to the fact that liquidity cannot be reduced to a single number but has to be calculated for all possible sizes.[93] This is done by calculating the weighted average price for which an order of a given size can be executed, i.e. the market impact costs of the order. Through variation of order size, the slope of the instantaneous offer and demand curves can be plotted.

Market impact measures are usually implemented as round-trip measures, i.e. computing costs of simultaneous buy and sell orders of the same size at a certain point in time, thus computing liquidity supply from the viewpoint of a market order trader. Round-trip costs measure the performance loss when opening and closing a position. Irvine/Benston/Kandel (2000) were the first to define this type of liquidity measure formally. They suggest its usage in the comparison of markets and urge exchanges to report it.[94] Similar measures were implemented by a variety of authors.[95]

---

[91] See Goldstein/Kavajecz (2000), p. 142 and p. 146. Jones/Lipson (2001), p. 274ff. also analyze the tick size reduction at NYSE in June 1997, but for institutional trades only. They find that execution costs increased for these (large) trades, concluding that spread alone is not sufficient to evaluate the results of a market structure change.

[92] See Kempf (1999), p. 30f. The economic meaning of a liquidity measure based on supply and demand schedules is the gap between an instrument's supply and demand schedules. If the gap is wide, liquidity is low and it is impossible to match orders. In that sense, it reflects the concession that an impatient trader has to make to achieve immediate execution. In fact, it is an inverse measure of liquidity.

[93] For the non-linearity of the function, see Cao/Hansch/Wang (2004), p. 6f., Griese/Kempf (2006), p. 405ff., Irvine/Benston/Kandel (2000), p. 16ff., and Kempf (1999), p. 27f.

[94] See Irvine/Benston/Kandel (2000), p. 7ff.

[95] See Beltran/Giot/Grammig (2005), p. 7f., Coppejans/Domowitz/Madhavan (2004), p. 7, Domowitz/Hansch/Wang (2005), p. 353f., and Kumar (2003), p. 6.

Gomber/Schweickert (2002a) have adapted the initial formula of Irvine/Benston/Kandel (2000), and Deutsche Boerse AG implemented it in the Xetra trading system as the so-called Exchange Liquidity Measure (XLM).[96] The XLM was introduced in July 2002 to provide market participants with the ability to identify the implicit transaction costs, to determine the trading parameters on Xetra, as well as to assess measures to improve the market model. The XLM calculates the costs of liquidity demand based on market impact: It represents an integrative view of liquidity and implicit transaction costs, as liquidity is determined through width, depth, and immediacy and implicit transaction costs are measured as market impact.[97]

As outlined in Exhibit 3-1, width is reflected in the liquidity premium (LP). However, orders with a volume exceeding the available volume at the spread require additional market depth; this dimension is reflected in the calculation of the adverse price movement (APM). Immediacy is reflected in the fact that the market impact calculates the costs of immediate demand for liquidity at a certain point in time.

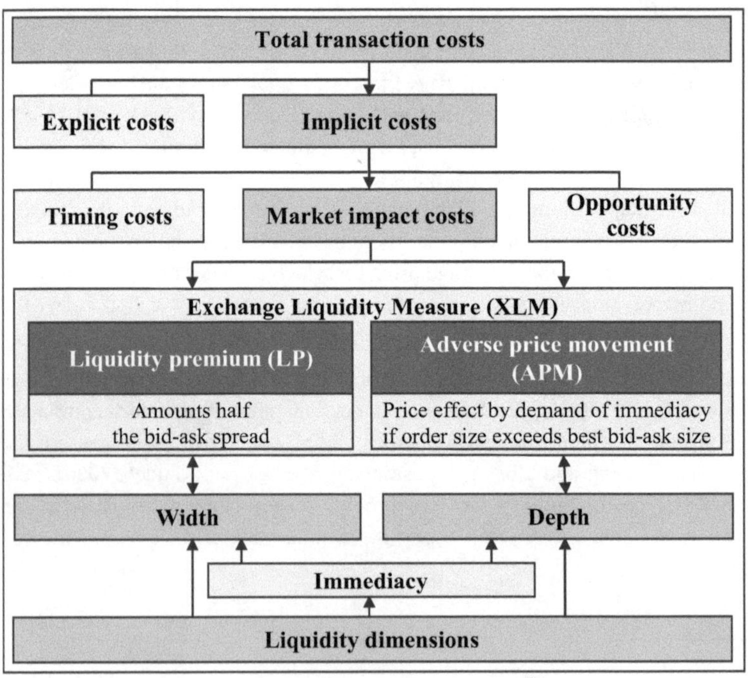

Exhibit 3-1: Integrative view of transaction costs and liquidity[98]

---

[96] See Gomber/Schweickert (2002a), p. 485ff. and Gomber/Schweickert/Theissen (2005), p. 6ff.

[97] Transaction costs are distinguished into explicit and implicit transactions costs. Explicit transaction costs are fees, commissions, or taxes; they are incurred with order-processing and settlement. In addition to market impact, implicit transaction costs include timing costs (costs that arise from price movement during the time of the transaction) and opportunity costs (any missed profit or loss arising if the complete order or parts of it remain unfilled at the end of the trading day).

[98] Exhibit 3-1 is adapted from Gomber/Schweickert (2002a), p. 486.

Market impact which measures liquidity costs is used to operationalize the concept of liquidity: It follows that the higher the liquidity the lower the implicit transaction costs (measured as market impact), and vice versa.[99] Implicit transaction costs are no source of revenue for the exchange but are redistributed between the market participants, those offering liquidity and those consuming it.[100]

Exhibit 3-2 provides a schematic introduction to the calculation of the XLM. Market impact is the sum of the liquidity premium (LP), i.e. the half bid-ask spread[101] and the adverse price movement (APM) measured as price effect if the order size exceeds the best bid-ask size. Both are separately calculated for each side of the book. The midpoint of the spread is the theoretical value of the instrument and serves as reference point. The sum of the market impacts on both sides of the order book results in the costs of a round-trip for a defined execution volume.

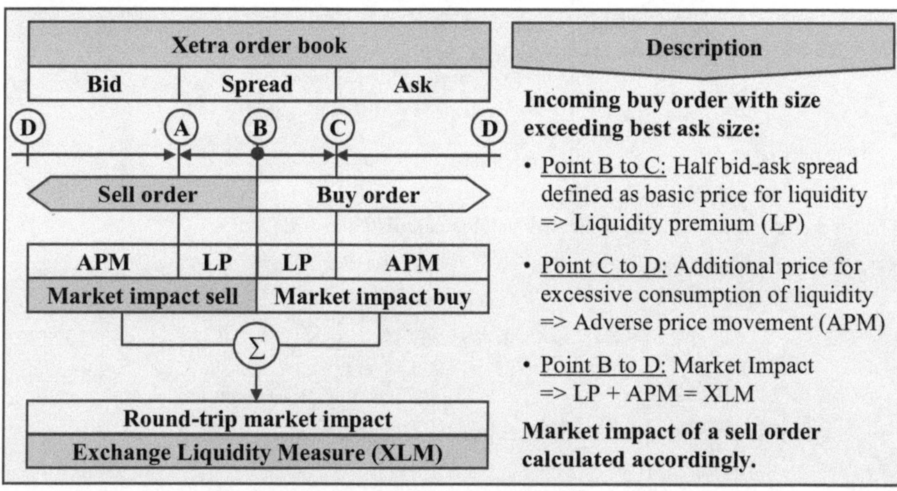

Exhibit 3-2: Basic concept of Exchange Liquidity Measure (XLM)[102]

Deutsche Boerse AG (2002) describes the formal calculation methodology based upon limit orders standing in the open limit order book as follows:[103]

The price limits of orders are denominated for buy orders as $L_{B_x} < ... < L_{B_3} < L_{B_2} < L_{B_1} < L_{B_0}$ and as $L_{A_0} < L_{A_1} < L_{A_2} < L_{A_3} < ... < L_{A_z}$ for sell orders with $x, z \in N_0^+$. L_{B_0} and L_{A_0} are the limits at the top of the order book, i.e. the best bid and best ask (BBA) available.

---

[99] See Gomber/Schweickert (2002a), p. 486.
[100] See Schwartz/Francioni (2004), pp. 63-66.
[101] The liquidity premium added for both sides of the order book is per definition similar to the relative quoted bid-ask spread.
[102] Exhibit 3-2 is adapted from Gomber/Schweickert (2002a), p. 486f.
[103] See Deutsche Boerse AG (2002), pp. 1-3.

For each price limit the corresponding quantity of shares is denoted as $N_{B_x},\dots,N_{B_3},N_{B_2},N_{B_1},N_{B_0}$ and as $N_{A_0},N_{A_1},N_{A_2},N_{A_3},\dots,N_{A_z}$ where N_{B_j} identifies the number of shares of the corresponding limit order(s) with rank j (j=0,1,2,3,…,x) for buy orders (bid side) and N_{A_k} the number of shares of the corresponding limit order(s) with rank k (k=0,1,2,3,…,z) for sell orders (ask side).

$\overline{N}_{B_j}(V)$ is an indicator variable. It denotes the number of shares which is executed from limit order(s) with rank j on the bid side when a marketable sell order of volume V (V>0) enters the order book. It is defined as:

$$\overline{N}_{B_j}(V)=\begin{cases} N_{B_j} & \text{if } V \geq \sum\limits_{i=0}^{j} N_{B_i}\cdot L_{B_i} \\ \left\lfloor \dfrac{V-\sum\limits_{i=0}^{j-1} N_{B_i}\cdot L_{B_i}}{L_{B_j}} \right\rfloor & \text{if } V > \sum\limits_{i=0}^{j-1} N_{B_i}\cdot L_{B_i} \text{ and } V < \sum\limits_{i=0}^{j} N_{B_i}\cdot L_{B_i} \\ 0 & \text{otherwise} \end{cases}$$

The market impact of a marketable sell order is calculated as follows:

$$MI_S(V)=LP_S(V)+APM_S(V)$$

$$=\frac{1}{V}\cdot\left|\sum_{j=0}^{x}\overline{N}_{B_j}(V)\cdot\left(\frac{L_{A_0}-L_{B_0}}{2}\right)\right|\cdot 10{,}000+\frac{1}{V}\cdot\left|\sum_{j=1}^{x}\overline{N}_{B_j}(V)\cdot\left(L_{B_0}-L_{B_j}\right)\right|\cdot 10{,}000$$

$$=\frac{1}{V}\cdot\left|\sum_{j=0}^{x}\overline{N}_{B_j}(V)\cdot\left(\frac{L_{B_0}+L_{A_0}}{2}-L_{B_j}\right)\right|\cdot 10{,}000$$

The result is multiplied by 10,000 to reflect basis points (BP), where 1 BP = 0.01%. The market impact for an incoming marketable buy order is calculated respectively. $\overline{N}_{A_k}(V)$ describes the number of shares which is executed from limit order(s) with rank k on the ask side when a marketable buy order of volume V (V>0) enters the order book. $\overline{N}_{A_k}(V)$ is defined as:

$$\overline{N}_{A_k}(V)=\begin{cases} N_{A_k} & \text{if } V \geq \sum\limits_{i=0}^{k} N_{A_i}\cdot L_{A_i} \\ \left\lfloor \dfrac{V-\sum\limits_{i=0}^{k-1} N_{A_i}\cdot L_{A_i}}{L_{A_k}} \right\rfloor & \text{if } V > \sum\limits_{i=0}^{k-1} N_{A_i}\cdot L_{A_i} \text{ and } V < \sum\limits_{i=0}^{k} N_{A_i}\cdot L_{A_i} \\ 0 & \text{other} \end{cases}$$

The market impact of a marketable buy order is calculated as follows:

$$\mathrm{MI_B(V)} = \mathrm{LP_B(V)} + \mathrm{APM_B(V)}$$

$$= \frac{1}{V} \cdot \left| \sum_{k=0}^{z} \overline{N}_{A_k}(V) \cdot \left(\frac{L_{A_0} - L_{B_0}}{2} \right) \right| \cdot 10{,}000 + \frac{1}{V} \cdot \left| \sum_{k=1}^{z} \overline{N}_{A_k}(V) \cdot \left(L_{A_0} - L_{A_k} \right) \right| \cdot 10{,}000$$

$$= \frac{1}{V} \cdot \left| \sum_{k=0}^{z} \overline{N}_{A_k}(V) \cdot \left(\frac{L_{B_0} + L_{A_0}}{2} - L_{A_k} \right) \right| \cdot 10{,}000$$

XLM calculates the market impact based upon order book snapshots taken every minute from the Xetra order book. These snapshots also include the hidden volumes of iceberg orders[104], providing a measure for committed rather than displayed liquidity.

A sample calculation for a round-trip of 1 million € is provided in Exhibit 3-3: It displays an order book snapshot taken from the Xetra trading system in Deutsche Telekom AG (DTE) on 15 May 2002, 12:02 pm. The fields in the table presented provide the limit prices (Bid or Ask), the corresponding number of shares (quantity) available at that limit price (BidQty or AskQty), and in addition, the number of orders (count) behind the limit price (BidCnt or AskCnt).

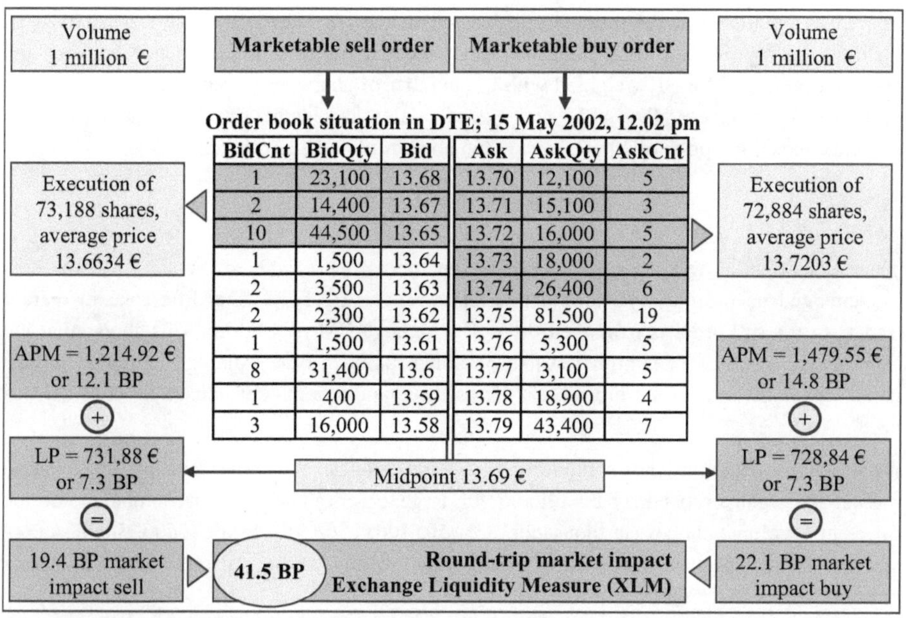

BidCnt	BidQty	Bid	Ask	AskQty	AskCnt
1	23,100	13.68	13.70	12,100	5
2	14,400	13.67	13.71	15,100	3
10	44,500	13.65	13.72	16,000	5
1	1,500	13.64	13.73	18,000	2
2	3,500	13.63	13.74	26,400	6
2	2,300	13.62	13.75	81,500	19
1	1,500	13.61	13.76	5,300	5
8	31,400	13.6	13.77	3,100	5
1	400	13.59	13.78	18,900	4
3	16,000	13.58	13.79	43,400	7

Exhibit 3-3: Sample calculation for a round-trip of € 1 million[105]

[104] For a description of iceberg orders, see Chapter 2.3. For instruments that require designated sponsors (liquidity providers) to be traded in continuous trading, two separate liquidity measures are calculated: the committed liquidity and the straight liquidity. The straight liquidity is the liquidity provided by all market participants except the designated sponsors. It is the basis for the categorization of instruments in liquidity classes. The committed liquidity includes the liquidity provided by the designated sponsors.

[105] Deutsche Boerse AG (2002), p. 3.

The midpoint at time t (MP_t) of 13.69 € is calculated based on the available BBA (BB = 13.68 € and BA = 13.70 €). If a sell market order of 1 m € enters the order book, it matches several bid limits until it is fully executed: At the time of order entry, 73,188 shares are executed at three limit prices ranging from 13.68 € to 13.65 €. This yields an average quantity weighted execution price of 13.6634 €, calculated as the ratio of order size and number of shares executed (1,000,000 € / 73,188 shares).

Implementing the above presented formula for a sell order of the given size of 1 m €, the calculated market impact yields 19.4 bp (approx. 1,945 €):

$$MI_S(V) = LP_S(V) + APM_S(V)$$

$$= \frac{1}{1{,}000{,}000} \cdot 73{,}188 \cdot \left(\frac{13.70 - 13.68}{2} \right) \cdot 10{,}000 +$$

$$\frac{1}{1{,}000{,}000} \cdot [14{,}400 \cdot (13.68 - 13.67) + 35{,}688 \cdot (13.68 - 13.65)] \cdot 10{,}000$$

$$= 7.3 + 12.1$$

$$= 19.4$$

The LP is calculated as the product of executed shares (73,188) and half the BBA (0.01 €) yielding 7.3 bp. The APM is calculated per executed limit as the difference between the executed limit and the BB weighted with the number of shares executed and yields as a sum 12.1 bp. Alternatively, the APM can be calculated implementing the average quantity weighted execution price of 13.6634 € and the number of executed shares:

$$APM_S(V) = \frac{1}{1{,}000{,}000} \cdot [73{,}188 \cdot (13.68 - 13.6634)] \cdot 10{,}000 = 12.1$$

The calculation of the market impact for the buy order of the given size of 1 m € is implemented accordingly, yielding a market impact of 22.1 bp. The difference in market impact to the sell order is explained through a higher APM of 14.8 bp. This shows that the liquidity for a sell order is higher at that particular point in time. Adding the market impact results for both sides of the order book yields the round-trip market impact or XLM of 41.5 bp.[106]

As the above example shows liquidity is a transaction size-specific concept; i.e. a liquid market for small orders may be illiquid for large orders. The XLM is computed for ten different € volume classes (in thousands): 25, 50, 100, 250, 500, 1,000, 2,000, 3,000, 4,000, and 5,000 for DAX instruments.[107] Plotting the results of the different volume classes

---

[106] For the case where the components of the market impact do not need to be calculated separately, Gomber/Schweickert/Theissen (2005), p. 7 have provided the following reduced formula that implements the quantity weighted average execution price $\overline{P}_{B,t}(V)$ and $\overline{P}_{S,t}(V)$ and the midpoint MP_t: $XLM_{B,t}(V) = 10{,}000 \frac{\overline{P}_{B,t}(V) - MP_t}{MP_t}$ and $XLM_{S,t}(V) = 10{,}000 \frac{MP_t - \overline{P}_{S,t}(V)}{MP_t}$ which leads to $XLM_t(V) = XLM_{B,t}(V) + XLM_{S,t}(V)$.

[107] Occasionally the order book is not deep enough to allow for calculation of all XLM sizes. This will be shown in part II, Chapters 6.2.1 and 7.1.2.

generates the liquidity supply function of a single instrument at a defined point in time. It is a monotone rising function, as liquidity offered for a larger order has to be more expensive than liquidity for a smaller order. As price determination follows price-time precedence, the price impact of a buy (sell) side trade is an increasing (decreasing) function of trade size.[108]

The non-linearity of the liquidity supply and demand function provides insight with respect to strategic trading activity. A uniform strategy of breaking up large trades into smaller ones and executing them continuously is more expensive than waiting for periods of high liquidity, i.e. timing orders. Open limit order books allow real time monitoring of the market and thus assessment of liquidity. This suggests active liquidity management to control implicit transaction costs, i.e. discretionary trading.[109]

3.3 Synopsis

This chapter starts with the definition of liquidity as a multi-dimensional concept based on Harris (1990). Although the theoretical and empirical literature has settled upon a common definition, there is little agreement concerning the optimal liquidity measure. The interrelation of the different dimensions (width, depth, immediacy, and resilience) determines the hurdles when trying to measure liquidity. Consequently, those measures that are able to capture several dimensions are preferred, suggesting the use of a multi-dimensional measure.

In addition, liquidity measures can be further distinguished concerning their calculation base (transaction or order data). While order based measures compute the ex-ante available liquidity, transaction based measures calculate the ex-post realized liquidity. As traders have the possibility to monitor the order book and Gomber/Schweickert/ Theissen (2005) provide evidence for discretionary trading in Xetra order based (ex-ante) measures are favored. Ex-post measures would overestimate liquidity, as they only measure liquidity when a transaction took place.

Deutsche Boerse AG has introduced the Exchange Liquidity Measure (XLM) that calculates the market impact of a hypothetical order size in basis points. It is an order based ex-ante liquidity measure that is able to capture three of the four liquidity dimensions directly. The fourth dimension resilience can be calculated through time.[110] This measure will be implemented in part II of this study, where detailed information is given on the XLM data table (Chapter 6.2.1) and the empirical results for the DAX instruments (Chapter 7.1). The analysis will also include the question of active transaction cost management (discretionary trading), which can only be addressed when comparing ex-ante and ex-post liquidity cost. For that question the ex-post liquidity cost will be operationalized, implementing the effective spread, and results will be compared to the XLM (Chapter 7.2).

---

108 An example is given in Chapter 7.1.1.

109 See Coppejans/Domowitz/Madhavan (2004), p. 9f., Domowitz (2001), p. 142, or Griese/Kempf (2006), p. 403.

110 The fourth dimension, resilience, is analyzed for Xetra by Gomber/Schweickert/Theissen (2005), for the Swedish Stock Index Futures Market by Coppejans/Domowitz/Madhavan (2004), and for Paris Bourse (prior to its merger to Euronext) by Degryse/de Jong/Ravenswaaij/Wuyts (2005).

4 Informed Trading

The objective of this chapter is to define the term *informed trading* and to determine the adequate measure for identifying informed trading on the trader level for this study. It starts with a brief introduction to the information paradigm, followed by a classification of traders along different motives for trading and the corresponding level of information. Common measures of informed trading will be briefly presented.[111] The choice of method follows (i) the need to identify the level of information for each transaction and (ii) data restrictions, i.e. there is no possibility to rebuild the order book.

Similar to the previous chapter, this chapter focuses solely on definitions and methods but not on their corresponding results. Thus, the role of informed trading for the liquidity in an equity market is not the subject of this chapter. Instead, the role will be discussed in Chapter 5, which presents the theoretical and empirical framework underlying this study.

4.1 Information Paradigm

The information paradigm in microstructure theory postulates that trades transfer information and induce a permanent price impact. Informed trading determines the informational efficiency[112] of markets by ensuring that private information is incorporated into prices through trading.[113] Bagheot (1971) is the first to introduce information as a trading motive. He distinguishes traders into three groups:[114]

(i) informed traders who possess information that is not reflected in market prices,

(ii) uninformed traders who do not posses any information and trade for liquidity reasons,

(iii) noise traders[115] who spuriously believe they possess information.

Informed traders have a reliable opinion on the fundamental[116] or true value of an asset, i.e. if the current market prices or BBA show undervaluation or overvaluation tendencies. An instrument is defined to be undervalued (overvalued) if the current market price is below (above) the true value of an asset. Informed traders impact prices permanently: When they

---

111 Measures for information asymmetry can be distinguished into two groups: (i) microstructure measures and (ii) corporate finance measures (e.g. analysts' forecasts, market-to-book or earnings-price ratio). This study solely focuses on microstructure measures. The latter have been additionally implemented by Clarke/Shastri (2000) and Van Ness/Van Ness/Warr (2001a).

112 Fama (1970), p. 383 distinguishes three forms of information efficiency depending on the level of information incorporated in prices (weak, semi-strong, strong market efficiency). According to Ross/ Westerfield/Jaffee (1996), p. 343ff. securities markets can be expected to be at least semi-strong efficient, meaning prices will reflect all publicly available information.

113 The initial contribution was made by Bagheot (1971). Copeland/Galai (1983) and Glosten/Milgrom (1985) show that asymmetric information alone is sufficient to explain the existence of bid-ask spreads. Kyle (1985) analyzes informed traders and their strategic trading behavior. Easley/O'Hara (1987) present a dynamic model for dealer behavior under the assumption of asymmetrically informed traders.

114 See Bagheot (1971), p. 13. The trisection did not prevail as consensus in the literature. In most of the theoretical and empirical literature, informed traders and uninformed (liquidity) traders are distinguished. Noise traders are included in the category of uninformed traders.

115 For an analysis of noise traders, see Black (1986).

116 The fundamental value of an asset is defined to be the value that all traders would agree upon if they had the same set of information and the same abilities to interpret the information.

buy an asset they push up prices, while prices decrease when they sell. As a consequence, their trading activity reflects their beliefs about fundamental values and prices consequently become more informative. Yet, they do not trade for this purpose but to profit from trading.

Uninformed traders lose when trading with informed traders. Those traders that provide liquidity (market makers or limit order traders) will increase spreads (BBA) by posting less aggressive price limits to cater for the risk of trading with an informed trader (adverse selection risk), leading to the general theoretical notion that informed trading and liquidity are inversely related.[117]

Information can be classified as public, private, or inside information, and traders can be categorized accordingly as informed traders (with private or insider information) and uninformed traders with public information only. Public information is readily available to all traders, though it does not have to be free of charge. Private information is information that an individual trader generates based on investigation and analysis. In contrast, insider information is a legal term: It is information that only a few individuals have, e.g. corporate officers, investment bankers, lawyers, and for which trading upon is forbidden in most securities markets.[118] Informed trading based upon private information is distinct from trading on inside information, as an insider has fiduciary obligations towards his shareholders.[119] This study focuses on informed trading based upon private information only.

4.2 Definition of Trader Types and Motives

The reasons why people trade are manifold, and traders can be categorized along their motives for trading into three general categories: profit-motivated traders, utilitarian traders, and futile traders. Profit-motivated traders trade to profit from their trading, while utilitarian traders try to realize benefits other than trading profits. Futile traders spuriously believe that they are profit-motivated traders.

Among utilitarian traders, investors or borrowers move money forward or back through time, while hedgers try to offload risk and gamblers imply to obtain entertainment from trading. They are considered uninformed, as they only know the price process but do not have any fundamental information. Consequently, they are not able to form a reliable opinion on the fundamental value of an asset. They trade for reasons unrelated to the underlying value but according to their liquidity needs. This is why they are often labeled as liquidity traders.[120]

Profit-motivated traders speculate on their information when buying undervalued and selling overvalued assets. Traders are considered informed if they know more about fundamental asset values than the other traders. Informed traders only trade when they possess information

---

117 See Harris (2003), p. 222ff.

118 See Hasbrouck (1990), p. 232. For Germany §§ 12-14 WpHG define what securities are eligible for insider trading and who insiders are, and finally prohibit insider trading. For a detailed description of these paragraphs, see Behr (2000), pp. 24-33.

119 See Madhavan (2000), p. 217. Chung/Charoenwong (1998), p. 15ff. study how trading of corporate insiders affects liquidity measured through the bid-ask spread. Results reveal that spreads increase with trading activity by insiders. Specialists increase their spreads depending on the size of incoming orders. This is in line with results for informed traders.

120 See Harris (2003), pp. 176-194.

and see profit opportunities. Dealers (market makers or specialists) also belong to the group of profit-motivated traders, as they try to profit from providing liquidity. Their service is most valued in illiquid markets.[121]

The described trading motives can be directly related to the trader categories described by Bagheot (1971). Profit-motivated traders are informed traders, utilitarian traders are uninformed traders, and futile traders are noise traders. Trading is a zero sum game[122], which is why informational frictions lead to wealth redistribution from uninformed to informed traders.[123] In trading both utilitarian traders and noise traders loose to profit-motivated informed traders. Thus in the following both are classified as uninformed traders.

Concerning their trading strategy, traders can be distinguished as implementing an active or passive trading strategy, i.e. immediacy demanding or immediacy supplying traders.[124] Active strategies are implemented with market orders, while passive strategies are based on limit orders. This transforms directly into the choice between liquidity provision and liquidity demand, where traders thus face the trade-off between price risk and execution risk when choosing among these order types (see Chapter 3.2).

Harris (1990) distinguishes between two types of liquidity providers: (i) passive liquidity providers that only trade when impatient traders demand liquidity (market makers or dealers) and (ii) pre-committed liquidity providers that trade via limit orders to reduce their transaction costs. These traders will eventually demand liquidity if they cannot fulfill their trading needs as liquidity providers.[125]

A special type of pre-committed trading is the so-called sunshine trading. These traders trade for reasons unrelated to information about future asset values. They can credibly signal (preannounce) that they are uninformed traders and display their orders and identities to attract more liquidity at lower costs.[126] Xetra, as a completely anonymous trading system, does not foresee any signaling; thus, sunshine trading does not play a role in this study.

Exhibit 4-1 provides trader taxonomy according to the identified motives and the corresponding level of information and resulting trading strategies. In this study, the focus is not on the trading motives but on the level of information of traders and their corresponding trading strategies.

---

121 See Harris (2003), pp. 222-243.

122 Bagheot (1971), p. 12 states: "Every time one investor benefits from a trade, after all, another loses."

123 In contrast to informational frictions, real frictions hinder all traders alike. See Stoll (2000), p. 1483.

124 See Hasbrouck/Schwartz (1988), p. 11 or Schwartz/Whitcomb (1988), p. 48.

125 See Harris (1990), p. 6f. Harris (1998), p. 3 finds evidence for uninformed traders acting as pre-committed traders when spreads are wide and the time frame until trading ends is still distant.

126 Admati/Pfleiderer (1991) provide a detailed theoretical analysis of sunshine trading, i.e. its effects on liquidity, volatility, and trader profits in a market with information asymmetry. Sunshine trading changes the nature of information asymmetry in the market, as sunshine traders, who can convince the other market participants that they are uninformed, receive better prices. However, uninformed traders that are not able to signal their status credibly are worse off as their costs increase.

Trader type	Motives	Information level	Trading strategy
Utilitarian traders	•Investors & borrowers •Hedgers, gamblers •Asset exchangers •…	**Uninformed traders**	**Market orders and limit orders (pre-committed traders)**
Futile traders	•Pseudo-informed traders		
Profit-motivated traders	•Value traders, news traders	**Informed traders**	**Market orders (and limit orders ?)**
	•*Dealers (market makers, specialists)**	*Uninformed traders*	*Limit orders (passive traders)*

* As Xetra provides a pure order driven market structure dealers are not relevant for the analysis.

Exhibit 4-1: Trader types and information level[127]

Utilitarian traders implement both market and limit orders, either implementing active trading strategies or acting as pre-committed traders. Futile traders that also belong to the group of uninformed traders act similarly.

Profit-motivated traders include dealers or market makers and value or news traders. Dealers want to profit from liquidity provision itself by implementing limit orders only (passive liquidity providers). As Xetra does not foresee any designated liquidity provision for trading in the DAX instruments, dealers are excluded from the discussion in this study. Value or news traders are informed traders. Their choice of trading strategy is the central research objective of this study: The question of whether they follow a pure active trading strategy based on market orders only or also choose to implement limit orders will be analyzed in the empirical part of this study.

In the literature, traders are often distinguished as individual or institutional traders based on the pure size of their transactions and the level of information gathered before trading. Large transactions and comprehensive research are usually attributed to institutional traders.[128] As an institutional trader can trade for several reasons, being either informed or uninformed, there is no link between this criterion and the level of information. Consequently, a distinction along these lines is not directly suitable for an analysis of informed trading behavior.

---

127 The trader types and motives follow Harris (2003), p. 199.

128 See Oesterhelweg (1998), p. 10. Dennis/Weston (2001), p. 1 explain that institutions are more likely to be informed than private investors as they generate an informational predominance through economies of scale in information processing and acquisition.

4.3 Measurement Methods

The preceding chapter showed that traders can be distinguished according to their trading motives and corresponding level of information. As informed traders do anything to disguise themselves, this chapter covers the most commonly applied measures of informed trading. Following the objective of this study, a method has to be chosen that allows the calculation of informed trading for the individual instruments but also for each individual transaction: The calculation ability on the instrument level is required to determine whether trading in Xetra's market structure evolves in a manner comparable to other markets based on cross-sectional results. The calculation on the basis of the individual transaction will allow the consolidation of the results for each individual trader and thus enable the identification of the level of information of an individual trader.

The data set implemented in the empirical part is described in detail in Chapter 6.2. The data include for the DAX instruments time-stamped information for all executed orders (trade and order information), including the responsible trader ID. Additionally, the data set includes the time-stamped BB and BA for each instrument as well as intraday data for the XLM for all size classes eligible for DAX instruments. For the choice of a measurement method, the following restriction has to be taken into account: There is no information available that would allow rebuilding the order book, i.e. no order entries and deletions of orders that did not execute.

There are different measures that allow identifying informed trading or adverse selection risk in an instrument or market. The most popular measures are presented in the following:

(1) spread decomposition models,

(2) structural models,

(3) ad hoc method.

Their common message based on the information paradigm is that liquidity (spreads) and informed trading are negatively (positively) related.

4.3.1 Spread Decomposition Models

The existence of the spread was first recognized by Demsetz (1968), who posited that trading has a time component. In that sense, the bid-ask spread is the price for the immediate execution service of the market maker and reflects an order processing cost.[129] Generalization of the order processing cost model has followed two different approaches, inventory models or information models.[130]

Inventory models focus on the costs that are incurred by order flow imbalances, as the market maker has to deviate from his optimum inventory to fulfill trading needs. Inventory models

---

[129] See Demsetz (1968), p. 35ff. He demonstrates that the bid-ask spread is the result of two equilibrium prices for buys and sells respectively.

[130] See Copeland/Galai (1983), p. 1457f. Hasbrouck (1988), p. 229 states that the inventory and the information paradigm are not competing, but both effects can be seen in practice. He models the simultaneous existence of both effects.

suggest that the bid-ask spread is positively related to the price and risk of the security and negatively related to trading volume and number of responsible market makers.[131]

Information models are based on the assumption of information asymmetry between traders. The dealer faces either uninformed liquidity-motivated traders or informed profit-motivated traders. The dealer expects to gain profits from trading with the uninformed traders by realizing the bid-ask spread. On the other hand, he expects to lose from trades with informed traders.[132]

Finally, three components of the bid-ask spread are identified in the literature: inventory costs, transaction costs, and adverse selection costs.[133] The inventory holding cost pays for the risk of price changes to unwanted inventory, the order processing cost reimburses immediacy services, and the adverse-selection cost compensates for losses incurred by trading with informed traders.

Inventory holding costs should not play a role in open limit order books, as there are no designated market makers that have to provide liquidity any time leading to unwanted inventory.[134] Consequently, spread decomposition models that explicitly model this component would not be suitable for the analysis of an open limit order book.

Spread decomposition models aim at identifying the different components. To estimate the adverse selection component, they build on the distinction of transitory and permanent price changes: Transitory price changes result from the trading activity of impatient uninformed traders, while permanent price changes are the response to informed traders that incorporate their information about changes to the underlying fundamental value. Generally these methods can be distinguished into two categories: (i) variance decomposition procedures (price reversal)[135] and (ii) trade indicator models.[136]

Price reversals are caused by traders' buying and selling activity. The most common is the bid-ask bounce when impatient traders buy and sell at the available BBA. These price changes reverse when an impatient trader on the opposite side of the market enters an order. The bid-ask bounce is reflected in the transaction cost component of the spread. Transitory price

---

131 While Demsetz (1968) and Tinic (1972) argued that the spread exists due to immediacy services, Stoll (1978) and Amihud/Mendelson (1980) formally modeled this component.

132 Based upon results provided by Bagheot (1971), Copeland/Galai (1983), Glosten/Milgrom (1985), and Easley/O'Hara (1987) provided theoretical models, while Glosten/Harris (1988) presented the first empirical analysis. Copeland/Galai (1983), p. 1459f. define the optimum spread of the market maker as a trade-off between reducing the costs of adverse selection when widening the spread and losing profitable trading opportunities with uninformed traders accordingly. Glosten/Milgrom (1985), p. 72 demonstrate that a spread exists even if the market makers' fixed and variable costs are zero and competition ensures that his profits are also zero. Easley/O'Hara (1987), p. 88f. include trade size as a signal for adverse selection in their model.

133 See Stoll (1978), p. 1153, Glosten/Milgrom (1985), p. 72, and Hasbrouck (1988), p. 230.

134 See Stoll (1989), p. 118f. Stoll (1989), p. 129 finds that the inventory holding cost is only 10% of the spread, although he analyzes a market with a specialist (NYSE). De Winne/Majois (2004) compare different spread decomposition models for Euronext and discuss problems arising from implementing models that explicitly compute an inventory component. They find that these models do not provide consistent results for the order-driven market structure of Euronext.

135 See Roll (1984), Stoll (1989), and George/Kaul/Nimalendran (1991).

136 See Glosten/Harris (1988), Lin/Sanger/Booth (1995), Huang/Stoll (1997), Madhavan/Richardson/Roomans (1997).

changes are indicated by negative serial correlation as price changes revert. Roll (1984) developed the initial framework for this model category.[137]

Trade indicator models compute spread components by regressing price changes on a trade indicator variable. Glosten/Harris (1988) present a model based on transaction prices and quote information and estimate the order processing and adverse selection components. They assume that the different spread components are a linear function of the trade size, and their model produces best estimates when the order processing cost is constant and the adverse selection cost increases with order size. This is in contrast to the variance decomposition procedures that assume a constant spread.[138]

Hasbrouck (1988) introduces vector autoregression (VAR) models to determine the different spread components starting a series of papers: Initially he computes the unexpected component of the trade (trade innovation) based on past trade series. Later he includes series of quote revisions and non-linear trade functions and extends his framework to a multi-market setting to estimate the contributions to price discovery of competing market places.[139]

Although designed initially for quote-driven or hybrid market structures, spread decomposition models have been successfully applied to order-driven market structures.[140] Brockman/Chung (1999) were the first to implement spread decomposition models to a market structure where liquidity is provided by limit orders only.[141] Spread decomposition models have also been applied successfully to the German equity market.[142]

---

137 Roll (1984), p. 1127 provides a model based on serial covariance of transaction prices. He presents a procedure that allows inferring the effective spread directly from a series of transaction prices. The model by Stoll (1989), pp. 116-123 introduces the concept of the realized spread, defined as the difference between the price at which a market maker buys at one point in time and the price at which he sells at a later point in time. Based on the covariance of the price change and the quote change, the realized spread is estimated as a fraction of the quoted spread of the market maker. George/Kaul/Nimalendran (1991), p. 628 and p. 635f. demonstrate that Roll (1984) and Stoll (1989) provide results that reveal a downward bias as they exclude any time variation in returns. Accordingly, they provide a spread decomposition method that includes time variation.

138 See Glosten/Harris (1988), p. 128. Lin/Sanger/Booth (1995) also provide a two-way decomposition. Huang/Stoll (1997) develop a three-way and a two-way decomposition model.

139 See Hasbrouck (1988, 1991a, 1991b, 1993, and 1995)

140 Van Ness/Van Ness/Warr (2001b), p. 3 demonstrate that the adverse selection component of the spread depends on the market structure of an exchange. Chung/Van Ness/Van Ness (2004), 269f. argue that - in line with their results on the proportions of limit orders that do not reflect a participation of the specialist (1999) - spread decomposition results for the bid-ask spread that include limit orders should be interpreted with care.

141 Brockman/Chung (1999), p. 235ff. find for a sample of 345 instruments traded at the Stock Exchange of Hong Kong (SEHK) that approx. 32% of the spread are due to adverse selection. They implement the model developed by Lin/Sanger/Booth (1995), which decomposes the spread into two components, the adverse selection component and order processing costs.

142 Iversen (1994) analyzes average spreads of DAX instruments in IBIS and on the floor for data in 1991. Treske (1996) investigates spread components in DAX instruments in IBIS. The adverse selection component is on average 22%, while small DAX companies reveal a component as high as two thirds of the spread. Wolff (2003) analyzes the spread components in Xetra comparing results for two different trading segments.

While popular among researchers[143], spread decomposition models reveal several critical points: firstly, they only take into account the costs for orders that are executed at the spread. However, for large orders that execute several limits in the order book, they do not provide an appropriate indication of adverse selection. When choosing the liquidity measure in the previous chapter, multi-dimensional measures that take into account order book depth beyond the BBA are strictly preferred over one-dimensional measures. Secondly, the different models find a broad range of results for adverse selection[144] and some of them reveal implausible results.[145] Finally, they compute average estimates for markets or instruments. Thus they do not provide a solution to measure informed trading for individual traders, which is the eliminating criterion. Accordingly, spread decomposition measures will not be implemented in this study.

4.3.2 Structural Models

One of the most popular structural models for a market with a market maker or specialist was developed by Easley/Kiefer/O'Hara/Paperman (1996), often referred to as EKOP.[146] In contrast to spread decomposition models, they do not infer informed trading from price changes but from buy and sell side imbalances, upon which the market maker forms his beliefs about the probability of informed trading (PINF).

The model assumes that prior to the beginning of each trading day nature selects whether an information event will occur (α) or not ($1-\alpha$). The information will be a bad (good) news event with entry probability δ ($1-\delta$). Uninformed traders arrive each day with probability ε. Informed traders only arrive on days with information events at the rate μ. Assuming independence across days, which is consistent with an informational efficient market, a direct estimate of α, δ, ε and μ is obtained, using a maximum likelihood function. Then, $PINF = \alpha\mu/(\alpha\mu+2\varepsilon)$. The formula reveals that the level of informed trading depends not only on the information environment (α and δ) but on the trading environment (ε and μ). The data input required for the maximum likelihood function is the number of buyer and seller initiated trades per trading day.[147]

---

[143] Daníelsson/Payne (2001), p. 1 explain the popularity of spread decomposition models due to the fact that the existing literature on the inventory and asymmetric information paradigm clearly defines the components of the spread and that most databases did not provide any information concerning the depth in the order book.

[144] The results vary between 8% and 40%: George/Kaul/Nimalendran (1991), 8-13%, Lin/Sanger/Booth (1995), approx. 35%, Huang/Stoll (1997), approx. 10%, Madhavan/Richardson/Roomans (1997), up to 40% and Glosten/Harris (1988), 25-40%.

[145] Clarke/Shastri (2000) analyze the models provided by Madhavan/Richardson/Roomans (1997) and Huang/Stoll (1997), concluding that the former yields implausible estimates 14% of the time and the latter about 60% of the time. Van Ness/Van Ness/Warr (2001a) support the analysis of Clarke/Shastri (2000), as they find implausible estimates for Madhavan/Richardson/Roomans (1997) 18% of the time and 50% for Huang/Stoll (1997). However, the Glosten/Harris (1988) model shows 0% implausible estimates and the Lin/Sanger/Booth (1995) model reveals implausible estimates only 0.5% of the time.

[146] The initial model as well as extensions have been implemented for different topics and markets by Easley/Kiefer/O'Hara (1996, 1997a and 1997b), Easley/O'Hara/Paperman (1998), Brockman/Chung (2000), Grammig/Schiereck/Theissen (2000 and 2001), Dennis/Weston (2001), Easley/Engle/ O'Hara/ Wu (2001), Easley/Hvidkjaer/O'Hara (2002 and 2004), Hanousek/Podpiera (2002), Heidle/Huang (2002), Chung/Li (2003), Jain/Jiang/McInish/Taechapiroontong (2003), Chung/Li/McInish (2005), Venter/De Jong (2004), Lei/Wu (2005), Brown/Hillegeist (2006), and Goldstein/Van Ness/Van Ness (2006).

[147] See Easley/Kiefer/O'Hara/Paperman (1996), pp. 1408-1415.

Although initially developed for market maker or specialist markets, the EKOP has been successfully implemented for order books.[148] The available data would allow calculating the PINF on the instrument level. While ε and μ could be obtained from intraday data, α and δ require multiple trading days to compute results.[149] Consequently, the model does not allow the determination of the level of information that each transaction entails. As with the spread decomposition models, this is an eliminating criterion.

The structural model provided by Glosten (1994) was the first model developed for a limit order book. He models a market with two types of traders: patient traders that provide liquidity with limit orders and impatient traders that demand liquidity through market orders. Traders that have private information use market orders only. The profitability of a limit order depends on its execution probability and the value of the asset. The execution probability of a buy order increases with its limit price (price priority), resulting in an increasing price schedule for buy limit orders and a decreasing price schedule for sell limit orders. The fundamental value of the asset depends on all publicly available information and changes when new information arrives. The next period's value is described as its initial value, a random innovation, and the expected change. A market order by a trader that knows the random innovation is informed and accordingly leads to a price impact (measured as adverse selection component). Liquidity providers incur an order processing cost and know the distribution of market order sizes and the adverse selection component; however, they do not know the value of the asset. They choose their limit prices to maximize their profits and accordingly determine their break-even conditions. Therefore, for each marginal bid and sell limit price, a break-even condition is computed. That is when profits from trading with uninformed traders are equal to losses from trading with informed traders. Combining these break-even conditions with moment conditions that reflect the market order distribution, the adverse selection cost can be estimated. To estimate the moment conditions, the different limits in the order book are required.

Sandas (2001) implements the model of Glosten (1994) but introduces discrete prices and time priority in precedence rules. His analysis of the Swedish Stock Exchange does not generate plausible results: transaction cost results are negative, while order book depth is overvalued.[150] Frey/Grammig (2006) apply a further adjusted version of the Glosten/Sandas type model and successfully estimate it for the DAX instruments in the Xetra trading environment.

The estimation procedure requires rebuilding the order book. As described in the introduction to this chapter, the data set does not allow rebuilding the order book. Thus the structural

---

[148] See, among others, Brockman/Chung (2000), Grammig/Schiereck/Theissen (2000) and (2001), Hachmeister/Schiereck (2006), and Ma/Hsieh/Chen (2001).

[149] Recent critics voiced by Boehmer/Grammig/Theissen (2007) based on trade misclassification due to implementing trade classification algorithms do not play a role in automated order-driven markets: Trades can only take place at the posted bid and ask prices, as per definition price improvement is not possible. The trade initiator of any trade can be identified through the available order entry and execution timestamps for all orders involved in the trade.

[150] See Sandas (2001), p. 721ff.

model cannot be estimated with the available data, which is an eliminating criterion. It will not be implemented in the empirical part of this study.

4.3.3 Ad hoc Method

The ad hoc method is a model free method that compares the execution price of a market order to a benchmark. This benchmark is the midpoint of the quoted spread in quote-driven markets or the midpoint of the BBA in order-driven markets.[151]

To calculate the effective spread (ES), the execution price is compared to the midpoint prevailing the order execution. For a buy (sell) order, it is the (negative) difference of the execution price and the corresponding midpoint. As such, it computes the real execution costs of an order.

Initially, the ES was calculated as trades often occurred inside quoted spreads. In that case, the quoted spread overestimated the execution costs. In open electronic limit order books, the trading algorithm foresees executions only at the BB or BA. Still, the effective spread needs to be calculated, as orders that require a larger quantity than provided at the BBA are allowed to walk up or down the book. In that case, the BBA underestimates the execution costs and the effective spread is larger than the BBA.

The realized spread (RS) is calculated similarly to the ES, but implementing a post-trade midpoint. The RS measures the difference between the execution price of an order and the estimated value after the trade. It determines the profits of liquidity provision net of adverse selection costs as it assumes that any information is absorbed by the market in the defined time period. As such, it reflects the temporary or non-informational impact of a trade.[152] While different time frames have been applied in research, the most common for the post-trade midpoint is five minutes.[153] This follows rule 11Ac1-5 ("Disclosure of Order Execution Information") by the Securities Exchange Commission (SEC), which foresees monthly reporting of trade execution costs by market centers based on the midpoint five minutes after the trade is implemented.[154]

The difference between the ES and the RS is the liquidity provider's loss to informed traders, referred to as price impact (PI). When informed traders trade, prices rise after they buy and fall after they sell. Consequently, the RS of informed traders is comparably smaller than their ES and the difference is larger. This difference reveals their successful speculation on their

---

151 See Huang/Stoll (1996b), p. 12f. Perold (1988), p. 5f. calculates the so-called implementation shortfall, where the relevant midpoint to be implemented is the midpoint at the time of the order entry decision and not the order entry itself. However, exchange databases do not include the time of the decision but the time of order entry. In a fully automated electronic trading system that allows order entry with no technical delays, the order entry timestamp can reflect the time of their decision. In that case, the results of the implementation shortfall and the effective spread would be similar.

152 See Huang/Stoll (1996b), p. 14 or Bessembinder (1999), p. 395.

153 Bessembinder (1999) and (2003b) implement a thirty-minute time frame, while Bessembinder (2003a) chooses a ten-minute difference. Huang/Stoll (1996b), pp. 22-27 implement five- and thirty-minute differences and find that thirty-minute price reversals are only slightly larger than price reversals calculated based upon the five-minute difference.

154 See www.sec.gov/rules/final/34-43590.htm. The rule became effective on 30 January 2001. To ensure comparability of results, especially to the US equity markets, this study follows the SEC rule.

information. Thus, the larger the PI the more informed the trader that entered the order. This is the key concept for the identification of informed traders, as the PI per trader reveals his absolute performance as well as his relative performance when comparing his PI result to the other traders' PI results, allowing identifying traders that are more informed than other traders. The three spread measures can either be implemented as round-trip or half-spread measures.[155] In addition, to ensure comparability across instruments, they can be computed as relative measures when divided by the corresponding midpoint at time t.

With this measurement method, the costs of an individual trade can be computed based on trade and BBA data and depending on the aggregation level chosen displayed as informed trading on the trader, instrument, or market level.[156] It has been frequently applied to different market structures[157] and is a standard reporting requirement by the SEC for US exchanges. Any issues in implementing the ad hoc method reported in US markets are not relevant for the Xetra trading environment.[158]

The ad hoc method fulfills the requirement for the calculation ability on the transaction level and can be estimated with the available data set. Consequently, it is the adequate measure for calculating informed trading in this study. It will be implemented in the empirical part of the study. Its data requirements and calculation procedure are described in detail in Chapter 7.2.1.

4.4 Synopsis

As presented in the introduction to this chapter, the choice of method for identifying informed trading follows (i) the need to identify the level of information for each transaction and (ii) data restrictions; i.e. there is no possibility to rebuild the order book. With the exception of the Glosten/Sandas type structural model, the presented information measures were initially designed to cater quote-driven or hybrid markets. However, they were successfully implemented to order-driven environments and specifically to the Xetra trading environment.[159]

When selecting an adequate measure to be implemented in this study, the spread decomposition measures as well as the structural model developed by Easley/Kiefer/O'Hara/Paperman (1996) are excluded, as they do not provide estimates at the transaction level (i). The structural model based on Glosten (1994) is excluded, as its data requirements exceed the available data set (ii).

---

155 While the round-trip measure calculates the result for a combined buy and sell order, the half-spread computes either the buy or sell order. The round-trip measure can be computed by multiplying half-spread results with two.

156 See Bessembinder (1999), p. 393.

157 Huang/Stoll (1996a, 1996b), Bessembinder (1999, 2003a, 2003b), Weston (2000), SEC (2001), Theissen (2002), Handa/Schwartz/Tiwari (2004), Boehmer (2005), Frey/Grammig (2006).

158 Bessembinder (2003b) discusses the issues for assessing trade execution costs for the US equity exchanges. The described issues, i.e. the estimation of trade direction or the general delay for quoted spreads, are not relevant for the Xetra trading systems. See Chapters 6.2.2 and 6.2.3.

159 Spread decomposition models were implemented by Wolff (2003), the structural models by Grammig/Schiereck/Theissen (2000 and 2001), Hachmeister/Schiereck (2006), and Frey/Grammig (2006), and the ad hoc method also by Frey/Grammig (2006).

The ad hoc method fulfills both conditions: Based on transaction and BBA data, it allows calculation of the level of information for each individual transaction. Consequently, it enables one to determine the level of information on the instrument as well as the trader level, depending on the aggregation standard chosen. Thus, it is the only measure of informed trading that enables both perspectives. It is not based on a specific theoretical model, but its choice can be further qualified. Frey/Grammig (2006) investigate whether their results from the adjusted structural Glosten (1994) model and the ad hoc method point in the same direction. They find cross-sectional correlation of the results of both methods of 0.95 significant at the 0.001 level. They conclude that on the one hand, this supports the robustness of the results of the structural model, while on the other hand, it provides a theoretical reasoning for implementing the model-free ad hoc method.[160]

The ad hoc method is calculated as the round-trip costs of any trade (effective spread), including the corresponding level of information (price impact). Its construction is thus comparable to the XLM (chosen measure for determining liquidity), the main difference being that it is not based on hypothetical (ex-ante) but on executed orders (ex-post). While the ad hoc method allows the determination of the level of information of the trader, a comparison of its outcome with the results for the XLM will reveal the trader's execution skills: If ex-post execution costs are lower than on average available ex-ante liquidity, the trader entered his order when liquidity was unusually high, revealing discretionary behavior.

Chapters 3 and 4 have provided definitions of liquidity and informed trading and selected the adequate methods for measuring both in this study. Both will be implemented in answering the question of whether trading in the open electronic limit order book Xetra is fairly normal - research objective (i). In addition, the ad hoc method will be implemented to answer whether and how informed traders can be identified - research objective (ii).

The next chapter will provide the theoretical and empirical framework, determining the research hypotheses tested in the empirical analysis.

---

160 See Frey/Grammig (2006), p. 1028. Chung/Li (2003), pp. 266-270 demonstrate that the adverse selection component of the spread estimated based on Glosten/Harris (1988) and Lin/Sanger/Booth (1995) and the results for PINF reveal a significant positive relation. Barclay/Hendershott/McCormick (2003) implement the Hasbrouck (1991a, 1991b) VAR method and the ad hoc method, with both results pointing in the same direction. Chung/Li/McInish (2005), p. 1667 analyze the PINF and Hasbrouck (1991a, 1991b) VAR model and find that results are comparable.

5 Informed Trading and Liquidity

The objective of this chapter is to develop the underlying research hypotheses for the second part of this study. Based on the existing theoretical, empirical, and experimental literature, testable hypotheses are developed to answer the questions (research objectives) as outlined in Chapter 1.2.

To provide the reference point for the interpretation of the results of the different trader categories and to determine whether the open electronic limit order book Xetra is comparable to other limit order books - research objective (i) - standard hypotheses on liquidity and informed trading in order-driven market structures are presented. Further, to provide evidence on whether informed traders do provide liquidity - research objective (iii) - hypotheses on the choice of market versus limit orders by informed traders are derived.[161]

The literature review presented in this chapter follows these research questions and can be distinguished into two parts. The first part covers the literature where informed traders implement market orders only acting as liquidity demanders deriving hypotheses sets for liquidity and informed trading in general. The second part focuses on the literature where informed traders' order type choice is endogenous and they are allowed to act as both liquidity demanders and liquidity providers, resulting in hypotheses sets that cover their liquidity demand and supply behavior as well as their general role.

The focus is on the literature for order-driven market structures. However, most of the initial literature was developed for quote-driven or hybrid market structures, and where suitable it will be presented additionally.[162]

5.1 Informed Liquidity Demand

This chapter derives the hypotheses for providing the reference point and determining if the anonymous open electronic limit order book Xetra reveals standard behavior of trading determinants and is comparable to other limit order books. The literature on informed liquidity demand is based on the information paradigm as introduced by Bagheot (1971). The theoretical literature on limit order books is relatively thin. However, as the role of limit order

---

161 The chapter does not provide any hypotheses for research objective (ii), the question of how informed traders can be identified. To give answers to this objective, the adequate measurement method was identified in Chapter 4. Its empirical implementation is presented in Chapter 8.

162 For a quote-driven market structure, theoretical models are provided by Copeland/Galai (1983) and Glosten/Milgrom (1985). Copeland/Galai (1983) formally analyze the trade-off of profits when trading with uninformed traders and the losses due to trading with informed traders. Glosten/Milgrom (1985) develop a model where the market maker is the sole provider of liquidity and quotes a bid-ask spread upon which one agent in each round can either submit a market buy or sell order. The informed trader's optimal order placement foresees that he enters a buy market order when his assumed value of the instrument is above the posted ask and a sell market order if his assumed value is below the posted bid. In any other case, the informed trader does not enter an order. Both Copeland/Galai (1983) and Glosten/Milgrom (1985) ignore the depth dimension of liquidity as they assume one unit size for all trades. Kyle (1985) provides a dynamic model with uninformed traders, one informed trader, and several market makers. As the informed trader does not face any competition, he gradually resolves his informational advantage. In contrast, Holden/Subrahmanyam (1992) introduce competitive informed traders, resulting in an aggressive trading strategy.

books has grown rapidly since the 1990s and high frequency data of electronic trading platforms is available, the empirical literature is broad.

5.1.1 Theoretical Work

The initial theoretical contribution for informed trading in order-driven market structures was made by Glosten (1994). See Chapter 4.3.2. He proves that adverse selection creates spreads also in this market structure, supporting the general notion of an inverse relation of liquidity and informed trading.[163] Due to the adverse selection risk, trading costs increase with order size; i.e. it is more costly to buy a large number of shares compared to a small number of shares.[164] As large orders are more likely to come from informed traders, the limit sell curve slopes upward and the limit buy curve downward; i.e. with increasing size of a buy order, the ask price (sell curve) increases, while with an increasing sell order the bid price (buy curve) decreases. As a consequence, order book depth and bid-ask spreads are a function of informed trading.[165] Glosten states that anonymity is key to his results as in contrast floor mechanisms would allow the identification of informed traders and consequently enable punishment in the form of discrimination.

Seppi (1997) provides a similar microstructure model for a specialist market, where the specialist competes with a limit order book. In his model, a hybrid market structure will cater the needs of small or large orders best while medium size orders are best executed in the open limit order book. Thus, competing market structures serve different types of investors preferring different order sizes.[166]

When deriving hypotheses for the liquidity in the DAX instruments, it should be noted that the XLM, the liquidity measure chosen in Chapter 3.2.2, reflects liquidity costs, and as such measures the inverse of liquidity. Based upon Glosten (1994), the following testable hypotheses are derived:

- *Liquidity (XLM) and informed trading are negatively (positively) related.*
- *Liquidity (XLM) is negatively (positively) related to order size; i.e. the XLM is an increasing function.*

In contrast to Glosten (1994) and Seppi (1997), where order type choice for both informed and uninformed traders is exogenous to the model, a separate branch in the literature endogenizes the decision between market orders and limit orders for uninformed traders. At the same time, the models either still assume that informed traders only implement market orders, i.e. order choice is exogenous to the model or they abstract from information asymmetry.

---

163 See Glosten (1994), p. 1139ff. (proposition 3).
164 See Glosten (1994), p. 1129.
165 Similar results are found by Chakravarty/Holden (1995), p. 216 and Daníelsson/Payne (2001), p. 5.
166 See Seppi (1997), p. 103. Parlour/Seppi (2003) analyze competition between a hybrid market structure and a pure order-driven market structure. They implement the limit order model of Seppi (1997) and model the economics of liquidity supply and demand.

Handa/Schwartz (1996b) model order type choice depending on the probability of informed trading. Transitory volatility[167] attracts limit orders as the gains from providing liquidity exceed the potential losses from trading with informed traders, while increased volatility due to informed trading (permanent volatility) decreases the possibility of limit orders. Therefore, volatility that is induced through informed trading is negatively related to liquidity.[168]

Parlour (1998) presents a dynamic model with symmetric information where order type choice is endogenously determined through the state of the limit order book. The general trade-off that traders face in this model is between the cost of market orders (price risk) and the execution risk of limit orders. Traders choose between immediate execution with a market order, delayed execution with a limit order, or no execution if they decide not to post any order. She finds that a trader that arrives at the market takes into account both sides of the order book when deciding upon the order type to implement.[169]

Following Parlour (1998), Foucault/Kadan/Kandel (2005) build a model with symmetric information based upon the initial idea of Demsetz (1968) of the trade-off between cost of delayed execution (execution risk) and the cost of immediacy (spread as price risk).[170] The key factors of the dynamics in the limit order book are the distribution of patient and impatient traders and the order arrival rate. Markets with a high (low) rate of patient traders and a low (high) arrival rate of orders are resilient (not resilient). Concerning intraday behavior, they assume that to the end of the trading day more traders become impatient, in turn increasing the order arrival of market orders and increasing spreads.[171]

Foucault (1999) also presents a dynamic model of market order and limit order placement strategies, allowing for divergences in valuation of the underlying asset based on public information. This introduces a winner's curse problem, for limit order traders as an order can become mispriced, which in turn increases its execution probability.[172] There are several predictions regarding volatility and order submission strategies: With increasing volatility, the proportion of limit orders increases. As limit order traders implement less aggressive limit prices to compensate for the increased risk of being picked off, market orders become more costly and more traders prefer limit orders. However, spreads also increase as traders post less aggressive limit prices. Consequently, limit order strategies are more often implemented when volatility is high while limit prices are less aggressive, which increases the spread in the market. Thus, volatility and spreads (liquidity) are positively (negatively) related.[173] In contrast to Handa/Schwartz (1996b), Foucault (1999) assumes that both transitory and permanent volatility are a direct determinant of order type choice and both yield the same result.

---

167 For an explanation of transitory and permanent volatility, see Footnote 68 in Chapter 3.1.

168 See Handa/Schwartz (1996b), p. 1860. See also Handa/Schwartz/Tiwari (1998), who describe order-driven market structures as ecological systems and Handa/Schwartz/Tiwari (2003), who provide evidence in accordance with Handa/Schwartz (1996b) for the CAC40 instruments at Paris Bourse.

169 See Parlour (1998), p. 793.

170 See Foucault/Kadan/Kandel (2005), p. 1172.

171 See Foucault/Kadan/Kandel (2005), p. 1197f.

172 See Foucault (1999), p. 105 and p. 110f. Winner's curse means that a buy (sell) limit order of an uninformed trader is executed because its limit price is too high (too low).

173 See Foucault (1999), p. 112 and p. 116 (corollary 2).

5.1.2 Empirical Work

As presented in Chapter 3.2, liquidity in an order-driven market can be displayed as a liquidity function based upon order book information (limits and corresponding quantities) beyond the BBA. Based on Glosten (1994), the initial hypothesis for liquidity is that it is negatively related to order size. This hypothesis can be detailed further.

Griese/Kempf (2006) demonstrate theoretically that the optimal trading strategies when splitting orders over a defined time period depend on the shape of the price impact function (liquidity function): While a linear price impact function supports equal splitting, concave (convex) functions support earlier (later) trading. Empirically they find that for the German equity market linear price impact functions have to be rejected.[174] Accordingly, the above hypothesis is refined:

- *Liquidity (XLM) is negatively (positively) related to order size, which is reflected in a monotone but non-linear increasing function of the XLM.*

In contrast to quote-driven and hybrid market structures where market makers or specialists stand ready to provide liquidity on both sides of the order book, in order- driven limit order books liquidity providers are not obliged to enter limit orders on both sides of the order book. Ahn/Bae/Chan (2001) find for the Stock Exchange of Hong Kong (SEHK) that bid and ask side volatility of the order book lead to different order submission strategies. This is consistent with limit order traders only providing liquidity to one side of the market. Accordingly, limit order books attract heterogeneous traders. Irvine/Benston/Kandel (2000) report for the Toronto Stock Exchange (order-driven market structure) a higher depth on the ask side. Chordia/Roll/Subrahmanyam (2002) analyze NYSE (hybrid market structure) and also discover an order imbalance with more market buy than sell orders, which implies higher depth on the ask side of the order book.[175] In contrast, Gomber/Schweickert/Theissen (2005) select the twelve most liquid instruments traded in Xetra and do not find significant differences between the buy and the sell side of the limit order book up to a hypothetical order size of 1 m €.[176] Kempf/Mayston (2005) find when analyzing commonality[177] in the order

---

174 See Griese/Kempf (2006), p. 403. For DAX instruments, they find that approx. half of the instruments reveal a convex function while the other half show a concave function. See p. 413.

175 See Ahn/Bae/Chan (2001), p. 782, Irvine/Benston/Kandel (2000), p. 22f. and Chordia/Roll/ Subrahmanyam (2002), p. 117. See also Beltran/Giot/Grammig (2005), p. 15 and Daníelsson/Payne (2001), p. 4, who find that depth for the buy and sell side depth are uncorrelated, i.e. liquidity suppliers enter limit orders only on one side of the market.

176 See Gomber/Schweickert/Theissen (2005), p. 10.

177 The presented theoretical and empirical literature focused on firm-specific determinants of liquidity. A unique research arm on commonality in liquidity has evolved. Commonality means a common variation or co-variation of liquidity across instruments, i.e. a systematic component of liquidity. The intuition for a liquidity risk factor is that other firm-specific attributes (risk and return) are influenced by systematic factors. Chordia/Roll/Subrahmanyam (2000), Hasbrouck/Seppi (2001), and Huberman/Halka (2001) analyze commonality in a market with designated liquidity providers, while Brockman/Chung (2002) and Domowitz/Hansch/Wang (2005) analyze the issue in a pure order-driven environment. Generally, all authors find affirmative results for a systematic component in liquidity. Chordia/Sarkar/Subrahmanyam (2005a) even find liquidity co-movement across asset classes (equities and bonds) and (2005b) analyze commonality across small and large firms.

book that both sides of the order book (bid and ask) reveal similar patterns, while the commonality effect is slightly stronger on the ask side.[178] As presented in Chapter 3.2.2, liquidity can be determined separately for both sides of the order book when implementing the XLM. The above results are mixed concerning differences between both sides of the order book and yield the following hypothesis:

- *Liquidity (XLM) on the buy and sell side of the order book does not systematically differ.*

Stoll (2000) argues that the cross-sectional relation between liquidity and trading characteristics as initially suggested by Demsetz (1968) is still a very strong empirical relation independent of market structure.[179] Demsetz (1968) originally suggests that a firm's trading characteristics provide a set of standard determinants of liquidity: trading volume and number of trades, volatility, firm size, and price. The rationale behind these determinants are order processing and inventory considerations. From an inventory perspective, trading activity measured by trading volume and number of trades should be positively related to liquidity, as an increase in trading activity allows the market maker to reduce his inventory risk, while volatility should have the opposite effect.[180] Along these lines, Tinic (1972) and Benston/Hagerman (1974) provide first empirical evidence for the positive relation for trading activity and liquidity and for a negative relation with volatility.[181]

In a world with asymmetric information, these relations still hold, although their rationale differs. Copeland/Galai (1983) provide a theoretical foundation for the negative relation between spreads and trading volume and the negative relation between spreads and volatility for a quote-driven market structure.[182] McInish/Wood (1992) analyze NYSE data and find that measures of trading activity (number of trades and trade size measured by number of shares per trade) are inversely related to the spread. Daníelsson/Payne (2001) prove that bid-ask spreads and volatility are positively related and depth decreases with increasing volatility. They confirm Foucault (1999) that increasing volatility increases the proportion of limit orders in the order flow but at the same time decreases the aggressiveness of limit order prices.[183]

Ahn/Bae/Chan (2001) investigate the relation of volatility and limit order submission in the SEHK. They find in line with Handa/Schwartz (1996b) that when transitory volatility increases, market depth also rises in turn, decreasing the transitory volatility; however, permanent volatility reveals the reverse result. Bae/Jang/Park (2003) analyze the choice of limit and market orders at NYSE. They find that transitory volatility increases limit order

---

178 See Kempf/Mayston (2005), p. 16. In this study, commonality will not be analyzed but the fact that Kempf/ Mayston (2005) find in line with existing empirical research for other hybrid and order-driven market structure commonality in Xetra (DAX instruments) is relevant for the first research question, if Xetra is comparable to other markets.

179 See Stoll (2000), p. 1480f.

180 See Demsetz (1968), p. 33ff.

181 See Tinic (1972), p. 81ff. and Benston/Hagerman (1974), p. 353 ff.

182 See Copeland/Galai (1983), p. 1464.

183 See Daníelsson/Payne (2001), p. 21f.

placement. However, the effect from informational volatility is unclear. They argue that some informed traders might implement limit orders and thus the net effect of an increase in informed volatility is indeterminate.[184] It is found by several authors that price reveals an inverse relationship to the spread.[185] The tick size defines the minimum available spread in an instrument. As Xetra foresees a minimum tick size of 0.01 € for all DAX instruments, a higher share price leads to a lower relative spread, inducing the negative relation of spread and price. Accordingly, the following hypothesis is defined:

- *Liquidity (XLM) is positively (negatively) related to trading volume and price but negatively (positively) related to volatility.*

Turning to the analysis of intraday patterns found in equity markets, Admati/Pfleiderer (1988) develop a theory where the behavior of strategic uninformed traders and informed traders results in the concentration of trading activities.[186] Any trader that has discretion over the timing of his trading needs will trade when his trading activity will have a minimal effect on market prices, i.e. when markets are most liquid.[187] Opening and closing of trading are both events where trading either before or after is not possible, which increases non-discretionary trading of uninformed traders. In turn, discretionary liquidity traders and informed traders will trade more heavily at these points. In addition, even for some discretionary traders, that do not rely on time of day, the end of the trading day determines their possibilities to trade as settlement periods schedule the delivery based on the trading day the transaction took place. This also explains the tendency for heavy trading towards the end of the trading day.[188]

As discussed earlier, volatility can be distinguished into transitory and permanent volatility. Both depend on trading activity, while the latter is induced by trading of informed traders. As informed traders reveal a concentration of their trading behavior, consequently, at these times volatility based on permanent price changes should be higher. This concentration based on discretionary trading behavior leads to specific trading patterns, i.e. the U-shaped distribution of trading of volume and volatility.

Admati/Pfleiderer (1988) support the empirical findings for equity markets, that trading volume is concentrated at the beginning and end of the trading day and that volatility reveals a similar pattern. Biais/Hillion/Spatt (1995) find a U-shaped pattern for trades and orders. Ahn/Bae/Chan (2001) demonstrate that volatility at SEHK follows a U-shaped intraday distribution.[189] For European exchanges, the morning trading of the US market increases

---

184 See Ahn/Bae/Chan (2001), p. 768f. and Bae/Jang/Park (2003), p. 535.

185 See, among others, Demsetz (1968), Tinic (1972), Benston/Hagerman (1974), Stoll (1978), and McInish/Wood (1992).

186 Admati/Pfleiderer (1988), p. 7ff. develop a basic model with one risk-neutral market maker and several informed and uninformed traders.

187 Admati/Pfleiderer (1988), p. 5. The authors use the term "thick market" instead of liquid market. As they refer to a market where trading activity has "little effect on prices", they refer to a liquid market, as defined in Chapter 3.1.

188 See Admati/Pfleiderer (1988), p. 34.

189 See Biais/Hillion/Spatt (1995), p. 1671f. and Ahn/Bae/Chan (2001), p. 773.

trading activity, due to market activities from the US, which could explain comparably larger trading volumes in the afternoon compared to the morning trading volume.[190]

The intraday variation in spreads (liquidity) can be explained through inventory and asymmetric information. Information based models foresee that liquidity providers (either market makers or limit order traders) widen their spreads in the presence of adverse selection risk. Information asymmetry is assumed strongest when the market opens, as overnight information is not yet incorporated into prices.

As described in Chapter 4.3.1, spread decomposition measures allow the identification of the different spread components. According to McInish/Wood (1992), spread components follow distinct intraday patterns: The transaction cost component is independent of the time of the day; i.e. it is constant. The adverse selection component is highest at the beginning of the trading day, and as information is gradually incorporated, it decreases until the end of the trading day.[191] The inventory component is small at the beginning and decreases until midday; however, it increases until the end of the trading day as the respective market maker does not want to hold inventory when trading ends. Combining these three elements yields a smile or U-shaped curve of the bid-ask spread.[192]

As in open limit order books without any designated liquidity provider, there is no inventory cost component, the smile distribution is softened, and it reflects a reverse J-shaped distribution. Therefore, it can be expected that spreads and informed trading reveal a similar pattern. McInish/Wood (1992) find a reverse J-shaped pattern for NYSE spreads and conclude that inventory is not a significant component of the spread.[193] Madhavan (1992) predicts that information asymmetry is gradually resolved through the trading day, i.e. spreads are highest when trading starts and smallest at the end of the trading day.[194] Foster/Viswanathan (1994) yield similar results. However, in their model it is competition between two informed traders that results in high volume, volatility, and spreads at the beginning of the trading day.[195] Nyholm (2002) presents for NYSE instruments a U-shaped pattern for spreads and a reverse J-shaped pattern for the level of informed trading.[196] Brockman/Chung (1998) find a U-shaped intraday pattern for the SEHK. They test several theoretical hypotheses for the intraday variation in liquidity and find that information asymmetry has the greatest explanatory power for the open electronic limit order book of the SEHK. As there are no designated market makers, the inventory management theory is rejected.[197]

---

190 See Beltran/Durée/Giot (2004), p. 13 and Ranaldo (2004), p. 56.

191 See Lin/Sanger/Booth (1995), pp. 1172-1176 and Madhavan/Richardson/Roomans (1997), p. 1055, who document that the adverse selection component of the spreads is highest at the start of trading and continuously declines throughout the trading day.

192 See McInish/Wood (1992), p. 759f.

193 McInish/Van Ness (2002) replicate the initial McInish/Wood (1992) study and find similar results. They implement spread measures to identify the intraday results for the different components of the spread.

194 See Madhavan (1992), p. 618f.

195 See Foster/Viswanathan (1994), p. 510f.

196 See Nyholm (2002), p. 497.

197 See Brockman/Chung (1998), p. 296f.

Giot/Grammig (2006) report for Xetra in 1999 that liquidity is lowest at the beginning of the trading day, increases during the next two trading hours, and remains constant until the end of the trading day - reflecting a reverse-J-shaped variation.[198] In contrast, Gomber/Schweickert/Theissen (2005) find a U-shaped pattern for DAX instruments in Xetra. However, their sample covers a time period when trading hours were extended until 8:00 pm and spreads increased only after the initial end of trading at 5:30 pm.

The above theoretical and empirical findings result in the following testable hypothesis:

- *Liquidity (XLM) is lowest (highest) at the beginning of the trading day, and increases (decreases) continuously while remaining stable at the end of the trading day; i.e. the XLM follows a reverse J-shaped pattern.*
- *Informed trading is highest at the beginning of the trading day and is gradually resolved through the trading day, revealing a reverse J-shaped pattern.*

In addition to the general theoretical notion of a negative relation between informed trading and liquidity brought forward by theories following the information paradigm, the literature on informed trading has developed theories and provided empirical evidence for informed trading in different contexts: The questions of which market structures are preferred by informed traders, what instruments are most affected by adverse selection risk, and what order sizes are frequently implemented are discussed in the following section.

Market design defines to what extent informed traders can exploit their private information and how this trading activity makes prices more informative. As discussed in Chapter 4.1, information is reflected in prices through trading by informed traders. These traders intend to trade profitably on their costly private information. If a market would fully reveal all informed traders, the price discovery process would go down as a consequence of the deteriorating profitability of collecting costly private information. On the other hand, if markets are fully anonymous, liquidity is reduced as uninformed traders reduce their liquidity provision. They do not want to lose to informed traders, which they are not able to identify in the anonymous set-up.[199]

In a specialist market, the specialist has the possibility to price discriminate traders previously acting on information. In contrast, in anonymous settings there is no possibility for market participants to identify informed traders, as trader IDs are not revealed. Informed traders prefer anonymous set-ups, as they do not want to announce their trading needs publicly and be identified as informed by other traders.[200] At the same time, uninformed liquidity traders do not have the possibility to signal their non-informational trading needs in the sense of sunshine trading[201] and prefer non-anonymous settings. Accordingly, informed trading is more pronounced in anonymous market structures. This rationale is in line with Glosten

---

198 See Giot/Grammig (2006), p. 879ff.
199 See Heidle/Huang (2002), p. 392.
200 See Glosten (1994), p. 1152f.
201 See Admati/Pfleiderer (1991), p. 444 and Chapter 4.2 for a description of sunshine trading.

(1994) and supported by empirical evidence.[202] As the Xetra trading system foresees pre-trade and post-trade anonymity, the following hypothesis will be tested:

- *Informed trading is significant in the anonymous open electronic limit order book (Xetra).*

For empirical results of the structural model developed by Easley/Kiefer/O'Hara/ Paperman (1996), see Chapter 4.3.2. These reveal, in addition to the general notion of a positive relation between probability of informed trading (PINF) and spreads, that PINF and firm size are positively related: Although high volume stocks reveal a higher probability for informational events and a higher arrival rate of informed traders, this is more than compensated by the even higher arrival rate of uninformed traders.[203] Empirical support for the role of firm size (measured by market capitalization and average trading volume) is found across quote-driven, hybrid, and order-driven market structures[204], leading to the following testable hypothesis:

- *Informed trading is negatively related to firm size, i.e. it is higher for smaller firms.*

Spread decomposition models posit that the adverse selection component of the spread increases with trade size, which is consistent with the results that informed traders prefer larger order sizes and larger orders induce a larger price impact.[205] Informed traders would implement large orders if they did not consider the price impact.[206] However, they are most likely to use medium size orders, as they wish to camouflage their trading motives.

Barclay/Warner (1993) explore whether trade size is distinct for informed traders, i.e. if they prefer certain sizes when trading. They assume that as informed traders try to hide their information, they prefer medium size orders often combined with order splitting strategies, which is labeled *stealth trading*.

---

202 Heidle/Huang (2002), p. 395 find that informed trading is more pronounced in the anonymous setting of NASDAQ compared to NYSE and AMEX. Barclay/Hendershott/McCormick (2003), p. 2653ff. demonstrate that informed trading is even higher in the anonymous trading environment of ECNs (electronic communication networks) than on NASDAQ. Grammig/Schiereck/Theissen (2001), pp. 388-401 analyze the German equity market. They compare floor and electronic trading system of FSE, concluding that informed trading is much higher in the electronic trading system IBIS. Theissen (2002), p. 48f. and (2003b), p. 24 also finds that adverse selection costs are higher in the anonymous electronic trading system compared to the non-anonymous floor trading system in Germany. Jain/Jiang/McInish/Taechapiroontong (2003), p. 32ff. find similar results for the LSE, where the anonymous SETS system and a non-anonymous dealer market are operated in parallel.

203 See Easley/Kiefer/O'Hara/Paperman (1996), pp. 1421-1428.

204 See Easley/Kiefer/O'Hara/Paperman (1996) for NYSE, p. 1422. See also Huang/Stoll (1997), p. 1010, Chakravarty (2001), p. 302, Chung/Li (2003), p. 264, Chung/Li/McInish (2004), p. 12 and, Nyholm (2002), p. 499f. For open limit order books, evidence is found by Brockman/Chung (2000), p. 137 and Frey/ Grammig (2006), p. 1026. Grammig/Schiereck/Theissen (2000), p. 631 do not find supporting evidence and explain their findings due to the relatively homogenous sample.

205 See Lin/Sanger/Booth (1995), p. 1164ff., Huang/Stoll (1997), p. 1004 and Glosten/Harris (1988), p. 128.

206 See Easley/O'Hara (1987), p. 81. Hasbrouck (1988), p. 250f. finds that order size conveys information and increases in size. Easley/Kiefer/O'Hara (1997b), p. 178 demonstrate that large orders convey more information than small orders.

The rationale behind the use of medium size orders is to minimize price impact of a trade by breaking up the trade. The block market is no alternative for informed traders, as in these markets anonymity is not given and uninformed traders have incentives to reveal that they are uninformed. Due to the fact that informed traders cannot reveal their trade motive, they will again face large price concessions. They implement the cumulative price changes as measure for information of trades and find that for a sample of NYSE stocks, more than 90% of the cumulative price change is caused by medium size orders. Thus, medium size orders reveal an unusually large cumulative price change in comparison to their overall proportion in trading volume.[207]

Hasbrouck (1995) finds for NYSE that medium size trades convey the most information, which is consistent with Barclay/Warner (1993).[208] Chakravarty (2001) links the cumulative price change and the initiator of the trade (institutions or individuals). He finds strong evidence that institutions are informed traders, as their medium size orders reveal a disproportionate cumulative price change, supporting the stealth trading hypothesis.[209]

The stealth trading hypothesis assumes that informed traders prefer medium size orders and consequently these trade sizes will reveal a higher level of information. The following hypothesis can be tested:

- *Informed trading and order size are related; i.e. medium size orders carry more information than small or large orders (stealth trading hypothesis).*

Within this chapter, different hypotheses that cover liquidity as well as informed trading are derived. These can be aggregated to form a hypothesis set (a) that analyzes liquidity in general and a second set (b) that analyzes informed trading in general. The connection between these two hypotheses sets is determined through the information paradigm that supports a negative relation between informed trading and liquidity. Testing these hypotheses sets will provide the context for analyzing the individual behavior of uninformed and informed traders and result in a qualified answer of whether trading in the DAX instruments in Xetra reveals trading patterns similar to other limit order books or even other market structures (hybrid or quote-driven).

5.2 Informed Liquidity Supply

In the above presented theoretical models (see Chapter 5.1.1), informed traders only implement market orders as they either do not have the choice between market orders and limit orders or are assumed impatient. Few authors relax this assumption and allow informed traders to choose between both order types. Their results are presented in the following section, starting with the theoretical literature and continuing with the experimental and empirical literature. Based upon this literature overview, hypotheses for informed traders' liquidity supply and demand behavior are derived for the second part of this study. The

---

207 See Barclay/Warner (1993), pp. 282, 285, and 302f.
208 See Hasbrouck (1995), p. 1196f.
209 See Chakravarty (2001), p. 299ff.

hypotheses will then be tested following the trader categorization and identification of informed traders.

5.2.1 Theoretical Work

The theoretical literature on informed traders' order type choice is rather small and mostly based on quote-driven or hybrid structures. Chakravarty/Holden (1995) model a quote-driven framework that includes competitive market makers, uninformed traders, and one informed trader. Both informed and uninformed traders are allowed to enter market and limit orders. As limit orders are allowed to cross market orders in the quote of the market maker, the market maker is not the defined counterparty to every trade. Informed traders determine their order choices depending on their expectations about the fundamental value of the underlying stock relative to the posted bid and ask quote: If the value is above the ask, the informed trader will strictly buy, whereas if it is below the bid he will sell. If the value is within the spread, a mix of market and limit orders will be implemented.[210]

Kaniel/Liu (2006) also develop a quote-driven model that consists of a market maker as well as uninformed and informed traders. Order type choice depends on the time horizon of the information as well as the magnitude of mispricing: Limit order use is positively related to the time horizon of the information; i.e. with long-lived information informed traders will favor limit orders over market orders. It is negatively related to the magnitude of mispricing; i.e. market orders are preferred to quickly realize profits by picking off mispriced orders. In that sense, informed traders' market orders are more profitable than market orders of uninformed traders as they do not face price risk when executing but realize gains from trading. In addition, informed traders camouflage behind uninformed traders; i.e. with an increasing rate of uninformed traders implementing limit orders, informed traders can more easily implement this order type without being detected. Accordingly, limit orders do transmit information. Kaniel/Liu (2006) theoretically and empirically demonstrate that limit orders convey more information than market orders.[211]

Harris (1998) analyzes order submission strategies in dynamic market structures and finds that informed traders who have short-lived information will implement market orders as an expression of the need for immediacy. In contrast, when spreads are wide, deadlines are distant, and information is long-lived, they will place limit orders. He concludes that most information is short-lived due to competition: Informed traders will prefer market orders over limit orders as they try to take advantage of their information. At the same time, uninformed traders will prefer limit orders over market orders depending on the remaining time to trade; i.e. the shorter the time frame the less likely the use of limit orders.[212]

Rindi (2002) theoretically studies the role of anonymity (trader or member information) in a central limit order book for the order type choice of risk-averse informed and uninformed

---

[210] See Chakravarty/Holden (1995), p. 233. In their single period model, the market makers first post a bid-ask quote, then both uninformed and informed traders simultaneously submit their orders, and lastly the orders are executed.

[211] See Kaniel/Liu (2006), p. 1871f. and p. 1892f.

[212] See Harris (1998), p. 3f. The major constraint to the results of his analysis is that it only applies to small orders that execute at the bid-ask spread and accordingly do not impact prices. See Harris (1998), p. 62.

traders as well as uninformed liquidity traders. She demonstrates that with endogenous (costly) information acquisition, the number of informed traders decreases when anonymity is abolished as the motivation to acquire information diminishes. In her model, this in turn reduces liquidity. Consequently, informed traders initially provide liquidity through limit orders in an anonymous environment, while they prefer not to do so in the non-anonymous set-up.[213]

The theoretical models described find that informed traders implement both market and limit orders depending on the state of the order book, the time horizon of their information (short- or long-lived information), and the level of anonymity. This general finding can be combined with the hypothesis on discretionary trading for market orders and the hypothesis on stealth trading for both order types, leading to the following testable hypotheses for market orders:

- *Informed traders prefer medium size market orders (stealth trading).*
- *Informed traders' market orders perform better than market orders of uninformed traders.*
- *Informed traders are discretionary market order traders.*

For limit orders testable hypotheses are:

- *Informed traders use limit orders as part of their trading strategies.*
- *Informed traders prefer medium size limit orders (stealth trading).*

5.2.2 Empirical and Experimental Work

Similar to the theoretical literature, only few experimental and empirical contributions that directly analyze informed traders' order type choice are made. While the experimental results are provided for an order-driven market structure, the empirical analyses focus on hybrid market structures only. This reveals the existing gap in the literature for an empirical analysis of an order-driven structure which is closed in the second part of this study.

Bloomfield/O'Hara/Saar (2005) simulate an experimental market to determine the evolution of liquidity modeled as the choice between market or limit orders. They implement a pure electronic limit order book with standard features that does not foresee any designated liquidity provision. Informed as well as small and large liquidity traders are the defined

---

[213] See Rindi (2002), p. 6. She stresses that the outcome of different transparency or anonymity regimes strictly depends on the underlying market structure. In a specialist structure, the disclosure of identities would help the specialist to reduce his adverse selection risk and accordingly liquidity would increase. In a centralized open limit order book with no dedicated liquidity provider, this effect differs significantly. Foucault/Moinas/Theissen (2004), pp. 30-34 provide evidence for the positive relation between pre-trade anonymity and liquidity for Euronext. Comerton-Forde/Frino/Mollica (2005) p. 534ff. find supporting results for the effects of pre-trade anonymity for Euronext, Tokyo Stock Exchange (TSE), and Korea Stock Exchange (KSE). Hachmeister/Schiereck (2006), p. 11f. provide analogous results for the relation between post-trade anonymity and liquidity for the Xetra trading system.

participants.[214] They investigate whether informed and uninformed traders differ in their implementation of market and limit orders, how order book depth and time left to trade influence this choice, and whether volatility affects these strategies. Major findings are: Informed traders implement limit orders as part of their trading strategies, even more extensively than uninformed traders. They switch their role as trading progresses and their information value reduces. Informed traders take liquidity earlier in the trading day and provide it later in the trading day.

The rationale behind informed traders providing liquidity in this market environment is that they are least subject to adverse selection. The liquidity providing role arises endogenously as when they enter a limit order they only face execution risk while uninformed traders additionally have to cope with adverse selection risk.[215] Informed traders implement market orders when the value of information is high, while they implement limit orders when prices draw nearer to the fundamental value, which is a dynamic adjustment to prices. Uninformed traders reveal the reverse behavior: They increase their use of market orders to reach their execution targets. The trade-off between price risk and execution risk evolves through time as execution risk becomes more important for the trader when trying to reach targets. The authors also find discretionary trading of large uninformed traders (institutional) as they trade later in the trading day and manage their trading costs through active strategies.[216] Critics can be applied as information is generated before trading starts and revealed after trading ends. In today's world, information is provided constantly, 24 hours a trading day.[217]

Anand/Chakravarty/Martell (2005) empirically study order type choice of informed and uninformed traders for NYSE data. They broach the issue of identifying informed traders, concluding that as informed traders are not readily observable, the researcher has to decide upon a sound proxy for informed traders. They distinguish informed and uninformed traders based on the criterion account type as institution or individual, assuming that the latter are uninformed.[218] They admit that institutions do frequently trade for liquidity reasons. To solve this issue, they analyze the cumulative price change[219] by order size, where a higher price change indicates a higher level of information.[220] In line with Bloomfield/O'Hara/Saar (2005), they provide evidence that informed traders (institutions) prefer market orders during the first half of the trading day compared to the second; i.e. they take liquidity in the morning and provide it in the afternoon, switching their role. When investigating the role of order size,

---

214 The trading protocol foresees continuous trading, price time priority, and the choice between market and limit orders. While the complete order book is visible ensuring pre-trade transparency, the traders remain concealed, foreseeing pre-trade anonymity. Bloomfield/O'Hara/Saar (2005), pp. 171-177 provide the details on experimental design and appendix A (pp. 194-197) provides the instructions given to the trading subjects.

215 See Bloomfield/O'Hara/Saar (2005), p. 168.

216 See Bloomfield/O'Hara/Saar (2005), pp. 186-189.

217 Bernhardt/Miao (2004) are an exception as they model how informed traders profit from their information when information is generated throughout the trading day.

218 Their database provides account type information for the individual trades, where I = Individual, A = Agent, P = Proprietary and P and A belong to institutions.

219 The cumulative price impact is calculated based on Barclay/Warner (1993), where the price change for the current trade is computed as the difference between the price of the current and the previous trade. These price changes are then cumulated for different classes of trades.

220 See Anand/Chakravarty/Martell (2005), p. 290f.

medium size orders reveal the highest price change, supporting the stealth trading hypothesis.[221] Concerning the aggressiveness of limit orders, they find that informed traders enter limit orders with limit prices set at or better than the available quote in approx. 78% of the cases, while uninformed traders show a lower level of aggressiveness as approx. 53% of their orders are entered at or better than the available quote.[222]

Critics to their analysis include having implemented a proxy to identify informed traders and having used a data set which is rather old (from 1991) in the light of several market structures changes in the last 15 years[223], the increase in operating efficiency of exchanges worldwide and the strong growth in trading volumes.[224] Kaniel/Liu (2006) implement the same data set as Anand/Chakravarty/Martell (2005) and reach similar conclusions.

Cao/Hansch/Wang (2004) do not directly asses order type choice of informed traders but indirectly assess whether informed traders implement limit orders. They evaluate the informational content of the open limit order book of the Australian Stock Exchange (ASX) and demonstrate that the order book conveys information beyond the BBA (estimated share of 30%). In addition, imbalances between demand and supply schedules are informative about future returns. In their analysis, they confront the common notion that limit orders are not as informative as market orders, which directly draws from the assumption that informed traders are more likely to use market orders. Their results are in contrast to the theoretical predictions of Glosten (1994) and Seppi (1997) but are in line with findings of Bloomfield/O'Hara/Saar (2005).[225] Finally, they observe that traders' order submission strategies are related to order book information beyond the BBA; i.e. the possibility to monitor the order book does influence traders' order submission strategies. This is direct evidence for discretionary trading.[226]

Harris/Panchapagesan (2005) analyze the information content of the limit order book at NYSE. They calculate the option value of the different limit orders and determine the imbalance of the buy and sell side. The analysis focuses on the time period where NYSE did not provide order book information to the market participants but specialists had exclusive information. They find evidence that specialist participation is higher in less active stocks, i.e. specialists provide liquidity when it is most needed. In line with Cao/Hansch/Wang (2004), order book asymmetry reveals a significant explanatory power for future price movements.[227] They find that specialists place more aggressive orders when spreads are wide. They do not

---

221 See Anand/Chakravarty/Martell (2005), p. 302ff.

222 See Anand/Chakravarty/Martell (2005), p. 295f.

223 Major market structure changes were the introduction of off-hour trading sessions on 13 June 1991, the reduction in the securities settlement period from five days to three days following the trade date on 7 June 1995, the reduction in tick sizes to sixteenths on 24 June 1997, the introduction of decimal pricing for all NYSE stocks on 29 January 2001, and the launch of NYSE OpenBook, which enables customers to view aggregate buy and sell limits in the order book. See http://www.nysedata.com/factbook, chronology of NYSE 1980-2002.

224 In 1990, the average daily volume measured in million shares was 157, compared to 1,602 in 2005. See http:// www.nysedata.com/factbook, overview statistics.

225 See Cao/Hansch/Wang (2004), pp. 14-18.

226 See Cao/Hansch/Wang (2004), p. 22f.

227 See Harris/Panchapagesan (2005), p. 46.

find the inventory component to be important.[228] Based on the results from the experimental set-up and the empirical results provided, the following additional hypothesis can be derived for limit orders:

- *Informed traders reveal stronger limit order aggressiveness.*

Hypotheses that concern the liquidity providing role of informed traders in general as well as from an intraday perspective are:

- *Informed traders are net liquidity providers.*
- *Informed traders show a net role change during the trading day; they prefer market orders earlier and limit orders later in the trading day, consequently switching from a liquidity demander to a liquidity provider role.*

The above presented hypotheses can be grouped to cater three hypotheses sets covering informed liquidity demand with market orders (c), informed liquidity supply with limit orders (d), as well as informed traders' net role and intraday behavior (e). Jointly these hypotheses sets address the question of informed traders' order type choice and corresponding trading strategies.

5.3 Synopsis

This chapter aims at deriving testable hypotheses for the empirical part of this study. Based upon theoretical, experimental, and empirical literature, these hypotheses are defined to address the research objectives of this study.

Following Glosten (1994) and Seppi (1997), initially uninformed and informed traders are differentiated by their patience. Informed traders will only implement market orders due to the higher benefit from immediate execution compared to the price impact, while uninformed traders prefer execution at a predetermined price with limit orders assuming that order type choice is exogenous for both trader types. Further studies by Handa/Schwartz (1996a, 1996b), Parlour (1998), Foucault (1999), and Foucault/Kadan/ Kandel (2005) change this restrictive assumption, modeling the choice between market and limit orders for uninformed traders. However, in these models order type is still exogenous for informed traders that only implement market orders. A major assumption of these models, in line with the information paradigm, is that liquidity and informed trading are inversely related. Based upon this branch of the literature, two hypotheses sets are derived: the first set (a) describes liquidity in general, i.e. the shape of the liquidity function, buy and sell side liquidity, intraday patterns of liquidity as well as standard determinants of liquidity. The second set (b) includes informed trading in general, i.e. the role of anonymity, firm size, and order size for informed trading, as well as the intraday distribution. This set also includes the connecting hypothesis that informed trading and liquidity are negatively related.

---

[228] See Harris/Panchapagesan (2005), p. 62.

A second branch of the literature models the same decision problem, but for informed traders. Chakravarty/Holden (1995), Harris (1998), and Kaniel/Liu (2006) present models where informed traders' order type choice is endogenous to the model, i.e. they are allowed to implement both market and limit orders. They demonstrate that informed traders use limit orders when spreads are wide, information is long-lived, and they trade in an anonymous trading environment.

Bloomfield/O'Hara/Saar (2005) provide a seminal paper, where they experimentally investigate the order choice of different trader types in an order-driven framework. Along their results, both Anand/Chakravarty/Martell (2005) and Kaniel/Liu (2006) provide empirical evidence for a hybrid market structure (NYSE). The authors illustrate that informed traders are liquidity providers, which evolves due to the fact that they are not subject to adverse selection when trading. Information asymmetry can benefit liquidity provision and help to preserve liquidity provision in times of uncertainty.

This branch of the literature results in three additional hypotheses sets that analyze informed traders' trading behavior: Hypotheses set (c) provides answers to the questions of whether informed traders use medium size market orders, how these orders perform, and if they act with discretion when trading. Hypotheses set (d) includes limit order use in general, preference for medium size orders, and limit order aggressiveness. Finally, hypotheses set (e) determines informed traders' net role as well as the relation between time of day and order choice. All hypotheses sets are presented jointly as the underlying framework for the empirical analysis in Chapter 6.4.

With this chapter, the theoretical part of this study concludes. Starting with the description of the underlying research object (Chapter 2), it has defined the adequate measurement methods implemented for liquidity and informed trading (Chapters 3 and 4) and then developed the underlying hypotheses for the empirical part of this study (Chapter 5).

Part II: Empirical Analyses

Based on the methods chosen and the hypotheses derived from existing theoretical, experimental and empirical literature in part I of the study, part II empirically investigates the central question of whether informed traders do provide liquidity in the open electronic limit order book Xetra: It starts with a description of the research design (Chapter 6) followed by a detailed market description that aims at answering whether the Xetra open limit order book is comparable to other exchanges (Chapter 7). Based on the results of the trader classification procedure (Chapter 8), the last part of the empirical analysis describes informed traders' liquidity demand and supply behavior (Chapter 9).

6 Research Design

This chapter starts with the research approach outlining the different steps in analyzing liquidity and informed trading in the DAX instruments, the classification of traders according to their level of information, and the analysis of their liquidity demand and supply behavior. What follows is a description of the data underlying the study, specifically any cleansing, selection, or enrichment measures taken. Initial descriptive statistics on the DAX instruments are presented and, finally, the set of hypotheses that will be analyzed in the empirical part is outlined.

6.1 Research Approach

The research approach is subdivided into three steps (see Exhibit 6-1). The first step provides an overall market description. It describes and measures liquidity and informed trading as well as their relation for the DAX instruments in general. The second step is the heart of the analysis and comprises the trader classification into informed and uninformed traders implementing the trader ID as unique identifier. Based on this trader classification, the third step analyzes the liquidity supply and demand behavior of informed and uninformed traders.

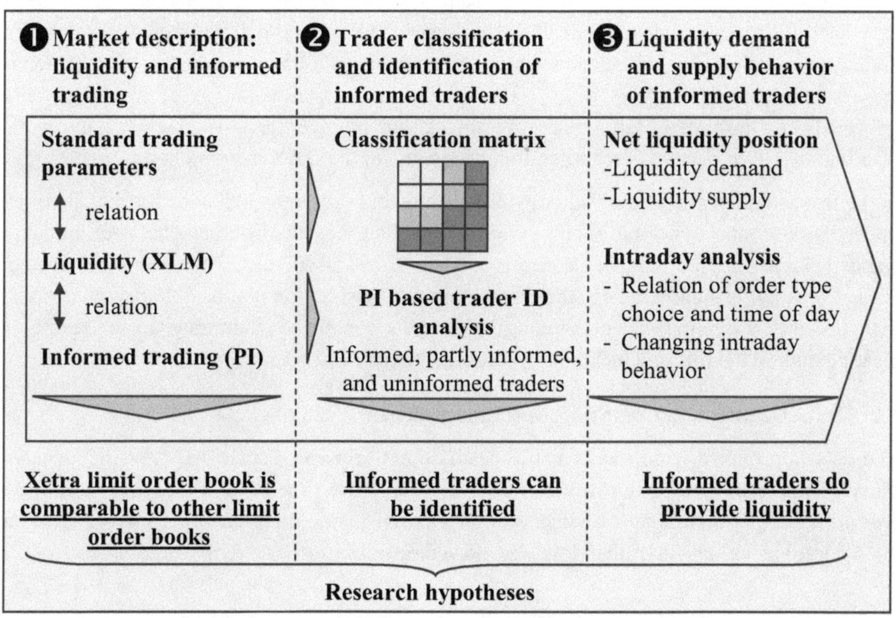

Exhibit 6-1: Research approach

In the first step, the XLM (see Chapter 3.2.2) is implemented to describe liquidity in the DAX instruments. The analyses include general and cross-sectional descriptions for all volume classes as well as a buy and sell side comparison. Based on general results and descriptive statistics on average order sizes in the DAX, the quoted spread and four volume classes representing small, standard, medium, and large orders are selected. For these classes, an intraday analysis and a regression analysis with standard determinants of liquidity are implemented. Next, to determine informed trading in the DAX instruments, the price impact (ad hoc method, see Chapter 4.3.3) is computed and results for the cross-section, instrument groups, order sizes, as well as the intraday distribution are presented. The results are then implemented in a correlation analysis with the XLM. This completes the first step of the analysis describing liquidity and informed liquidity demand in the Xetra open limit order book, providing the reference point for the interpretation of results of the trader categories. If the analysis yields the expected results, the Xetra open limit order book for liquid instruments is comparable to other open limit order books, such as Euronext, LSE, or SEHK. The results generated in the third part of the analysis can then be transferred to markets with a similar market design and regulatory framework.

The second step of the analysis includes the identification and selection of a key identifier for informed trading and its subsequent implementation for the analysis of informed liquidity supply and demand in the third part. The trader ID classification follows a stepwise approach. Initially, trader IDs are classified in accordance to their relative importance measured in terms of liquidity demanding (aggressor) trading volume and in terms of total trading volume. This leads to a classification matrix. Based on this matrix, a first set of trader IDs is excluded from the analysis as not relevant. In the next step, the average price impact per trader ID is calculated for the remaining trader IDs: The larger the price impact, the more information a trade contains; thus, the higher the average price impact of a trader ID, the more informed is the respective trader (trader ID).[229] Trader IDs are classified as uninformed, partially informed, and informed, following different classification criteria, such as the trader ID distribution and respective percentiles and the results for the DAX instruments.

In the third step, an analysis of liquidity demanding and providing behavior for the classified trader IDs is conducted. First, their overall net position, i.e. the difference between liquidity demanded and supplied will be determined. Then, a test is conducted to determine whether the net position is significant for the demand or supply side. Finally, an intraday analysis of their liquidity providing and demanding behavior is conducted. Summing up the results, a clear picture on the role and behavior of informed traders emerges.

6.2 Data Description, Cleansing, and Enrichment

The data is provided from the StatistiX database of Deutsche Boerse AG.[230] It includes all thirty instruments constituting the DAX index during the time from 1 September until 30 November 2005.[231] Although trading is conducted on the German National Day (3 October 2005), trading volume is rather low and not comparable to the average trading day. As a

---

[229] Technically, it is not the trader ID but the trader behind the ID that makes any decisions when trading. Throughout this study, the terms *trader ID* and *trader* are implemented as synonyms.

[230] StatistiX is an internal database which combines data from the different trading systems of Deutsche Boerse AG (DBAG) as well as data from other German stock exchanges. It is the source for all statistics that are published by DBAG.

[231] During that time, there were no changes to the index composition, i.e. no deletions or additions. The last change had been implemented on 19 August 2003, when Continental AG replaced MLP AG.

consequence, this trading day was excluded from the data set leading to a data set covering 64 trading days for thirty instruments.[232]

During this timeframe, 260 Xetra trading members with 2,413 admitted traders actively participated in trading on Xetra. The number of admitted but inactive traders is quite high; a further 6,530 traders were admitted but did not participate in trading.[233]

The data set consists of three different tables: (1) XLM, (2) Trades, and (3) BBA. The XLM table includes the calculation of the liquidity measure for all volume classes per instrument and defined time interval. The Trades table includes all transactions executed during auctions and continuous trading and provides both sides of each transaction, i.e. the liquidity demanding traders, so-called aggressors, and the liquidity supplying counterparties, so-called originators. The BBA (Best Bid and Ask) table includes all updates of BBs and BAs and respective quantities during the trading day. It serves together with the Trades table as a basis for the price impact calculation.

6.2.1 XLM Table

Due to its extensive calculation effort, the XLM is not directly calculated in the Xetra trading system but in a related module of the StatistiX database based on order book data extracted from the Xetra trading system.

In Exhibit 6-2, the data fields of the XLM table are described. The table reflects that the LP, the APM, and the XLM are calculated separately (i) for the buy and sell side of the order book (BUY_SELL_ID), (ii) per instrument (MR_ISIN), (iii) per size of hypothetical order (VOLUME_CLASS), and (iv) per time interval (SLICE_ID) of the individual trading day (FACT_DATE).

Field name	**Description**
FACT_DATE	Date of the trading day, provided as YYYY:MM:DD.
MR_ISIN	ISIN of any instrument, e.g. DE0008404005 for Allianz AG.
SLICE_ID	The ID corresponds to a defined time slice during the trading day. The trading is divided into 11 separate slices, with hourly slices from 9:00:00 am to 3:00:00 pm and half-hour slices from 3:00:01 pm to 5:30:00 pm Thus SLICE_ID = 1 covers the time period from 9:00:00 until 10:00:00 am.
AGG_SLICE_FROM	Defines the start of each slice in HH:MM:SS.
AGG_SLICE_TO	Defines the end of each slice in HH:MM:SS.

Exhibit 6-2: XLM table – data fields and description

232 An internal DBAG analysis revealed that trading volume is only 60% of the average trading volume on the German National Day.

233 There is no restriction to the number of traders a Xetra member can have admitted. During the time of the analysis, the largest number of active traders admitted for one individual member was 98 actively participating traders.

Field name	Description
BUY_SELL_ID	Defines if a hypothetical buy (B) or sell (S) order was run against the order book.
VOLUME_CLASS	Defines the size of the hypothetical order. For DAX instruments, ten different volume classes (in thousand €) ranging from 25 to 5,000 are calculated.
NOOF_AGGR_ROWS	The XLM is calculated based on order book snapshots taken every minute during the trading day. This field provides the number of values that enter the average calculations per slice.
LP_BP	Average liquidity premium (LP) measured in basis points (bp).
APM_BP	Average adverse price movement (APM) measured in bp.
XLM	Exchange Liquidity Measure (XLM) measured in bp, calculated as the sum of LP and APM.

Exhibit 6-2 (continued): XLM table – data fields and description

The SLICE_ID is introduced based on the provided start (AGG_SLICE_FROM) and end point (AGG_SLICE_TO) of the slices. As described, the trading day is originally divided into eleven slices that differ in terms of their length – either hour or half-hour slices (see Exhibit 6-2).When determining daily averages, these are adjusted for the differing lengths of the slices by applying weighting factors.[234]

For all subsequent intraday analyses, nine slices are distinguished (SLICE_ID_2 is introduced), hourly slices from 9:00 am until 5:00 pm and one half-hour slice until 5:30 pm. The half-hour slices from 3:00 pm to 5:00 pm are weighted to reflect two hourly slices. Following the Xetra trading model that schedules an intraday auction at 1:00 pm, the trading day can be split into a morning and an afternoon trading session. These two again differ in their length, i.e. 4 hours for the morning trading session (9:00 am to 1:00 pm) and 4.5 hours for the afternoon trading session (1:00 pm to 5:30 pm). Calculation of averages for each session is again based on weighting factors to account for the different length in slices, i.e. for the morning session with four hourly slices a simple average can be calculated, while for the afternoon session the different lengths (two hour slices and five half-hour slices) are incorporated through weighting factors ($0.\overline{22}$ and $0.\overline{11}$ respectively).

The XLM can only be calculated during continuous trading and not during auctions. It is computed based on order book snapshots that are extracted from the order book every 60 seconds. Calculation of the XLM is not always possible. This is due to the fact that the Xetra trading model for high liquids foresees scheduled opening, intraday, and closing auctions as well as volatility interruptions that depend on the course of trading (Chapter 2.3). This is reflected in the field NOOF_AGGR_ROWS that counts the number of values available for the

234 The weighting factor for the hourly slices is 0.11765, and for the half-hourly slices it is 0.05882, adding up to 1.0 for the complete trading day.

calculation of the average per slice. The maximum number of values is 60 for slices with a duration of an hour and 30 for slices that span only half an hour.

The number of values for XLM calculation is further reduced when the available order book is not thick enough to allow for calculation of a larger volume class. In that case, the calculated XLM is an overestimate of the available liquidity in that instrument, due to the fact that the average only includes those order book situations when calculation is possible. Consequently, the results of the XLM have to be interpreted in the context of the number of values entering the average calculations. The volume classes that are implemented for XLM calculation measured in thousand € are 25, 50, 100, 250, 500, 1,000, 2,000, 3,000, 4,000, and 5,000. The table provides separate results for the components of the XLM, i.e. results measured in basis points for the average liquidity premium (LP_BP) and the average adverse price movement (APM_BP). Summing up the two components yields the XLM.[235]

The only cleansing activity of the initial data set is the exclusion of the results of 3 October 2005. The initial XLM table includes 425,987 data sets, while the cleansed table includes 419,422 data sets. All descriptive calculations and respective statistical analyses presented in Chapter 7.1 are provided based on this table.

6.2.2 Trades Table

The Trades table provides both sides of all transactions during the trading day, i.e. transactions during auctions and continuous trading.[236] For each completed transaction, it includes transaction and order information. Thus, only executed orders are part of the Trades table. Orders that were entered but did not execute, either being deleted before their execution or remaining in the limit order book are not included in the data set. The Trades table provides extensive information, but only those fields that are needed for the analysis are described in Exhibit 6-3.

Field name	**Description**
FACT_DATE	Date of the trading day, provided as YYYY:MM:DD.
MR_ISIN	ISIN of any instrument, i.e. DE0008404005 for Allianz AG.
TRADER_ID	Unique identifier for the individual traders of a trading member.
MBR_ID	Unique identifier for the individual trading member, i.e. DBKFR is the trading member code of Deutsche Bank (DBK) Frankfurt (FR).

Exhibit 6-3: Trades table – data fields and description

[235] The formula for the calculation is presented in Chapter 3.2.2.

[236] The Xetra trading system also provides an OTC trade facility, which would be reflected in a respective indicator in the field TRADE_TYPE_ID. However, the data was already provided without OTC trades, so no cleansing was needed.

Field name	Description
BUYSELL_ID	Defines if the order entered is a buy (B) or sell (S) order.
ORDER_NO	Each order that enters the Xetra trading system is given an order number, which is a unique identifier with 18 digits.
ORDER_TYPE_ID	Defines the order type of the individual order.
ORDER_ENTRY_TIMESTAMP	Provides order entry information, i.e. the trading day (YYYY:MM:DD) and the entry time in hours, minutes, and seconds (HH:MM:SS).
ORDER_ENTRY_MILLISECONDS	Provides order entry information in milliseconds and can only be interpreted jointly with the ORDER_ENTRY_TIME-STAMP.
REGIONAL_TIMESTAMP	Provides order execution information, i.e. the trading day (YYYY:MM:DD) and the execution time in hours, minutes, and seconds (HH:MM:SS).
MILLISECONDS	Provides execution information in milli-seconds and can only be interpreted jointly with the REGIONAL_TIMESTAMP.
ORDER_EXEC_TYPE_ID	Provides information on the type of the trade, i.e. full or partial match.
RATE_PRICE_TYPE_ID	Provides a denominator for the trading form a transaction takes place in, e.g. continuous trading, (opening, intraday, closing) auctions, volatility interruptions, etc.
PRICE	Execution price of the transaction.
TXN_AMT	Transaction amount, i.e. execution volume measured in €.
NBR_OF_UNITS	Number of units executed at the defined price. Multiplying price and number of units provides the execution volume.

Exhibit 6-3 (continued): Trades table – data fields and description

When an order is entered into the Xetra trading system, it receives an order number (ORDER_NO) as unique identifier for which additional information is logged: the order entry date and time (FACT_DATE, ORDER_ENTRY_TIMESTAMP, and ORDER_ENTRY_ MILLISECONDS), whether it is a buy or sell order (BUY_SELL_ID), the order type (ORDER_TYPE_ID), the instrument for which the order is entered (MR_ISIN), and the identification of the responsible trader (TRADER_ID and MBR_ID). Once the order is executed, additional information is provided: the order execution date and time (FACT_DATE, REGIONAL_TIMESTAMP, and MILLISECONDS), the execution price (PRICE), the executed trading volume in € (TXN_AMT), the number of shares executed (NBR_OF_UNITS), during which trading form, e.g. continuous trading or auctions, it was executed (RATE_PRICE_TYPE_ID), and whether it was partially or fully executed (ORDER_EXEC_TYPE_ID). The basis of the further analysis is the distinction between counterparties into liquidity providers (originators) and liquidity demanders (aggressors). However, the counterparties of transactions during auctions cannot be distinguished as aggressors and originators; thus transactions during auctions (either scheduled or volatility interruptions) are separated from the data set based on the value of the field RATE_PRICE_TYPE_ID.[237]

The remaining transactions are split into an aggressor and an originator table. This split is done based on the following splitting algorithm: Transactions, where the order execution (REGIONAL_TIMESTAMP) and order entry timestamp (ORDER_ENTRY_ TIMESTAMP) including the milliseconds (ORDER_ENTRY_MILLISECONDS) are identical, are classified as aggressor trades; for transactions where the two timestamps differ, i.e. the order entry timestamp was earlier than the order execution timestamp, the trade party is classified as originator.[238] Aggressor orders are per definition market orders or marketable limit orders as they trigger an execution when they enter the book as reflected in the equality of timestamps. Originator orders are orders that provide liquidity as they are standing in the order book waiting to be hit by an aggressor order.

The initial Trades table included 13,878,901 data sets and was reduced by 163,368 transactions that were executed on 3 October 2005. The remaining transactions were first split into transactions during auctions (600,518 trades) and continuous trading (13,115,015). Trades during continuous trading were further split into aggressor (6,618,802) and originator (6,496,213) trades following the outlined algorithm.

In addition, after the split, all orders where the counterparties could not be identified unambiguously (the counterparty volume was missing partially or completely) were excluded from the sample. The final aggressor and originator tables include only corresponding trades, i.e. only transactions where both sides of the transactions were available; thus, as can be seen in Exhibit 6-4, the total traded volume for both aggressor and originator is equal at 227,197 million €.

[237] The field RATE_PRICE_TYPE_ID can be found in different tables in StatistiX and allows differentiation between trading phases (pre-trade or trade information), type of information (price or quote information), and trading forms (continuous trading, auctions etc.). ID = 31 stands for trades during continuous trading. See Appendix 1.

[238] Per definition, the order execution cannot have an earlier timestamp than the order entry.

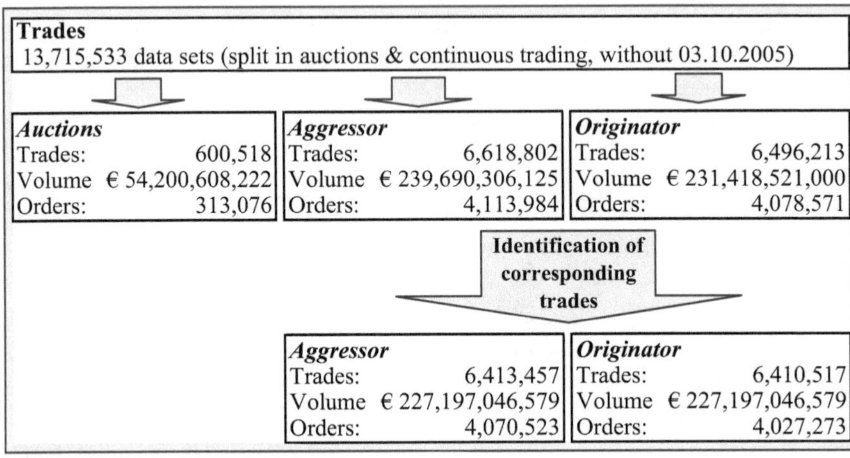

Exhibit 6-4: Splitting and cleansing of Trades table

As outlined in Chapter 2.3, an order can be executed fully or partially, leading to several trades. The Trades table reflects all details of an order execution, allowing direct identification of the counterparties of each trade. It does not provide any aggregated data on order level. The analysis will not focus on trades but on orders; thus for orders that are partially executed, the different parts of the order can be identified based on the field ORDER_NO and average execution prices and the full trading volume are calculated based on the Trades table. Exhibit 6-4 provides the splitting results for number of trades, number of orders, and total traded volume. From this data, the partial execution (PE) ratio of orders can be calculated. During the analyzed time span, the PE ratio calculated as the ratio of trades to orders was on average 1.58 during continuous trading (aggressor PE ratio = 1.576 and originator PE ratio = 1.592) and 1.92 during auctions.[239]

The final aggressor and originator tables are extended by additional fields based on the XLM table. The SLICE_ID and the corresponding SLICE_ID_2 are implemented to allow for intraday results. In addition, based on the ten volume classes, all orders are classified into six size classes (SIZE_ID). Class 1 includes all orders (measured in thousand €) that are smaller than 25; Class 2 includes all orders that are equal to or larger than 25 while being smaller than 50, and so on. Class 6 includes all orders that are larger than 500.[240]

6.2.3 BBA Table

The order book reflects all orders that are available for matching but are not executable immediately. The BBA is the minimum spread available in the order book, i.e. the highest bid (buy) and the lowest ask (sell) limit order. The BBA table does not provide the BBA spread

---

[239] Partial executions result from the matching algorithm implemented in Xetra. They do not have any impact on the pricing of transactions as the pricing schedule is based only on orders and their corresponding volume.

[240] SIZE_ID (measured in thousand €): 1: orders < 25; 2: orders ≥ 25 and < 50; 3: orders ≥ 50 and < 100; 4: orders ≥ 100 and < 250; 5: orders ≥ 250 and < 500; 6: orders ≥ 500.

itself but the individual best bids and asks that are recorded from the start of the trading phase till it ends. The bids and asks are written to the table whenever changes take place. These changes occur either if a new limit order enters at the top of the order book (BB or BA), an order is modified or deleted at the BB or BA, or a marketable order enters the order book and executes against the BB or BA. Both sides of the book update independently.

The table as presented in Exhibit 6-5 provides information on the instrument (MR_ISIN), whether it is a bid or ask limit (BID_ASK_FLAG), the limit of the order (PRICE), the available quantity (UNITS), and its validity start (TSTAMP and HSEC).

Field name	Description
MR_ISIN	ISIN of any instrument, e.g. DE0008404005 for Allianz AG.
TSTAMP	The timestamp provides the trading day (YYYY:MM:DD) and the start of validity in hours, minutes, and seconds (HH:MM:SS).
HSEC	This field provides start of validity in hundredth seconds and can only be interpreted jointly with the TSTAMP.
PRICE	Limit order price of the best bid or ask.
UNITS	Units available at the current best bid or ask.
BID_ASK_FLAG	Defines if the price and units belong to a bid (buy) or ask (sell) limit order or an indicative price during auctions.

Exhibit 6-5: BBA table – data fields and description

The data is cleansed for 3 October 2005 and for BBAs during auctions as these are only indicative BBAs (BID_ASK_FLAG = I). It is further extended to provide the starting and ending time of each individual BBA. The validity of each BB and BA based on start and end time of the respective BB and BA is needed to determine the quoted spread and respective midpoint, when an order enters the order book or is executed against an incoming order.

The BBA table serves together with the aggressor data from the Trades table as a basis for the price impact calculation; midpoints (BBA table) are matched with the execution prices (Trades table). In addition, the BBA table is combined with originator data from the Trades table to determine the order aggressiveness of limit orders, i.e. if orders are entered at/better as or behind the BBA at order entry.[241]

Due to the fact that in the Xetra trading system order and trade confirmations have priority over any statistical information, the BBA file that is written directly from Xetra can at times have missing or invalid values. To allow matching with the Trades table, the timestamp is adapted to reflect milliseconds. Details on the matching and calculation procedure are given in Chapters 7.2.1 and 9.2.2. After the cleansing activities, the table includes 12,313,615 data sets, thereof 6,234,675 bids and 6,078,940 asks.

---

[241] This is done by combining order execution timestamps of buy (sell) orders from the Trades table with the BA (BB) calculated from the BBA table.

6.3 Descriptive Statistics

The analysis outlined in the research design is based on the distinction between aggressor and originator; thus, the focus will be on transactions during continuous trading only. Based on the cleansed Trades table, continuous trading reflects 89.3% in terms of average daily trading volume and 95.5% in terms of average daily trades.[242]

6.3.1 Cross-sectional Results

Based on the aggressor table, Exhibit 6-6 reports single count results (i.e. only one side of the transaction) of transactions during continuous trading for the cross-section of instruments of the DAX: means and standard deviations for average daily trading volume in million €, average daily number of trades, average price, and average volatility.

Volatility is defined as the average daily volatility measured as a logarithm of the highest and lowest price during each 30-minute trading interval of the trading day. Market capitalization in million (m) € is reported as of 30 November 2005 with respective index weight. The index weight is determined based on free float factor, number of shares, and actual closing price.[243] Market capitalization of the full set of DAX instruments is 559.4 billion (bn) €.[244]

The results demonstrate that the market for blue chip stocks is active. On average, 3,340 trades are executed per day with a corresponding average volume of approx. 35,400 € per trade. The statistics also document that the sample of instruments differs with respect to the reported parameters which is reflected in the relatively high standard deviations. The average daily number of trades of the most active instrument Allianz AG with 7,196 trades per day is 5.5 times higher as the instrument with the least trading activity Fresenius Medical Care AG (1,312 trades per day). The same holds true for traded volume with a factor of 15.6 and for market cap with a factor of 20.1, although E.ON AG instead of Allianz AG is the instrument with the highest market cap. The average price ranges from 7.97 € (Infineon Technologies AG) to 145.49 € (Adidas Salomon AG), with a factor of 18.2, and volatility ranges from 0.31% (Henkel KGaA) to 0.49% (Volkswagen AG), with a factor of 1.6.

---

242 I.e. during auctions 10.7% of trading volume and 4.5% of trades are executed. Thus the average size per trade is much higher during auctions (approx. 90,300 €) in comparison to continuous trading (approx. 35,400 €). All results are rounded to the next hundred.

243 The index weight of any single company in the DAX is capped at 10% of the index capitalization.

244 If Exhibit 6-6 had been presented incorporating both sides of the transaction (i.e. double count), the volume would have been exactly double and number of trades 2.02 times, due to the slightly higher PE ratio on the originator side. Price, volatility, and market cap would remain unchanged.

Instruments	Avg. daily volume (m €)		Avg. daily trades		Avg. price		Volatility		Market cap (m €)	Index weight
	Mean	Standard deviation	Mean	Standard deviation	Mean	Standard deviation	Mean	Standard deviation	End of month	End of month
ADIDAS-SALOMON AG O.N.	67.8	44.6	2,381	945	145.49	3.55	0.36%	0.12%	6,837	1.22%
ALLIANZ AG VNA O.N.	391.1	144.1	7,169	1,801	113.95	6.29	0.34%	0.10%	48,889	8.74%
ALTANA AG O.N.	30.1	26.5	1,759	836	46.19	0.97	0.35%	0.12%	3,146	0.56%
BASF AG O.N.	153.7	42.2	4,548	1,015	60.65	1.53	0.37%	0.07%	32,831	5.87%
BAY.HYPO-VEREINSBK.O.N.	77.4	38.2	2,241	825	23.93	1.14	0.41%	0.11%	14,903	2.66%
BAY.MOTOREN WERKE AG ST	91.6	43.4	3,218	1,124	37.38	0.93	0.40%	0.11%	12,400	2.22%
BAYER AG O.N.	99.8	36.0	3,633	928	30.45	1.60	0.44%	0.08%	24,729	4.42%
COMMERZBANK AG O.N.	99.3	94.8	3,019	1,249	22.36	1.11	0.46%	0.13%	13,680	2.45%
CONTINENTAL AG O.N.	52.4	23.8	2,190	637	67.37	2.39	0.40%	0.10%	10,463	1.87%
DAIMLERCHRYSLER AG NA O.N	220.6	86.4	5,688	1,599	42.27	1.17	0.48%	0.11%	37,358	6.68%
DEUTSCHE BANK AG NA O.N.	268.6	80.3	5,646	1,339	77.90	3.07	0.36%	0.08%	43,007	7.69%
DEUTSCHE BOERSE NA O.N.	47.2	20.0	1,725	522	78.55	2.70	0.37%	0.10%	8,844	1.58%
DEUTSCHE POST AG NA O.N.	68.0	36.7	2,620	874	19.12	0.55	0.37%	0.09%	11,425	2.04%
DT.TELEKOM AG NA	304.7	135.7	5,521	1,212	14.92	0.37	0.32%	0.06%	37,290	6.67%
E.ON AG O.N.	243.7	83.3	5,805	1,431	76.96	2.23	0.42%	0.09%	55,921	10.0%
DAX Mean or Sum	**118.3**	**96.0**	**3,340**	**1,634**	**55.45**	**35.49**	**0.39%**	**0.05%**	**559,380**	**100%**
DAX Min	25.0		1,312		7.972		0.49%		2,776	
DAX Max	391.1		7,169		145.49		0.31%		55,921	

Exhibit 6-6: Descriptive statistics

Instruments	Avg. daily volume (m €)		Avg. daily trades		Avg. price		Volatility		Market cap (m €)	Index weight
	Mean	Standard deviation	Mean	Standard deviation	Mean	Standard deviation	Mean	Standard deviation	End of month	End of month
FRESEN.MED.CARE AG O.N.	25.0	11.8	1,312	461	77.19	2.19	0.32%	0.10%	2,776	0.50%
HENKEL KGAA VZO O.N.	26.2	16.1	1,412	554	75.96	2.63	0.31%	0.09%	4,858	0.87%
INFINEON TECH.AG NA O.N.	58.0	27.6	2,356	683	7.97	0.21	0.47%	0.10%	4,646	0.83%
LINDE AG O.N.	28.8	10.4	1,563	443	60.74	1.41	0.37%	0.09%	4,920	0.88%
LUFTHANSA AG VNA O.N.	38.7	18.1	1,980	650	11.28	0.26	0.41%	0.10%	4,767	0.85%
MAN AG ST O.N.	36.7	15.7	1,957	590	41.14	1.65	0.44%	0.11%	5,963	1.07%
METRO AG ST O.N.	39.6	19.3	1,928	640	39.29	1.77	0.36%	0.09%	5,474	0.98%
MUENCH.RUECKVERS.VNA O.N.	184.2	67.4	4,482	1,170	98.33	6.26	0.35%	0.07%	20,420	3.65%
RWE AG ST O.N.	163.5	56.1	4,606	1,156	54.97	2.05	0.43%	0.08%	27,314	4.88%
SAP AG O.N.	166.2	76.8	4,363	1,304	143.64	3.04	0.38%	0.08%	32,617	5.83%
SCHERING AG O.N.	45.7	20.2	1,957	631	52.11	1.28	0.32%	0.06%	9,532	1.70%
SIEMENS AG NA	253.0	80.1	5,825	1,349	63.12	1.25	0.38%	0.08%	53,835	9.62%
THYSSENKRUPP AG O.N.	53.2	29.5	2,406	831	16.94	0.55	0.38%	0.10%	7,034	1.26%
TUI AG NA	47.4	30.2	2,367	894	17.01	0.66	0.48%	0.14%	3,683	0.66%
VOLKSWAGEN AG ST O.N.	167.9	158.9	4,536	2,582	46.45	2.59	0.49%	0.19%	9,817	1.8%
DAX Mean or Sum	**118.3**	**96.0**	**3,340**	**1,634**	**55.45**	**35.49**	**0.39%**	**0.05%**	**559,380**	**100%**
DAX Min	25.0		1,312		7.972		0.49%		2,776	
DAX Max	391.1		7,169		145.49		0.31%		55,921	

Exhibit 6-6 (continued): Descriptive statistics

6.3.2 Order Size Results

As described in Chapter 6.2.2, an additional field SIZE_ID was computed for the aggressor and originator tables. Based on this field, an analysis of order size distribution is implemented.

Exhibit 6-7 shows for the aggressor side that the number of orders belonging to a size class decreases with increasing order size; almost half of all orders (47%) are smaller than 25,000 €, but these orders only generate 9% of the total trading volume. The average order size for all orders is approx. 55,800 €[245], while the average order size in class 6 is about 797,000 €. Xetra does not provide a direct indicator for retail and wholesale order flow, but assuming based on order size that all orders assigned to class 1 are retail order flow and the other orders (classes 2 to 6) belong to wholesale traders the average order size for retail orders is approx. 10,500 €, while it is approx. 96,500 € for wholesale orders.[246]

SIZE_ID	In thousand €	Number of orders	Orders % share	Total trading volume	Volume % share
1	< 25	1.924.389	47,3%	20.174.960.624	8,9%
2	≥ 25 and < 50	821.940	20,2%	29.881.270.101	13,2%
3	≥ 50 and < 100	724.524	17,8%	51.050.347.313	22,5%
4	≥ 100 and < 250	473.755	11,6%	71.095.748.092	31,3%
5	≥ 250 and < 500	98.292	2,4%	32.989.471.116	14,5%
6	≥ 500	27.623	0,7%	22.005.249.334	9,7%
Total		**4.070.523**	**100%**	**227.197.046.579**	**100%**

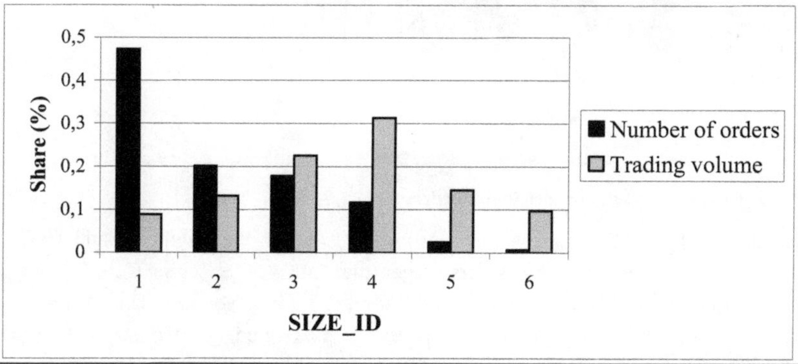

Exhibit 6-7: Order size distribution of aggressor orders

In addition, the largest executed order per trading day is identified separately for all instruments: The largest order in the sample is 12.3 m € in Siemens AG with a corresponding

---

245 The average order size of approx. 55,800 € transforms into the average trade size of approx. 35,400 € when adjusting for the PE ratio of 1.576 on the aggressor side.

246 Markets in Financial Instruments Directive (MiFID) determines the average retail order size to be 7,500 €; see CESR (2005), p. 68.

average of the largest order per day of 1.8 m €. The smallest order of Siemens AG in this sample is 0.7 m €.[247]

The same statistics are computed for the originator orders as displayed in Exhibit 6-8. Class 1 constitutes more than 50% of all orders while generating 10% of total trading volume. The average order size is 56,400 €[248] which is slightly higher than the aggressor side. Class 6 has an average order size of 890,000 €.

SIZE_ID	In thousand €	Number of orders	Orders % share	Total trading volume	Volume % share
1	< 25	2.055.351	51,0%	23.458.179.487	10,3%
2	≥ 25 and < 50	774.135	19,2%	27.797.072.558	12,2%
3	≥ 50 and < 100	666.154	16,5%	46.764.617.576	20,6%
4	≥ 100 and < 250	393.465	9,8%	58.998.734.491	26,0%
5	≥ 250 and < 500	96.212	2,4%	32.804.942.082	14,4%
6	≥ 500	41.956	1,0%	37.373.500.385	16,4%
Total		**4.027.273**	**100%**	**227.197.046.579**	**100%**

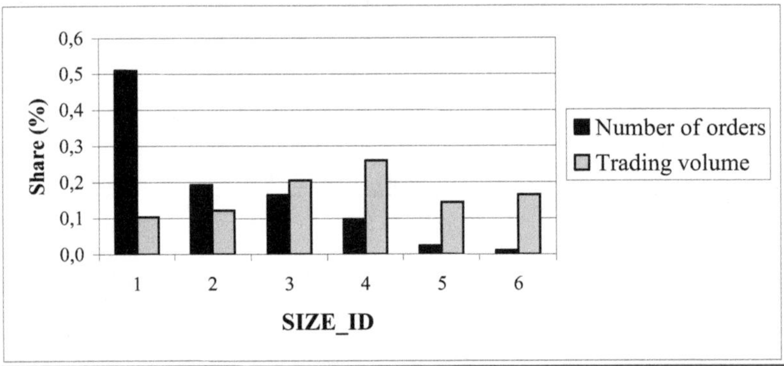

Exhibit 6-8: Order size distribution of originator orders

Comparing the results for the aggressor and originator side, on the originator side 16.4% of the trading volume is generated by orders larger than 500,000 € (class 6), while on the aggressor side this class only accounts for 9.7% of the trading volume. This difference is explained (i) through the higher number of orders implemented (41,956 originator orders compared to 27,623 aggressor orders) and (ii) through the larger average order size (approx. 890,800 € for originator orders and approx. 796,600 € for aggressor orders). Paired t-tests comparing the aggressor and originator results for average order size and number of orders

247 The second largest order is 8.3 m € in Allianz AG, with an average order size of 2.4 m € and smallest order of 1.04 m €. Compared to Siemens AG, both smallest and average of the largest order per day are higher supporting that the 12.3 m € order in Siemens AG is exceptional. Appendix 2 provides the individual results for the DAX instruments.

248 The average order size of approx. 56,400 € transforms into the average trade size of approx. 35,400 € when adjusting for the PE ratio of 1.592 on the originator side.

across instruments show that both are significantly higher for the originator side (t-statistics are -3.91 and -9.28 respectively at the 0.001 significance level).[249]

These results reflect the differences between order types. In comparison to marketable orders that ensure immediacy while facing potential price risk, limit orders are executed at the defined limit price but face execution risk. The larger the order the larger the price risk of marketable orders; thus, it is expected that orders of a size ≥ 500,000 € are more often implemented as limit orders; the actual factor comparing the results for aggressor and originator orders is that originator orders are implemented 1.5 times more often.

Taking the largest executed order per trading day per individual DAX instrument, the largest order is 9.6 m € in Allianz AG with 3.8 m € as average and 1.5 m € as smallest order of the sample.[250]

6.3.3 Intraday Results

With the availability of intraday data, empirical studies focused on intraday patterns of trading variables, e.g. trading volume, price, variability of return (volatility). Theories for endogenously determined patterns followed. For trading volume and volatility, a U-shaped pattern, also known as smile-distribution, is found across different market structures.[251]

Based on the field SLICE_ID_2, intraday results are computed for average daily trading volume and for average daily volatility. The time of day in the graphs relates to the starting point of SLICE_ID_2 and reflects the average result during that defined time interval; e.g. SLICE_ID_2 = 1 is defined as the time interval from 9.00 am to 10.00 am and is reflected in the value for 9.00 am.

The average trading volume (single count) is calculated for the defined nine time intervals as follows: Initially, it is calculated per time interval per instrument as daily average (64 observations) and then aggregated to reflect the DAX average (30 observations). Each point in the graph represents 1,920 (= 30x64) observations. Finally, it is adjusted to display the average volume per minute during the hourly intervals until 5:00 pm (divided by 60) and the half-hour interval from 5:00 pm to 5:30 pm (divided by 30) to allow comparability of the different lengths of time intervals. See Exhibit 6-9. Average trading volume starts relatively high at 0.295 m € per minute during the first slice (9:00 am to 10:00 am) and decreases until the fifth slice (1:00 pm to 2:00 pm), while it increases continuously until the end of trading at 5:30 pm with its highest trading volume of 0.422 m € per minute during the last slice (5:00 pm to 5:30 pm).

---

249 Only Deutsche Telekom AG reveals a comparable average order size and number of orders (the difference being less than 0.5%). Lufthansa AG reveals a slightly smaller average order size for originator orders but five times as many originator as aggressor orders of that size. Bae/Jang/Park (2003), p. 533f. find for NYSE that large orders are more likely to be limit orders and conclude that order size is an important determinant of order type.

250 Appendix 3 provides the individual results for the DAX instruments based on the originator table.

251 Admati/Pfleiderer (1988) developed a theory where intraday patterns arise endogenously as a consequence of strategic trading behavior of informed and (uninformed) liquidity traders. Key to their model is the assumption of discretionary liquidity traders; see Admati/Pfleiderer (1988), p. 5.

The Friedman test that allows comparing more than two related samples yields significant differences at the 0.001 significant level (Chi-Square = 221.7) and corresponding pair-wise Wilcoxon tests reveal significant differences for all slices at least at the 0.01 significance level (corresponding z-statistics range from -2.746 to -4.782).[252]

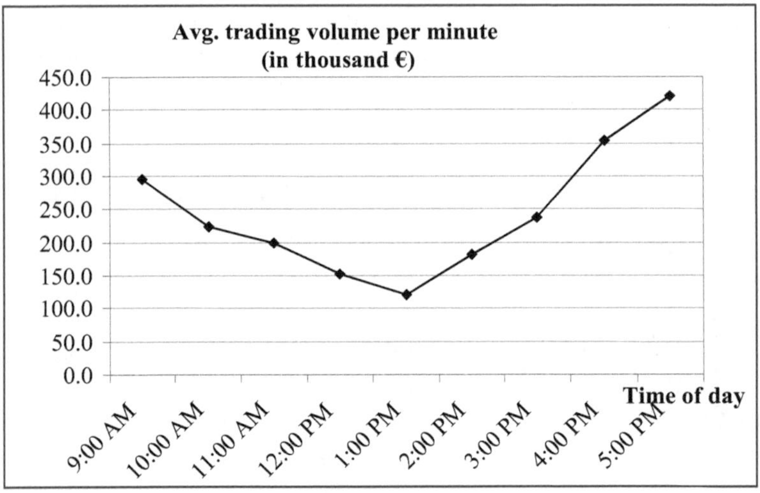

Exhibit 6-9: Intraday distribution of average trading volume

In addition, morning and afternoon trading are compared. As explained in Chapter 6.2.1, the Xetra trading model foresees an intraday auction as a natural split at 1:00 pm. As a consequence, the two trading sessions have different lengths that have to be accounted for. First, the average daily trading volume for all DAX instruments is aggregated separately for the two trading sessions.[253] During the morning session, 52.2 m € are traded, while during the afternoon session 66.1 m €; these add to the average daily trading volume of 118.3 m €, as presented in Exhibit 6-6. To compare the two sessions, the results for the second sub-period are adjusted for their longer duration of half an hour; this is done by multiplying the second half with the factor $0.\overline{88}$ (= 4/4.5), yielding 58.8 m €.

Wilcoxon test statistics show that even after adjustments, the average trading volume is significantly higher during the afternoon trading session than during the morning session (0.001 significance level with z-statistic = -4.35). The results demonstrate that trading is more active in the afternoon, for which one common explanation is the parallel opening of the US equity markets after 3:30 pm. As the graph shows, the trading volume is already higher during

---

[252] According to the Kolgomorov-Smirnov test statistics, the intraday results show a normal distribution (z-statistics ranging from 0.98 to 1.18) but the data show outliers. As non-parametric median tests are more robust to outliers, only Friedman test results and corresponding Wilcoxon signed-rank tests are presented. The results of the corresponding parametric tests (tests of within-subjects effects and pair-wise t-tests) are in line with the results of the non-parametric tests.

[253] Again, the daily average is calculated in two steps, first as daily average per instrument (64 observations) and then computed as DAX average (30 observations).

the time interval from 4:00 pm to 5:00 pm (approx. 350,000 € per minute) compared to the beginning of the trading day.

Exhibit 6-10 shows the intraday distribution of volatility in the DAX instruments. Volatility is measured as a logarithm of the highest and lowest price during 30-minute trading intervals. For the hourly intervals from 9:00 am to 5:00 pm, averages of the two values per hour are calculated, while for the last interval the initial value is employed. Average volatility is highest at the beginning of the trading with 0.63%, decreases similar to the average trading volume until the fifth interval (1:00 pm to 2:00 pm) with 0.27%, and increases until again the end of trading to 0.47% but does not reach its initial level.

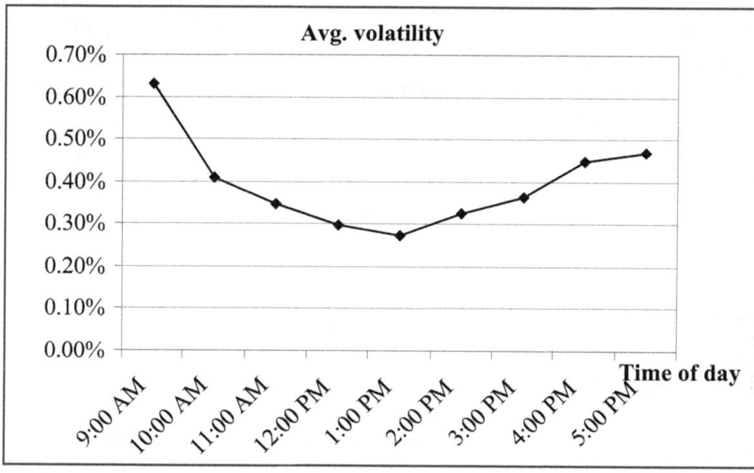

Exhibit 6-10: Intraday distribution of average volatility

Friedman test results demonstrate significant differences at the 0.001 level (Chi-Square = 223.3) and corresponding pair-wise Wilcoxon test show significant differences for all slices at the 0.01 significance level.[254] Morning and afternoon trading sessions are compared: The afternoon trading session yields a significantly lower volatility (z-statistic = -4.74, significant at 0.001 level).[255]

Both intraday patterns follow the expected standard distribution that is common in other limit order books as well as in specialist markets and market making systems.[256] Therefore, the above results are a first indication that the Xetra open limit order book yields similar trading patterns as other equity markets. See Chapter 5.1.2.

---

[254] Differences between slice 3 (11:00 am to 12:00 pm) and slices 6 and 7 (2:00 pm to 3:00 pm and 3:00 pm to 4:00 pm respectively) are only significant at the 0.05 level.

[255] As volatility is initially calculated for half-hour intervals, simple means are calculated for the morning (8 observations) and afternoon session (9 observations).

[256] Similar results have been reported for Euronext by Foucault/Moinas/Theissen (2004), p. 30 f. and Beltran/Durée/Giot (2004), p. 13; for SEHK by Ahn/Bae/Chan (2001), p. 773; for NYSE by Lee/Mucklow/ Ready (1993), p. 360f.

6.4 Hypothesis Framework

The hypothesis framework follows the results from Chapter 5 concerning existing theoretical, empirical, and experimental results for trading in open limit order books. The hypotheses are tested during the different steps of the research approach.

As described in Exhibit 6-1, the first step analyzes the research objective (i) that the Xetra electronic open limit order book displays similar characteristics to other limit order books. This is broken down into several sub-hypotheses that will be tested separately. The second step does not analyze a hypothesis per se but determines that trader IDs are the unique identifier for distinguishing informed and uninformed traders, research objective (ii). The general theoretical notion of an inverse relation of liquidity and informed trading implies that informed traders are on the liquidity demanding side implementing market orders. Against this notion, the third step tests the research objective (iii) that informed traders do provide liquidity. Again, several sub-hypotheses are tested.

6.4.1 Characteristics of the Xetra Limit Order Book

To provide the reference point for the interpretation of results of the different trader categories as well as to analyze the Xetra limit order book in comparison to other electronic limit order books, the following sub-hypotheses are tested based on the XLM and PI calculation. The hypotheses follow the results as derived in Chapter 5.1. It should be noted that the XLM calculates the cost of liquidity; i.e. it is the inverse of liquidity, meaning the higher the XLM results the lower the liquidity and vice versa.

Hypotheses set (a): Liquidity in general

(i) Liquidity (XLM) is negatively (positively) related to order size, which is reflected in a monotone but non-linear increasing function of the XLM.

(ii) Liquidity (XLM) on the buy and sell side of the order book does not systematically differ.

(iii) Liquidity (XLM) is lowest (highest) at the beginning of the trading day, and increases (decreases) continuously while remaining stable at the end of the trading day; i.e. the XLM follows a reverse J-shaped pattern.

(iv) Liquidity (XLM) is positively (negatively) related to trading volume and price but negatively (positively) related to volatility.

Hypotheses set (b): Informed trading in general

(v) Informed trading is significant in the anonymous open electronic limit order book (Xetra).

(vi) Informed trading is negatively related to firm size, i.e. it is higher for smaller firms.

(vii) Informed trading and order size are related; i.e. medium size orders carry more information than small or large orders (stealth trading hypothesis).

(viii) Informed trading is highest at the beginning of the trading day and is gradually resolved throughout the trading day, revealing a reverse J-shaped pattern.

(ix) Liquidity (XLM) and informed trading are negatively (positively) related.

6.4.2 Informed Liquidity Supply and Demand

Following the trader classification and identification of informed traders, the following hypotheses are analyzed for informed traders comparing their results to the other trader categories (uninformed and partly informed traders) and to the average results across all orders. The hypotheses follow the results as derived in Chapter 5.2. The analyses will help to form a picture on the evolution of liquidity in the Xetra limit order book, especially on how informed and uninformed traders differ in their choice of order type.

Hypotheses set (c): Informed liquidity demand

(x) Informed traders prefer medium size market orders (stealth trading).

(xi) Informed traders' market orders perform better than market orders of other trader categories.

(xii) Informed traders are discretionary market order traders.

Hypotheses set (d): Informed liquidity supply

(xiii) Informed traders use limit orders as part of their trading strategies.

(xiv) Informed traders prefer medium size limit orders (stealth trading).

(xv) Informed traders reveal stronger limit order aggressiveness.

Hypotheses set (e): Net position and intraday results

(xvi) Informed traders are net liquidity providers.

(xvii) Informed traders show a net role change during the trading day:

(a) Informed traders prefer market orders earlier in the trading day.

(b) Informed traders prefer limit orders later in the trading day.

(c) Informed traders switch from a net liquidity demander to a net liquidity provider role.

6.5 Synopsis

In this chapter, the research approach underlying the empirical analysis is presented. It is composed of three consecutive steps: (1) market description, (2) trader classification and identification of informed traders, and (3) analysis of liquidity demand and supply behavior of informed traders.

The relevant data set (XLM table, Trades table, BBA table) is described in detail including any additional data fields introduced and cleansing activities performed. The split of the Trades table into aggressor and originator orders and transactions is explained.

Descriptive statistics of the DAX instruments are provided based on the cleansed aggressor data set. These include instrument specific information concerning trading volume, number of trades, volatility, and market capitalization. The intraday distributions of trading volume and volatility are computed, both following the expected standard U-shaped distribution.

In addition, the order size distribution comparing aggressor and originator order is provided. The main difference is found for orders larger than 500,000 €, where originator orders reveal a significantly larger average order size as well as higher number of orders across the DAX instruments.

Finally, the hypothesis framework for steps (1) and (3) is derived. The remaining chapters of the empirical part will follow the outlined research approach.

7 Market Description: Liquidity and Informed Trading

This chapter covers the first step of the empirical analysis. See Exhibit 7-1. It is subdivided into separate descriptions and tests of common hypotheses of liquidity and informed trading as well as their relation. It lays the foundation for the interpretation of results on informed traders' behavior, which are presented in the third step. The synopsis summarizes the results in comparison to the results found in other electronic limit order markets.

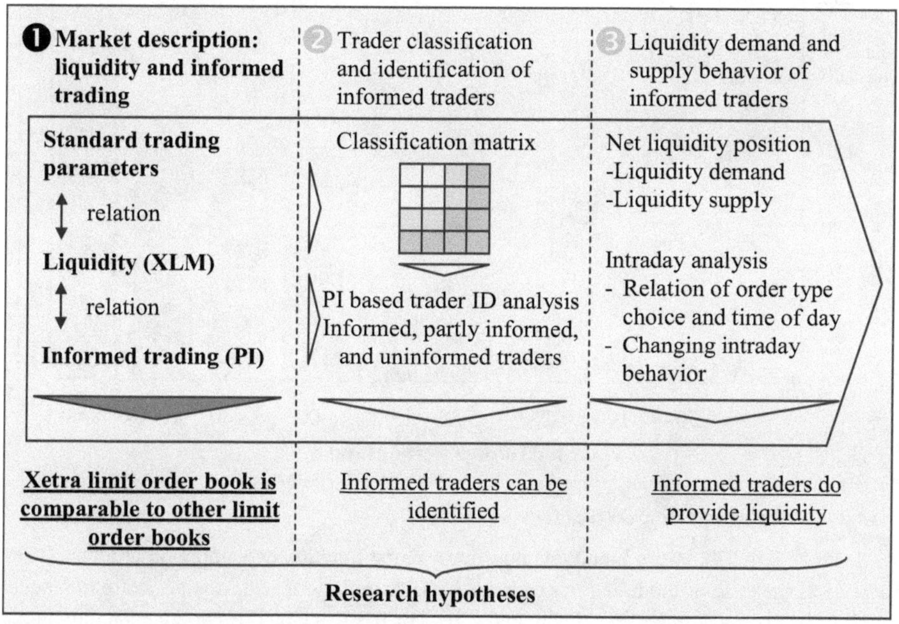

Exhibit 7-1: Research approach step 1

7.1 Liquidity

As presented in Chapter 3.2.2, the XLM is implemented to measure the liquidity of the DAX instruments. XLM results are provided for the different hypothetical order sizes. Initially it is calculated separately for both sides of the order book (see Chapter 6.2.1). But for most analyses the XLM is presented as round-trip market impact costs, taking both sides of the order book into account. The results presented include the liquidity function, cross-sectional results, a comparison of bid and ask liquidity, intraday liquidity, as well as regressions with standard determinants of liquidity. Results cover hypotheses set (a) and are tested for hypotheses (i) to (iv).

The following notation is applied throughout this chapter: When referring to a specific XLM volume class, XLM(V), the volume (V) is measured in 1,000 €, i.e. XLM(250) corresponds to an order size of 250,000 €.

7.1.1 Liquidity Function

Exhibit 7-2 presents the average round-trip costs (XLM) for the DAX instruments during the research period. Based on daily averages per instrument for each XLM volume class, the data is further aggregated to provide the average of the DAX instruments. Results are presented for all volume classes for which the XLM is calculated.

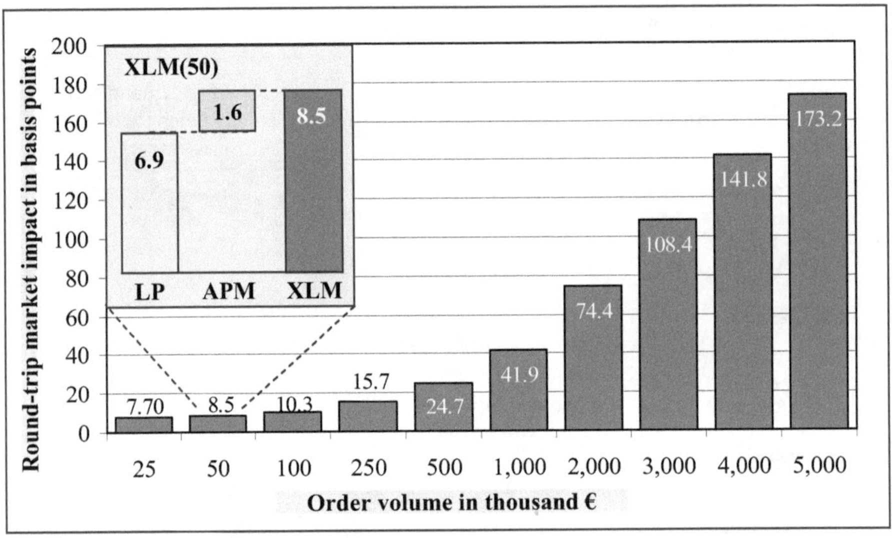

Exhibit 7-2: XLM results for average of DAX instruments

As illustrated, the XLM is a monotone non-linear rising function depending on order size. The LP reflects the state of the function and is the basis or minimum cost. It is per definition equal for all order sizes as it measures the quoted spread or BBA, which does not depend on volume class.

The slope of the function is reflected in the APM, the marginal cost of liquidity demand. The APM increases with order size, as larger orders move further into the order book when executed. During the research period, the average basis cost (LP) is 6.9 bp. As the XLM(25) is 7.7 bp, the LP of 6.9 bp reflects that on average orders up to a size of 22,300 € are executed at the available spread (BBA), incurring implicit costs of 15.39 € (= 22,300 € x 6.9 bp). Adding the LP and the APM yields the XLM.

Taking XLM(50) as an example (see Exhibit 7-2) the total cost of 8.5 bp (42.5 €) can be split into the LP (6.9 bp) and the APM (1.6 bp) with the APM reflecting approx. 19% of the total cost. In comparison, for XLM(100) the ratio of the APM is 33% (3.4 bp) of the total cost, and for XLM(500) it is 72% (17.8 bp), increasing to over 90% (35 bp) for XLM(1,000) and larger showing the increasing marginal cost of liquidity demand. The results confirm hypothesis (i) Liquidity (XLM) is negatively (positively) related to order size, which is reflected in a monotone but non-linear increasing function of the XLM.

7.1.2 Cross-sectional Results

In Chapter 6.3.1, large differences between market capitalization and trading volume were reported for the sample of DAX instruments. These differences suggest large differences in execution costs. This assumption is supported by the data presented in Exhibit 7-3. The table presents for the LP and selected volume classes from XLM(50) to XLM(5,000) the individual (round-trip) results as well as the DAX minimum, maximum, and mean (equal results as in Exhibit 7-2). Furthermore, the average computed only for instruments where calculation of the XLM is always possible are presented as DAX Avg. (100% availability). Results are sorted in ascending order by XLM(1,000).

The cross-sectional results illustrate that liquidity varies considerably. The LP is smallest for Allianz AG with 3.6 bp and highest for Infineon Technologies AG with 14.0 bp. Allianz AG remains the instrument with the highest liquidity until XLM(500), while Telekom AG, which accounts for a LP that is twice as high at 7.2 bp, takes the lead for XLM(1,000) and larger order sizes. Thus, there is no instrument that provides the highest liquidity independent of order size. A ranking based on XLM(V) would always depend on the volume class underlying the ranking results. Exhibit 7-3 is displayed as a heat map with a color scheme suggesting a segmentation for instruments and the respective XLM volume classes for highly liquids (≤ 50 bp), liquids (> 50 ≤ 100 bp), medium liquids (> 100 ≤ 200 bp), and less liquids (> 200 bp).[257]

In addition, the values displayed in italics reflect that these volume classes could not be calculated all the time. As described in Chapter 6.2.1, the XLM can only be calculated when two conditions are fulfilled: (i) trading is continuous and (ii) the volume provided by the orders standing in the book is large enough to allow execution of the hypothetical order size (see Chapter 6.2.1, field explanation for NOOF_AGGR_ROWS). For 28 out of 30 instruments, calculation of XLM(1,000) is always possible, and for XLM(2,000) 25 instruments still allow full calculation which then reduces to 11 instruments that allow for regular calculation of XLM(5,000).

---

[257] The DAX instruments are generally classified as highly liquid instruments, as they do not require any liquidity provider (see Chapter 2.3 and Exhibit 2-4). The heat map classification in different liquidity levels does not imply that any of these instruments are not highly liquid. It only foresees a further distinction of these instruments depending on liquidity.

	XLM in basis points (bp) per volume class								
Instrument	**LP**	**50**	**250**	**500**	**1,000**	**2,000**	**3,000**	**4,000**	**5,000**
DT.TELEKOM AG NA	7.2	7.4	8.3	9.4	11.6	16.1	20.5	24.9	29.3
ALLIANZ AG VNA O.N.	3.6	4.2	6.2	8.4	12.3	19.4	26.1	32.8	39.5
DEUTSCHE BANK AG NA O.N.	4.2	4.9	7.5	10.6	16.3	26.9	37.4	48.0	58.3
SIEMENS AG NA	4.2	4.9	7.5	10.8	17.2	30.0	42.8	55.4	67.3
MUENCH.RUECKVERS.VNA O.N.	4.6	5.4	8.6	12.6	20.4	35.5	50.1	64.1	77.6
E.ON AG O.N.	4.4	5.2	8.4	12.4	20.5	36.5	51.5	65.4	77.9
DAIMLERCHRYSLER AG NA O.N.	5.1	6.0	9.5	13.8	22.3	39.6	56.8	72.5	85.9
SAP AG O.N.	4.8	5.8	9.7	14.6	24.3	42.9	59.3	73.7	86.5
BASF AG O.N.	4.5	5.4	9.2	14.3	24.6	44.9	63.9	80.2	*94.5*
RWE AG ST O.N.	5.2	6.2	10.6	16.1	27.1	49.0	68.6	85.0	99.4
BAYER AG O.N.	6.7	8.1	13.6	20.2	33.5	60.3	83.1	102.7	120.9
BAY.MOTOREN WERKE AG ST	5.7	7.1	12.9	20.4	35.2	63.7	88.0	111.0	134.6
VOLKSWAGEN AG ST O.N.	6.0	7.4	13.2	20.7	35.7	63.5	86.1	*107.0*	*129.4*
DEUTSCHE POST AG NA O.N.	7.6	9.0	15.2	23.2	38.8	67.5	93.3	119.3	*147.7*
COMMERZBANK AG O.N.	8.0	9.7	16.6	24.7	40.3	69.2	95.7	123.8	*157.4*
INFINEON TECH.AG NA O.N.	14.0	15.4	21.0	28.6	44.1	73.0	98.2	*123.6*	*152.0*
ADIDAS-SALOMON AG O.N.	6.0	7.6	14.9	24.7	44.2	79.2	111.5	*146.6*	*189.6*
THYSSENKRUPP AG O.N.	8.3	10.2	17.8	27.2	45.2	80.5	114.2	150.4	*194.2*
SCHERING AG O.N.	6.4	8.4	16.5	26.2	46.0	81.8	115.1	153.1	*200.7*
BAY.HYPO-VEREINSBK.O.N.	9.4	11.1	18.1	27.5	47.7	*87.2*	*117.6*	*157.8*	239.6
DEUTSCHE BOERSE NA O.N.	7.1	8.9	17.1	27.9	*49.1*	*83.2*	*113.6*	*147.1*	*180.8*
CONTINENTAL AG O.N.	6.6	8.6	17.2	27.8	49.1	86.0	*120.1*	*155.9*	*198.9*
METRO AG ST O.N.	7.2	9.8	20.0	32.0	55.3	98.9	142.6	*192.0*	*255.4*
LUFTHANSA AG VNA O.N.	11.1	13.4	22.5	34.0	56.2	96.1	136.3	185.0	*251.1*
TUI AG NA	10.1	13.1	24.3	38.1	63.2	105.4	148.1	*198.1*	*259.7*
MAN AG ST O.N.	7.9	11.0	24.0	39.1	67.8	117.7	*178.9*	*282.0*	*332.6*
ALTANA AG O.N.	6.7	10.2	23.8	40.0	69.2	118.1	177.7	255.5	353.9
LINDE AG O.N.	7.3	10.3	23.8	41.7	74.8	*144.7*	*256.0*	*345.3*	*293.4*
HENKEL KGAA VZO O.N.	7.6	10.7	26.8	46.1	79.1	*139.7*	*222.4*	*324.8*	*456.5*
FRESEN.MED.CARE AG O.N.	8.4	11.3	27.3	48.5	*86.1*	*176.9*	*277.1*	*259.4*	*160.5*
DAX Min	3.6	4.2	6.2	8.4	11.6	16.1	20.5	24.9	29.3
DAX Max	14.0	15.4	27.3	48.5	86.1	176.9	277.1	345.3	456.5
DAX Mean	6.9	8.5	15.7	24.7	41.9	74.4	108.4	141.4	170.8
DAX Avg. (100% availability)	6.9	8.5	15.7	24.7	40.1	64.1	85.6	100.2	102.6

≤ 50	>50 ≤ 100	>100 ≤ 200	> 200

Exhibit 7-3: Cross-sectional heat map for selected volume classes

Whenever the calculation availability is below 100%, the liquidity will be overestimated only taking the order book into account, when it is deeper than usual. Results for Fresenius Medical Care AG visualize this relation. The XLM results increase up to 277.1 bp for XLM(3,000) where calculation is at least possible 75% of the time. However, results decrease for larger order sizes reaching a level of 160.5 bp for XLM(5,000) where calculation is only possible approx. 20% of the time. As the XLM is an increasing function of order size, the interpretation of XLM(V) results depends on the calculation availability. A comparison of results of different instruments is only feasible for volume classes with similar calculation availability: The DAX instruments can only be compared directly for volume classes until XLM(500). Exhibit 7-3 presents the average for each volume class across all instruments (DAX mean) as well as average results only for those instruments per volume class, where the calculation availability was 100% (DAX Avg. with 100% availability). The DAX average taking into account those instruments where calculation availability is 100% is always smaller than the DAX mean: For XLM(1,000) this difference is only 1.8 bp but increases to 68.2 bp for XLM(5,000). This demonstrates that even within the DAX instruments, which are the most liquid stocks in Germany, a distinction between instruments classified as highly liquid and those that reveal a lower liquidity can be made.

The results suggest a possible grouping of instruments along their liquidity, i.e. along their results for different volume classes. The ten most liquid instruments show results in the high liquid field (below 50 bp) for both XLM(1,000) and XLM(2,000), while the next twelve instruments also display high liquid results for XLM(1,000) and the last eight only for XLM(500). As described in Chapter 6.3.2, only 0.7% of the orders that enter the order book as aggressive (liquidity demanding) orders belong to SIZE_ID = 6, i.e. orders that are equal to or larger than 500,000 € with an average order size in this group of approx. 797,000 €. In addition, as shown, the calculation ability of the XLM reduces with increasing volume classes reducing the accuracy of the results from XLM(1,000) and larger. Thus, these volume classes are excluded from further analysis.

Correlation analysis for the cross-section of instruments supports the strongly negative (positive) relation between trading volume and the different volume classes of the XLM (liquidity). The Pearson correlation coefficient computed for traded volume and XLM(V) is significant at the 0.001 level and ranges from -0.63 for LP, -0.76 for XLM(50) to -0.86, and -0.85 for XLM(250) and XLM(500) respectively.[258] The DAX instruments are finally distinguished into three groups, each including ten instruments. For the distinction, two rankings are computed: (i) average daily trading volume (see Chapter 6.3.1.) and (ii) XLM(V). Trading volume is preferred over XLM(V), as different volume classes would suggest different groupings. The results for XLM(500) support the group clustering for 26 out of 30 instruments; the remaining instruments are displayed in italics: Volkswagen AG is included in group 1, although only ranked 13th based on XLM(500). It replaces BASF that ranked 8th in terms of liquidity but only 11th in terms of trading volume. In addition, Infineon Technologies AG ranked 22nd in terms of liquidity but 18th in terms of trading volume replaces Schering AG that was ranked 17th in terms of liquidity but only 23rd in terms of trading volume.[259] The detailed results are presented in Exhibit 7-4.

---

[258] Spearman rank correlation coefficients range from -0.69 (LP) to -0.97 (XLM(500)) significant at the 0.001 level.

[259] Gomber/Schweickert (2002b), p. 6 implement a similar approach comparing trading volume and XLM(100). In contrast to the presented results, their sample (five trading days in March 2002) reveals stronger differences between the rankings.

Instruments	Avg. daily volume (m €)	XLM (500)	Rank volume	Rank XLM(500)	GROUP_ID
ALLIANZ AG VNA O.N.	391,1	8,4	1	1	1
DT.TELEKOM AG NA	304,7	9,4	2	2	1
DEUTSCHE BANK AG NA O.N.	268,6	10,6	3	3	1
SIEMENS AG NA	253,0	10,8	4	4	1
E.ON AG O.N.	243,7	12,4	5	5	1
DAIMLERCHRYSLER AG NA O.N.	220,6	13,8	6	7	1
MUENCH.RUECKVERS.VNA O.N.	184,2	12,6	7	6	1
VOLKSWAGEN AG ST O.N.	*167,9*	*20,7*	*8*	*13*	*1*
SAP AG O.N.	166,2	14,6	9	9	1
RWE AG ST O.N.	163,5	16,1	10	10	1
BASF AG O.N.	*153,7*	*14,3*	*11*	*8*	*2*
BAYER AG O.N.	99,8	20,2	12	11	2
COMMERZBANK AG O.N.	99,3	24,7	13	15	2
BAY.MOTOREN WERKE AG ST	91,6	20,4	14	12	2
BAY.HYPO-VEREINSBK.O.N.	77,4	27,5	15	19	2
DEUTSCHE POST AG NA O.N.	68,0	23,2	16	14	2
ADIDAS-SALOMON AG O.N.	67,8	24,7	17	16	2
INFINEON TECH.AG NA O.N.	*58,0*	*28,6*	*18*	*22*	*2*
THYSSENKRUPP AG O.N.	53,2	27,2	19	18	2
CONTINENTAL AG O.N.	52,4	27,8	20	20	2
TUI AG NA	47,4	38,1	21	25	3
DEUTSCHE BOERSE NA O.N.	47,2	27,9	22	21	3
SCHERING AG O.N.	*45,7*	*26,2*	*23*	*17*	*3*
METRO AG ST O.N.	39,6	32,0	24	23	3
LUFTHANSA AG VNA O.N.	38,7	34,0	25	24	3
MAN AG ST O.N.	36,7	39,1	26	26	3
ALTANA AG O.N.	30,1	40,0	27	27	3
LINDE AG O.N.	28,8	41,7	28	28	3
HENKEL KGAA VZO O.N.	26,2	46,1	29	29	3
FRESEN.MED.CARE AG O.N.	25,0	48,5	30	30	3

Exhibit 7-4: Definition of Group_ID

Finally, GROUP_ID = 1 includes the ten most actively traded and most liquid instruments, while GROUP_ID = 3 contains the ten instruments with lowest trading volume and highest XLM.

7.1.3 Bid and Ask Liquidity

The XLM is initially calculated separately for each side of the order book and then summed up to provide the round-trip costs. As a consequence, it is possible to compare liquidity on the bid and ask side of the order book and test for significant differences. The liquidity on the bid side reflects the liquidity available to sell market orders while the liquidity on the ask side reflects the liquidity available to buy market orders.

Exhibit 7-5 presents averages for the bid and ask side for the XLM for all volume classes. The results show that the XLM for market sell orders that execute against the bid side is always higher than for market buy orders that execute against the ask side. For XLM(25) results for market sell orders are 0.11% higher (0.004 bp), while this difference increases to 2.79% for XLM(1,000). As described in the previous chapter, results for volume sizes larger than XLM(500) should be interpreted with care. Cross-sectional test statistics for the equality of mean yield no significant results for order sizes up to XLM(250).

XLM(V)	Bid (sell orders)	Ask (buy orders)	Difference (Bid - Ask)	t-statistic	
XLM(25)	3.852	3.848	0.004	-0.534	ns
XLM(50)	4.282	4.266	0.016	-1.090	ns
XLM(100)	5.169	5.131	0.038	-1.474	ns
XLM(250)	7.925	7.804	0.121	-1.787	ns
XLM(500)	12.479	12.236	0.243	-2.102	*
XLM(1,000)	21.246	20.654	0.592	-2.676	*
XLM(2,000)	38.207	36.227	1.980	-3.242	**
XLM(3,000)	57.610	50.819	6.791	-2.233	*
XLM(4,000)	78.378	63.460	14.918	-2.448	*
XLM(5,000)	96.130	77.053	19.077	-2.988	**

** = significant at 0.01 level; * = 0.05 level; ns = not significant

Exhibit 7-5: XLM for bid and ask side

These findings partly support earlier results found for Xetra based on data during August 2002, where no significant differences were found for a selection of DAX instruments up to XLM(1,000). However, it should be noted that Gomber/Schweickert/Theissen (2005) selected the twelve most liquid instruments of the DAX.[260] Implementing the GROUP_ID and repeating the paired t-tests, for GROUP_ID = 1, which includes the ten most liquid instruments in the DAX, no significant differences are found until XLM(1,000) supporting their results. Thus, the results partly confirm hypothesis (ii) Liquidity (XLM) on the buy and sell side of the order book does not systematically differ. However, they contrast to results for other markets (e.g. NYSE), where order book depth is generally significantly higher for the ask side than for the bid side.[261]

7.1.4 Intraday Results

In Chapter 6.3.3, intraday patterns for trading volume and volatility are described and evaluated in comparison to other limit order markets. These descriptive variables show distinct intraday patterns. The relation between the two descriptive variables and liquidity will be further tested with a regression analysis in the following chapter.

In line with hypothesis (iii) XLM(V) is expected to display a reverse J-shaped pattern. The intraday analysis is implemented for different order sizes to demonstrate that results are

[260] See Gomber/Schweickert/Theissen (2005), p. 10.

[261] See Irvine/Benston/Kandel (2000), p. 22f. Chordia/Roll/Subrahmanyam (2002), p. 117 find an order imbalance with more market buy than sell orders which implies higher depth on the ask side of the order book. Ranaldo (2004), p. 55f. discovers that buyers more frequently submit limit orders within the quote.

independent of order size. Intraday results are presented for LP and three additional volume classes, classified as small, standard, medium, and large orders: LP, XLM(50), XLM(250), and XLM(500), respectively. The choice of these four liquidity measures for the numerical analysis is based on the following assumptions: First, the LP captures small orders up to a size of approx. 22,300 €; thus, XLM(25) should not yield differing results and is excluded from the reporting. Second, XLM(50) is chosen as standard order size, reflecting the average aggressor order size (55,800 €) as reported in Chapter 6.3.2. Third, all measures larger than XLM(500) are excluded due to the calculation validity of below 100%, classifying XLM(500) as large.[262] Finally, XLM(250) is defined as medium order size in comparison to XLM(50) and XLM(500).

Exhibit 7-6 displays the intraday distribution of the chosen liquidity measures. Results are generated as averages per SLICE_ID_2 (see Chapter 6.2.1) in two steps: first, calculation of average based on 64 daily observations per instrument and then aggregation as average for all DAX instruments. Thus, each point in the graph represents 1,920 (= 30x64) observations. The time of day in the graphs relates to the starting point of SLICE_ID_2 and reflects the average result during that defined time interval, e.g. SLICE_ID_2 = 1 is defined as the time interval from 9.00 am to 10.00 am and is reflected in the value for 9.00 am.

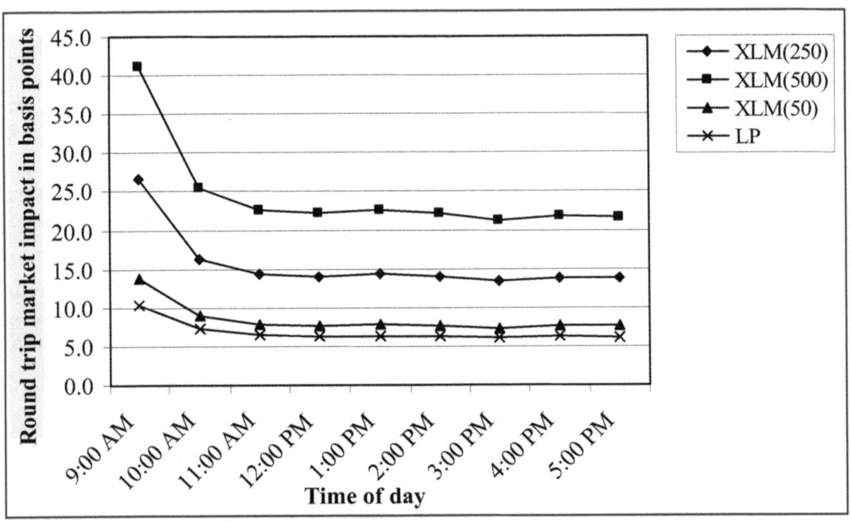

Exhibit 7-6: Intraday distribution of LP and XLM(V)

The graphs display reverse J-shaped patterns. The XLM provides the highest value at the start of continuous trading and decreases until the 12:00 pm interval. After a slight increase until the 2:00 pm interval, the XLM decreases again until the 3:00 pm interval, finally increasing slightly until the end of the trading day. The lowest results for the LP and the order sizes

---

262 In addition, Gomber/Schweickert/Theissen (2005), p. 14 have shown that large orders are timed, i.e. they are entered when order book depth is exceptionally large. The authors chose the 100 largest transactions during one month; their average size is 899,402 € for the sell and 866,337 € for the buy side.

chosen are found for the time interval 3:00 pm to 4:00 pm. During this time, the NYSE opens at 3:30 pm, allowing for additional liquidity from the US.

As Friedman test results for the LP and the different XLM(V) show significant differences between the results of the different time intervals at the 0.001 level, pair-wise Wilcoxon tests are computed.[263] Wilcoxon test results compute significant differences between most of the time intervals, especially between the morning and afternoon intervals, also indicating that liquidity remains stable for the last two time intervals. Test results are reported in detail in Appendix 4. In addition, means for the morning and afternoon trading sessions are tested for significant differences.[264] For all four liquidity measures, means are significantly larger (0.001 significance level) for the morning trading session, i.e. liquidity is lower during the morning trading session compared to the afternoon. Pair-wise t-statistics are presented in Exhibit 7-7.[265]

Liquidity measure	Morning session	Afternoon session	Difference	t-statistic
LP	7.569	6.240	1.329	9.49 ***
XLM(50)	9.564	7.641	1.923	9.31 ***
XLM(250)	17.823	13.853	3.970	8.31 ***
XLM(500)	27.808	21.928	5.880	8.19 ***

*** = significant at 0.001 level

Exhibit 7-7: Comparison of liquidity during morning and afternoon trading session

The intraday distribution is very similar for all four liquidity measures, which is confirmed by the high correlation between these measures. The Pearson correlation coefficients are significant at the 0.001 level and range from 0.616 (LP and XLM(500)) to 0.989 (XLM(250) and XLM(500)) for the cross-section.[266]

The initial hypothesis (iii) that the XLM shows a reverse J-shaped pattern, being highest at the beginning of the trading day, is confirmed. This outcome contrasts to existing results for Xetra: Gomber/Schweickert/Theissen (2005) present a data set including twelve DAX instruments for 22 trading days in August 2002 that displayed a distinct U-shaped pattern. However, trading hours extended until 8:00 pm at that time and the increase in the XLM(V) that lead to the U-shaped pattern is reported to take place after 5:30 pm. The authors explain the sharp increase in XLM with institutional investors closing their book after the auction at

---

263 Friedman tests are conducted similar to the intraday analysis for trading volume and volatility as the liquidity measures show a normal distribution but some outliers. Test statistics for the four liquidity measures show significant results at the 0.001 level with Chi-Square statistics ranging from 157.8 for XLM(500) to 170.7 for XLM(50).

264 For the morning trading session, a simple mean can be calculated, while for the afternoon trading session, weighting factors are applied for the four hourly time intervals and the half-hour interval ($0.\overline{22}$ and $0.\overline{11}$ respectively).

265 Wilcoxon signed-ranks test results are significant at the 0.001 level with an identical z-statistic of -4.78; i.e. for all thirty instruments the results are smaller (30 negative ranks) in the afternoon trading session.

266 Spearman rank correlation coefficients are comparable and range from 0.764 to 0.986, with a 0.001 significance level.

5:30 pm.[267] Looking at the intraday distribution of the XLM until 5:30 pm, their results are comparable to those presented in Exhibit 7-6, explaining the divergences in results with the difference in trading hours. The fact that the authors explain the decrease in liquidity with institutional investors leaving the market is an indication for institutional investors providing liquidity. As presented in Chapter 4.2, institutional investors are often assumed to be informed traders.[268] Following this assumption, these results are a first hint that informed traders provide liquidity.

7.1.5 Regression with Standard Determinants

Previous research shows that liquidity is a function of price, volume, and volatility: traded volume and price are inversely related to (quoted or effective) spread, while volatility has a positive relation. See Chapter 5.1.2.[269] Therefore, these variables are tested for the cross-section (N = 30) with the following regression:

$$Liquidity_i = \alpha + \beta_1 Volume_i + \beta_2 Volatility_i + \beta_3 Price_i + \varepsilon$$

Liquidity$_i$ as dependent variable is defined as quoted percentage spread (LP) or XLM(V) for the volume classes 50, 250, and 500 of the *i*th instrument. The choice of liquidity measures follows the same rationale as implemented in the intraday results ensuring that the regression results are robust to changes in order size.

The three independent variables are determined identical to the initial descriptive statistics presented in Chapter 6.3.1 and Exhibit 6-6: *Volume$_i$* is the average daily trading volume in m € per instrument (*i*). It is calculated as total aggressor trading volume per day and then averaged across the 64 trading days. *Volatility$_i$* is defined as the average daily volatility per instrument (*i*). It is measured as a logarithm of the highest and lowest price during each 30-minute trading interval of the trading day, computed as average per trading day, and further aggregated across the 64 trading days. *Price$_i$* is the average daily trade price per instrument (*i*). It is computed as the average of all transaction prices per trading day and further averaged across the 64 trading days.

The regression is estimated using standard OLS estimation on the log regression equation to ensure normal distribution of all regression parameters. Exhibit 7-8 displays the results of the regression analysis. It presents the means of the coefficients and standard t-statistics for the defined regression equation. The results of the adjusted R square range from 0.87 to 0.972, increasing with volume class. F-statistics show that the different regressions fit the data rather well.

---

[267] See Gomber/Schweickert/Theissen (2005), p. 11 and p. 37. Following discussions with the Xetra members, trading hours were reduced to 5:30 pm in November 2003. For the floor trading hours still extend until 8:00 pm. Wolff (2003), pp. 151-155 finds a U-shaped distribution for the DAX instruments during June to September 2001. McInish/Wood (1992), p. 760 find a reverse J-shaped distribution for NYSE spreads.

[268] See Dennis/Weston (2001), p. 4 and p. 19f., Chakravarty (2001), p. 291, and Anand/Chakravarty/Martell (2005), p. 290.

[269] See Stoll (2000), p. 1482. Chung/Chaeronwong (1998), p. 5, who analyze NYSE and AMEX data, implement average daily trading volume, price, and risk as regression variables and report that using other measures of trading activity, such as the number of trades, yields similar results.

		LP		XLM(50)	
		Estimate of coefficient	t-statistic	Estimate of coefficient	t-statistic
Intercept	α	8.881	7.14 ***	11.275	11.05 ***
Volume	$\beta1$	-0.227	-8.40 ***	-0.314	-14.15 ***
Volatility	$\beta2$	0.174	0.96 ns	0.254	1.71 ns
Price	$\beta3$	-0.252	-7.79 ***	-0.196	-7.40 ***
Adjusted R^2		0.87		0.924	
F-Statistic		65.68	***	118.8	***

		XLM(250)		XLM(500)	
		Estimate of coefficient	t-statistic	Estimate of coefficient	t-statistic
Intercept	α	16.922	18.60 ***	20.409	22.28 ***
Volume	$\beta1$	-0.512	-25.90 ***	-0.611	-30.70 ***
Volatility	$\beta2$	0.461	3.47 **	0.668	4.99 ***
Price	$\beta3$	-0.057	-2.39 *	0.023	0.95 ns
Adjusted R^2		0.964		0.972	
F-Statistic		260.6	***	338.0	***

*** = significant at 0.001 level; ** = 0.01 level; * = 0.05 level; ns = not significant

Exhibit 7-8: Results of the multivariate analysis

The coefficient of the controlling variable *Volume* displays the expected negative sign and is significant at the 0.001 level for all four liquidity measures.

Results for the variables *Volatility* and *Price* are mixed: *Volatility* has the expected positive sign but is not significant for the smaller order sizes, LP and XLM(50), while it yields significant results at least at the 0.01 level for the larger order sizes, XLM(250) and XLM(500). *Price* shows the expected reverse behavior to *Volatility*. The average price of an instrument directly influences the LP of the instrument as the minimum price increment is defined as 0.01 €. As explained in Chapter 7.1.1, the APM increases with increasing order size; thus, its percentage share of the XLM increases while the percentage share of the LP decreases accordingly. The explanatory power of the variable *Price* thus decreases with increasing order size, which is reflected in the results.

As LP and XLM(V) do not measure liquidity but the costs of liquidity, the independent variables reflect the inverse relation. In summary, the multivariate tests support the initial hypothesis (iv) Liquidity (XLM) is positively (negatively) related to trading volume and price but negatively (positively) related to volatility.

7.2 Informed Trading

As presented in Chapter 4.3.3, (ad hoc method) informed trading can be determined on the level of the individual trade based on different spread measures, the effective (ES) and realized spreads (RS) with the difference defining the price impact (PI) as a measure for informed trading.

The effective spread reflects the difference between the average price of the transaction and the midpoint at the time of order entry, while the realized spread is computed similarly using the midpoint five minutes after the order was executed. Thus the calculation of the realized spread is based on the assumption that any informational advantage of a trader's order is absorbed fully by the market five minutes after the initial order's execution.[270] The price impact calculates the difference between the effective spread and realized spread. It is a measure for informed trading as compared to the effective spread a relatively smaller or even negative realized spread reflects informed trading.

$$ES = \frac{2D(P_t - MP_t)}{MP_t},$$

$$RS = \frac{2D(P_t - MP_{t+5\,min})}{MP_t},$$

$$PI = \frac{2D(MP_{t+5\,min} - MP_t)}{MP_t} = ES - RS,$$

where D is the trade direction, taking the value 1 for buyer initiated trades and -1 for seller initiated trades, P_t is the average (weighted) price of the executed order, and MP_t is the midpoint prevailing the order's execution. MP_{t+5min} is defined as the midpoint five minutes after the order's execution. Comparability across instruments is ensured when computing the spread measures relative to the midpoint prevailing at order entry.

Results are provided for the cross-section of instruments, Group ID, order sizes, intraday and in relation to liquidity. They cover hypotheses set (b) and are tested for hypotheses (v) to (ix).

7.2.1 *Calculation Methodology*

For the price impact calculation, the aggressor orders extracted from the Trades table have to be combined with the BBA table. Based on the order entry timestamp of each aggressor order, the respective midpoint at order entry (MP_t) and five minutes after order entry (MP_{t+5min}) are determined. As described in Chapter 6.2.3, the best bid (BB) and best ask (BA) are updated independently of each other, leading to different validity times. Technically, the BBA Table is split into two separate tables, one including only the ask side and the other the bid side values.

TSTAMP and HSEC determine the START_TIME of the validity of a BB or BA, while the END_TIME is determined through the start of validity of the respective update on the same

---

270 Implementing a midpoint five minutes after the order execution is common practice and in line with rule 11Ac1-5 as introduced by the SEC. See Chapter 4.3.3 and Footnote 154.

side of the book: END_TIME = START_TIME(update). The start and end of the validity are transformed to reflect milliseconds (HSEC multiplied with 10).

When an aggressive buy (sell) order enters the limit order book, it instantaneously affects the sell (buy) side, i.e. BA (BB), of the order book. Thus the order entry timestamp is equal to the START_TIME of the BA (BB) update. When identifying the respective BA (BB), the following matching procedure ensures that the BBA and its corresponding midpoint (MP_t) prevailing the order entry are identified:

ORDER_ENTRY_TIMESTAMP > START_TIME and ≤ END_TIME.

Exhibit 7-9 provides an excerpt from the BBA Table, providing the START_TIME, the determined END_TIME, the limit price, and corresponding units of the BB and BA separately.

Panel A: Best Bid (BB) for ADIDAS-SALOMON AG O.N.

START_TIME (MSEC)	END_TIME (MSEC)	PRICE	UNITS
2005-09-01 09:00:28 5900	2005-09-01 09:00:34 9000	145.50	1,000
2005-09-01 09:00:34 9000	2005-09-01 09:00:37 5400	145.51	108
2005-09-01 09:00:37 5400	**2005-09-01 09:06:39 9000**	**145.52**	**300**
2005-09-01 09:00:39 9000	2005-09-01 09:00:46 5700	146.00	20
2005-09-01 09:00:46 5700	2005-09-01 09:00:48 2900	146.20	223
...	...	...	...
2005-09-01 09:05:10 4700	**2005-09-01 09:06:29 7500**	**145.23**	**134**

Panel B: Best Ask (BA) for ADIDAS-SALOMON AG O.N.

START_TIME (MSEC)	END_TIME (MSEC)	PRICE	UNITS
2005-09-01 09:00:28 5900	2005-09-01 09:00:02 5200	146.01	315
2005-09-01 09:00:29 5200	2005-09-01 09:00:31 2000	146.00	560
2005-09-01 09:00:31 2000	2005-09-01 09:00:32 2000	146.04	560
2005-09-01 09:00:32 2000	**2005-09-01 09:00:39 5000**	**146.20**	**1,000**
2005-09-01 09:00:39 5000	2005-09-01 09:00:48 2900	146.29	613
2005-09-01 09:00:48 2900	2005-09-01 09:00:56 8000	146.20	277
...	...	...	...
2005-09-01 09:05:27 6000	**2005-09-01 09:05:52 8000**	**145.50**	**921**

Exhibit 7-9: Excerpt from BBA table

From the Trades table, it is known that a buy market order with a quantity of 1,000 units entered the order book on that trading day at 09:00:39 and 5000 milliseconds (MSEC) and is immediately executed for 146.20 €, leading to a transaction volume of 146,200 €. With its execution, the order changes the BA in the order book from 146.20 to 146.29 by executing the first limit in the order book.

To determine the relevant BA (panel B, Exhibit 7-9) for this order, the above matching procedure selects the BA with START_TIME 09:00:32 2000 and END_TIME 09:00:39 5000 (fulfilling both criteria), determining the BA prevailing the order entry to 146.20 €. The same procedure is applied to the BB (panel A, Exhibit 7-9), identifying the BB prevailing the order entry at 145.52 € with START_TIME 09:00:37 5400 and END_TIME 09:00:39 9000. Thus, the relevant spread prevailing the order entry is 145.52 € to 146.20 € with MP_t = 145.86 €.

The midpoint five minutes after the transaction is identified based on the same matching procedure, adding 300 seconds to the ORDER_ENTRY_TIMESTAMP (transforming to 09:05:39 5000): MP_{t+5min} = 145.365 € with corresponding BBA of 145.23 € to 145.50 €. The effective spread (ES) yields 46.62 bp and the realized spread (RS) 114.49 bp, leading to a PI of -67.87 bp. The results reflect that the market turned against the trader, as the PI is negative. It can be assumed that the trader was uninformed and trading for liquidity reasons, the order size suggesting a wholesale trader. In addition, the order was entered directly after the opening auction, when liquidity is lowest in the DAX instruments (see Chapter 7.1.4), supporting the assumption that this trader had no discretion concerning the timing of order entry and execution.

When calculating the different spread measures, it has to be kept in mind that orders are allowed to walk up or down the order book, which is reflected in the PE ratio of 1.58 for aggressor orders (see Chapter 6.2.2). Thus, for orders that are executed more than once, the average execution price (P_t) of an order has to be computed, implying that the effective spread is equal to or larger than the BBA.[271]

As the BBA table might have missing or invalid values, the matching and calculation procedure yielded invalid results for 220,494 orders; i.e. for 5.42% of all aggressor orders PI calculation was not possible. The data set was thus reduced to 3,850,029 orders that reflected 95.5% of initial cleansed aggressor trading volume.

It should be noted that the calculation methodology to determine the BBA and MP presented in this chapter is new to the empirical literature for the Xetra open limit order book: To determine the BBA and order book depth, the order book is usually rebuilt in real-time sequences and snapshots are then taken. This procedure requires extensive data, including all order entries and cancellations as well as order execution information. In addition, the Xetra trading algorithms have to be implemented to rebuild the order book at any time during the trading day.[272] In contrast, the XLM table provides information on the order book depth, the BBA table allows the determination of the BBA and respective MP at any point in time, and the combination of the BBA and the Trades table allows calculation of price impact. As a consequence, this reduces the amount of data required as well as the computation effort tremendously.

---

271 For NYSE and NASDAQ, effective spreads have been reported to be smaller than the quoted spread (BBA). The results reflect any price improvement granted by the specialist or market makers. See Bessembinder/Kaufman (1997), p. 296f., SEC (2001), p. 15, and Boehmer (2005), p. 567. Electronic limit order books do not offer the opportunity to trade inside the spread; thus, effective spreads cannot be smaller than the BBA.

272 See Frey/Grammig (2006), p. 1014, Grammig/Heinen/Renfigo (2004), p. 5f., and Beltran/Giot/Grammig (2005), p. 24.

7.2.2 Cross-sectional Results

Exhibit 7-10 provides average results of the ES, the RS, as well as the PI for the DAX instruments. Results are computed as daily averages per instrument and are aggregated to reflect the average price impact for each instrument during the analyzed period.[273]

Instrument	Effective spread	Realized spread	Price impact	Number of orders
ADIDAS-SALOMON AG O.N.	4.864	-0.090	4.954	91,812
ALLIANZ AG VNA O.N.	3.073	0.411	2.662	284,158
ALTANA AG O.N.	5.718	0.067	5.650	65,766
BASF AG O.N.	3.791	0.138	3.653	174,241
BAY.HYPO-VEREINSBK.O.N.	7.753	2.435	5.318	93,981
BAY.MOTOREN WERKE AG ST	4.777	-0.062	4.840	123,722
BAYER AG O.N.	5.815	0.699	5.116	137,227
COMMERZBANK AG O.N.	7.097	1.185	5.912	111,047
CONTINENTAL AG O.N.	5.461	-1.084	6.545	82,853
DAIMLERCHRYSLER AG NA O.N.	4.563	0.110	4.454	213,157
DEUTSCHE BANK AG NA O.N.	3.591	0.484	3.107	223,049
DEUTSCHE BOERSE NA O.N.	5.354	-0.616	5.970	67,688
DEUTSCHE POST AG NA O.N.	6.970	2.106	4.864	95,880
DT.TELEKOM AG NA	7.148	3.912	3.236	216,554
E.ON AG O.N.	3.777	0.327	3.450	223,676
FRESEN.MED.CARE AG O.N.	6.345	0.948	5.397	55,169
HENKEL KGAA VZO O.N.	5.719	0.227	5.492	55,176
INFINEON TECH.AG NA O.N.	13.582	6.537	7.045	86,031
LINDE AG O.N.	5.925	-0.674	6.599	59,985
LUFTHANSA AG VNA O.N.	10.304	3.478	6.826	73,369
MAN AG ST O.N.	6.570	-0.733	7.303	75,969
METRO AG ST O.N.	5.686	-0.265	5.951	73,981
MUENCH.RUECKVERS.VNA O.N.	3.668	0.311	3.357	174,414
RWE AG ST O.N.	4.415	-0.488	4.903	174,291
SAP AG O.N.	3.689	-0.299	3.987	173,693
SCHERING AG O.N.	5.177	0.233	4.944	74,062
SIEMENS AG NA	3.628	0.365	3.263	223,138
THYSSENKRUPP AG O.N.	7.773	2.492	5.281	87,458
TUI AG NA	8.923	2.572	6.351	89,126
VOLKSWAGEN AG ST O.N.	5.052	0.225	4.827	169,356
DAX Mean	**5.874**	**0.832**	**5.042**	**3,850,029**
DAX Min	3.073	-1.084	2.662	
DAX Max	13.582	6.537	7.303	

Exhibit 7-10: Effective spread, realized spread, and price impact measured in basis points

---

[273] Calculating the average price impact per instrument directly, i.e. the average of all transactions per instrument, yields comparable results.

Similar to the results for average trading volume and XLM, results differ across instruments. The relative effective spread ranges from 3.1 bp for Allianz AG to 13.6 bp for Infineon Technologies AG, with a mean of 5.9 bp for the DAX. In comparison to the effective spread, the realized spread is considerably smaller, ranging from -1.1 bp for Continental AG to 6.5 bp for Infineon Technologies AG, with an average realized spread of 0.8 bp. This leads to a relatively large average price impact of 5.0 bp, meaning that the major part of the spread is a result of informational order flow.

Spread decomposition models compute three components of the spread - inventory costs, operational costs, and costs of adverse selection (see Chapter 4.3.1). As Xetra is organized as an open electronic limit order book without market makers in high liquid instruments (e.g. DAX instruments), there is no reason for inventory costs that can be associated with market making or a monopolistic power of a market maker.[274] In addition, operational costs, i.e. submission and execution fees, are considerably small. It follows that adverse selection costs are the major source for the spread supporting hypothesis (v) Informed trading is significant in the anonymous open electronic limit order book (Xetra).

As the effective spread is an ex-post liquidity measure, it reflects the cost of liquidity for the order execution, while the XLM(V) as a hypothetical ex-ante measure provides the average available liquidity. Results for the effective spread of 5.9 bp are smaller than the average results for LP (6.9 bp) and any XLM(V). The average aggressor order size is approx. 55,800 € with corresponding liquidity costs of more than 8.5 bp as estimated for XLM(50).[275] The lower ex-post liquidity costs reflected in a difference of at least 2.6 bp demonstrate that traders time their order entries, meaning these orders are able to realize lower costs than average ex-ante liquidity costs.

This is in line with theoretical and empirical results for discretionary trading. The open limit order book allows traders to assess the available liquidity at any point in time (during continuous trading), making the available liquidity a decision criterion in investors' choice when to trade.[276]

7.2.3 Group ID Results

The general notion is that adverse selection risk is higher for smaller capitalized and less frequently traded instruments.[277] For the cross-section of instruments, the Pearson correlation coefficient between market capitalization and price impact is -0.83 and between average daily

---

[274] Even for specialist and market maker markets, empirical studies have demonstrated that the inventory cost component is insignificant for high volume stocks. See Harris/Panchapagesan (2005), p. 61, Hasbrouck (1988), pp. 243-247, Madhavan/Panchapagesan (2002), p. 107 and, Stoll (1989), p. 132. McInish/Van Ness (2002), p. 508 analyze intraday spread components for NYSE instruments, disregarding inventory costs based upon the results of the aforementioned authors.

[275] It should be noted that XLM(50) is still an underestimate of the ex-ante liquidity as it is smaller than the average order size of 58,000 €.

[276] Admati/Pfleiderer (1988), p. 5 introduce the concept of discretionary trading. Biais/Hillion/Spatt (1995), p. 1657 find that traders monitor the order book and submit orders depending on the state of the order book. Gomber/Schweickert/Theissen (2005), p. 17ff. discover timing of large orders in Xetra.

[277] See Hasbrouck (1991a), p. 199; Easley/Kiefer/O'Hara/Paperman (1996), p. 1407; Huang/Stoll (1997), p. 1010.

trading volume and price impact -0.85 (both significant at the 0.001 level), supporting the above notion.[278]

Following the categorization of the DAX instruments based on trading volume into three sets each including ten instruments (see Chapter 7.1.2), results for the different measures based on GROUP_ID including results for paired t-tests are presented in Exhibit 7-11. As presented in panel A, the effective spread increases with decreasing trading volume from 4.2 bp for the ten most frequently traded instruments to 6.7 bp for the ten least frequently traded instruments. Price impact follows a similar pattern, increasing across all instrument groups, ranging from 3.7 bp to 6.1 bp.

The ratio of price impact and effective spread is computed to reflect the different levels of liquidity in the three instrument groups, showing that although effective spread and price impact both increase across the three groups, the share of price impact is smaller for GROUP_ID = 2 compared to the other groups.

Panel A: GROUP_ID means

GROUP_ID	Effective spread	Realized spread	Price impact	PI/ ES
1	4.218	0.581	3.637	86%
2	6.439	1.251	5.188	81%
3	6.684	0.599	6.085	91%
DAX Average	5.874	0.832	5.042	85.8%

Panel B: Paired samples test statistics

GROUP_ID differences	Effective spread	Realized spread	Price impact	PI/ ES
1 - 2	-2.43 *	-1.08 ns	-4.11 **	0.61 ns
1 - 3	-3.54 **	0.02 ns	-10.66 ***	-0.69 ns
2 - 3	0.22 ns	1.26 ns	-1.92 ns	-1.64 ns

*** = significant at 0.001 level; ** = 0.01 level; * = 0.05 level; ns = not significant

Exhibit 7-11: Results based on GROUP_ID

Paired samples t-tests are conducted and panel B presents the respective t-statistics and their corresponding significance levels. The difference in effective spreads is significant at least at the 0.05 level between group one and the two other groups, while it is not significantly different between groups two and three. This relation is even stronger for price impact where the difference is significant at least at the 0.05 level between group one and the two other groups, while it is not significantly different between groups two and three. However, the relative importance of price impact (PI/ES) is not significantly different between the

[278] Results for Spearman Rank correlation are comparable: -0.82 for the correlation between market capitalization and price impact and -0.84 between average daily trading volume and price impact (both significant at the 0.001 level).

groups.[279] The test results reflect the inverse relation of price impact and trading volume, supporting existing evidence that adverse selection risk is higher for smaller capitalized and less frequently traded instruments. Thus, results support hypothesis (vi).

7.2.4 Order Size Results

In the literature, order volume or size are assumed to carry information revealing whether an order is entered by an uninformed or informed trader. Theoretical and empirical research posit that informed traders will implement medium size orders to profit from their information gradually while hiding among other traders, which is labeled stealth trading.[280] Based on the order size classification introduced in Chapter 6.3.2, the means of effective and realized spread, price impact, and the ratio of price impact to effective spread are presented in Exhibit 7-12.[281] As expected, the effective spread increases with increasing order size from 5.8 bp for orders smaller than 25,000 € to 11.2 bp for orders with a volume larger than 500,000 €. However, one exception should be noted: the effective spread for SIZE_ID = 2 is smaller than for SIZE_ID = 1, suggesting that orders that belong to SIZE_ID = 2 are handled with discretion.[282]

SIZE_ID	In thousand €	Effective spread	Realized spread	Price impact	PI/ ES
1	< 25	5.779	1.983	3.796	66%
2	≥ 25 and < 50	5.620	-0.103	5.723	102%
3	≥ 50 and < 100	5.886	-0.682	6.568	112%
4	≥ 100 and < 250	6.851	-1.252	8.103	118%
5	≥ 250 and < 500	8.779	-2.244	11.023	126%
6	≥ 500	11.157	-2.305	13.462	121%

Exhibit 7-12: Results based on SIZE_ID

The cross-sectional results reported in Chapter 7.2.2 provided an indication for active order handling when comparing ex-ante and ex-post execution costs, suggesting lower execution costs for active order handling. The results imply that for orders smaller than 25,000 €, traders either do not value active order handling or these orders are entered by investors that do not have the possibility for active order handling through monitoring of order book liquidity. Usually, retail order flow that does not have access to order book information is attributed to SIZE_ID = 1.

---

279 Test results are based on a low number of cases (N=10); thus the significant differences found are a strong indicator. Computing the t-test with N=640, i.e. daily values for each instrument in each group, test results are inflated, showing significant differences of the price impact for all groups at the 0.001 level. In addition, Wilcoxon signed-ranks tests are computed and support the results of the t-statistics.

280 Barclay/Warner (1993), p. 292 empirically demonstrate that medium sized orders display a disproportionately large price impact. Chakravarty (2001), p. 301 link order size and trader type, confirming that institutional in contrast to individual traders are much more likely to use medium sized orders, identifying them as informed.

281 Average results for SIZE_ID are calculated in two steps: first, daily averages per instrument for each SIZE_ID are computed and then aggregated as average per SIZE_ID.

282 Comparing the results for SIZE_ID 1 and 2, t-statistics of 3.812 reveal significant differences at the 0.001 level.

At the same time, price impact increases continuously from 3.8 bp to 13.5 bp. Paired samples t-tests show significant differences between all size classes at the 0.001 level (corresponding t-statistics ranging from -6.24 to -15.37). As both measures (effective spread and price impact) increase with increasing order size, the ratio of price impact and effective spread is additionally calculated, illustrating the relative importance of informed trading. This ratio increases until size class five but decreases for class six reaching comparable levels to class four. Paired samples t-tests show significant differences at the 0.001 level between size classes one to four, though for orders with a volume larger than 100,000 € (SIZE_ID ≥ 4) no significant differences are found; i.e. the relative importance of price impact remains stable.

The six order size classes can be aggregated further to reflect small, medium, and large orders, i.e. SIZE_ID = 1 and 2 reflecting small orders, SIZE_ID = 3 and 4 medium, and SIZE_ID = 5 and 6 large orders. Medium size orders then include all orders larger than 50,000 € and smaller than 250,000 €, reflecting 29.4% of orders and 53.8% of trading volume.[283] These orders did not have the highest absolute price impact or the highest relative price impact. However, as the results for the relation of price impact to effective spread show, medium size orders are relatively more informed than small orders but are comparable to large orders. The results only partly support hypothesis (vii) Informed trading and order size are related; i.e. medium size orders carry more information than small or large orders (stealth trading hypothesis).

It should be noted that results depend on the definition of small, medium, and large orders. In the previous chapter, the negative relation of informed trading and trading volume was demonstrated. The classification of instruments followed their overall trading volume. The difference between the thirty DAX instruments concerning their trading characteristics, i.e. liquidity and trading volume, support the assumption that a distinction between small, medium, and large orders might vary between the different instruments.

Exhibit 7-13 illustrates that 67% of the trading volume is executed in group one, 23% in group two, and only 10% in group three. The use of order sizes differs accordingly. Small orders account for 60% of orders in group one, 72% in group two, and 82% in group three.[284]

This indicates that results should be interpreted taking into account the differing order size distribution. The ratio of price impact and effective spread increases accordingly except for GROUP_ID = 1. In this group the ratio increases from 60.4% up to 111.1% for SIZE_ID = 4 and decreases again until it reaches the level of SIZE_ID = 2 of approx. 100%. Thus, GROUP_ID = 1 is the only group that unambiguously reflects the stealth trading hypothesis, where medium size orders (SIZE_ID = 3; 4) show a higher relative importance of price impact compared to both small and large orders. For the two other groups, this relation is not confirmed. Hypothesis (vii) will be further analyzed in Chapters 9.1.1 and 9.2.1 when informed traders are identified and their choice of order size is analyzed.

---

283 These results can be calculated from Exhibit 6-7 in Chapter 6.3.2.

284 Analyzing the individual trading days for each instrument and size class, it is shown that in GROUP_ID = 1 at least one order per day was executed in all size classes. For GROUP_ID = 2 this is only true for the size classes 1 to 5, while for GROUP_ID = 3 it is only true for size classes 1 to 4. E.g. for Altana AG and Henkel KGaA order(s) larger than 500,000 € were executed on 15 of the 64 trading days.

GROUP_ID	SIZE_ID	Effective spread	Realized spread	Price impact	PI/ES	Number of orders	Orders % share	Volume (m €)	Volume % share
1	1	4.184	1.656	2.528	60.4%	889,450	40.4%	9,512	6.3%
	2	4.023	0.036	3.987	99.1%	438,331	19.9%	16,069	10.6%
	3	4.145	-0.289	4.434	107.0%	448,406	20.3%	31,775	21.0%
	4	4.628	-0.515	5.142	111.1%	329,560	15.0%	49,747	32.9%
	5	5.756	-0.334	6.090	105.8%	75,515	3.4%	25,411	16.8%
	6	7.961	-0.021	7.982	100.3%	23,065	1.0%	18,753	12.4%
Average or total		**5.114**	**0.089**	**5.025**	**98.3%**	**2,204,327**	**54.2%**	**151,266**	**66.6%**
2	1	6.712	2.795	3.917	58.4%	587,731	51.5%	6,106	11.6%
	2	6.497	0.321	6.176	95.1%	237,817	20.8%	8,575	16.3%
	3	6.731	-0.389	7.121	105.8%	186,873	16.4%	13,107	24.9%
	4	7.538	-0.767	8.305	110.2%	107,245	9.4%	15,995	30.4%
	5	9.544	-1.345	10.889	114.1%	18,159	1.6%	6,061	11.5%
	6	12.578	-2.996	15.574	123.8%	3,788	0.3%	2,708	5.2%
Average or total		**8.157**	**-0.331**	**8.488**	**104.1%**	**1,141,613**	**28.0%**	**52,552**	**23.1%**
3	1	6.440	1.498	4.942	76.7%	447,208	61.7%	4,557	19.5%
	2	6.339	-0.665	7.005	110.5%	145,792	20.1%	5,237	22.4%
	3	6.782	-1.367	8.149	120.2%	89,245	12.3%	6,168	26.4%
	4	8.387	-2.475	10.862	129.5%	36,950	5.1%	5,354	22.9%
	5	11.307	-5.386	16.692	147.6%	4,618	0.6%	1,518	6.5%
	6	15.661	-6.155	21.816	139.3%	770	0.1%	545	2.3%
Average or total		**8.423**	**-1.973**	**10.396**	**123.4%**	**724,583**	**17.8%**	**23,378**	**10.3%**

Exhibit 7-13: Combined results for GROUP_ID and SIZE_ID

7.2.5 Intraday Results

The intraday analyses of effective spread and price impact are similar to those analyses computed in Chapters 6.3.3 and 7.1.4: ES and PI results are generated as averages per SLICE_ID_2 per instrument and are further aggregated across the trading days to represent one observation per time interval for all DAX instruments.

As presented in Exhibit 7-14, the effective spread displays a reverse J-shaped pattern comparable to the LP and XLM(V). Cross-sectional results presented in Chapter 7.2.2

revealed that the effective spread as an ex-post liquidity measure is smaller than the related XLM(50). As there is no difference in the intraday distribution itself, this difference is attributed to a different level of liquidity costs only.

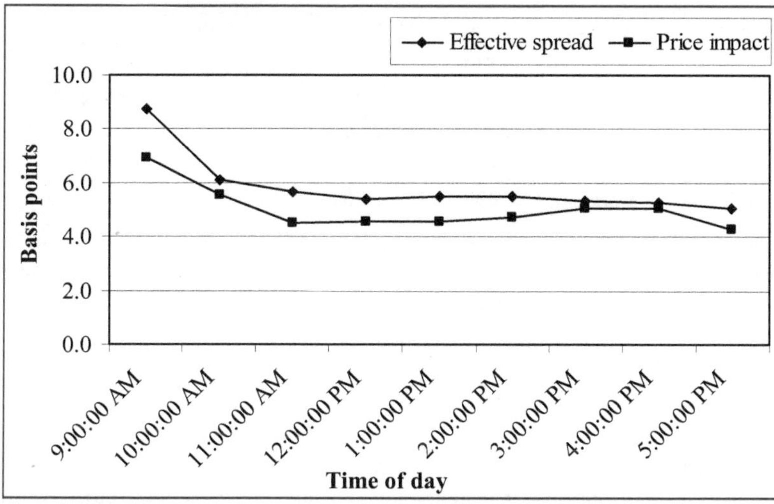

Exhibit 7-14: Intraday distribution of effective spread and price impact

As Friedman test results show significant differences between the results of the different time intervals at the 0.001 level (Chi-Square = 181.8) for the effective spread, Wilcoxon signed-ranks were computed. Z-statistics show significant differences between some of the time intervals, especially between the morning and afternoon intervals, also showing that the effective spread remains stable during the last three time intervals. Test results are reported in detail in panel A, Appendix 5.

The intraday distribution of the price impact also shows its highest results at the beginning of the trading day decreasing until the 11:00 am to 12:00 pm interval, increasing again until the 3:00 to 4:00 pm interval but staying below the initial levels of price impact during the first two time intervals, finally decreasing until the end of the trading day. Friedman test results find significant differences between the different time intervals at the 0.001 level (Chi-Square = 99.2). Wilcoxon test results show significant differences between some of the intervals, especially the morning and afternoon trading session. Results are presented in panel B of Appendix 5. The described outcome supports hypothesis (viii) Informed trading is highest at the beginning of the trading day and is gradually resolved throughout the trading day, revealing a reverse J-shaped pattern.

Comparing morning and afternoon sessions, the effective spread and price impact are significantly higher during the morning trading session. Pair-wise t-statistics are presented in Exhibit 7-15.[285]

Means and t-statistics	Morning session	Afternoon session	Difference	t-statistic
Effective spread	6.466	5.357	1.109	9.19 ***
Price impact	5.369	4.780	0.589	3.61 ***

*** = significant at 0.001 level

Exhibit 7-15: Comparison of morning and afternoon trading sessions

This result is in line with the above results, as the intraday distribution of the effective spread and price impact are quite similar, which is also reflected in a Pearson correlation coefficient of the two measures of 0.682 significant at the 0.001 level.[286]

7.3 Relation of Liquidity and Informed Trading

An increase in informed order flow should lead to a decrease (increase) in liquidity (XLM). The rationale behind this is that in the presence of informed traders, liquidity providers tend to widen the spread to account for the risk of trading with an informed trader. Initial results were provided for specialist or market maker markets but also hold for open limit order books where liquidity is provided by the limit orders standing in the order book.

To test hypothesis (ix), correlation coefficients for price impact and LP and XLM(V) are calculated. Exhibit 7-16 shows that price impact is significantly positively related to the liquidity measures, with correlation coefficients ranging from 0.766 to 0.898 at the 0.001 level. As LP and XLM(V) measure the liquidity cost and price impact is a direct measure of the level of informed trading, the negative relation with liquidity described in hypothesis (ix) holds for the DAX instruments.

	Liquidity measures			
Price impact	LP	XLM(50)	XLM(250)	XLM(500)
Pearson Correlation	0.766 ***	0.863 ***	0.848 ***	0.801 ***
Spearman Rank Correlation	0.796 ***	0.878 ***	0.898 ***	0.892 ***

*** = significant at the 0.001 level

Exhibit 7-16: Correlation coefficients of price impact and liquidity measures

---

285 For the morning trading session, a simple mean can be calculated, while for the afternoon trading session, weighting factors are applied for the four hourly time intervals and the half-hour interval ($0.\overline{22}$ and $0.\overline{11}$ respectively). Wilcoxon signed-rank tests provide similar results significant at the 0.001 level with a corresponding z-statistic of -4.78 and -3.10 respectively.

286 The Spearman rank correlation is slightly higher at 0.72 and significant at 0.001 level.

7.4 Synopsis

The first step of the research approach provides a detailed market description for highly liquid instruments in the electronic open limit order book Xetra. The chapter is distinguished in three parts that describe and test general hypotheses for liquidity (1), for informed trading (2), and for the relation of liquidity and informed trading (3). It positively answers the question of whether trading in Xetra is comparable to other exchanges (see Chapter 1.2, research objective (i)). In addition, results will function as a reference point for the interpretation of the results of the trader categories.

The description of liquidity is based on the XLM as presented in Chapter 3.2.2. The different analyses for LP and XLM(V) confirm standard hypotheses: liquidity (i) is negatively related to order size, (ii) does not differ significantly for the buy and sell side of the order book for orders smaller than 500,000 €, (iii) is lowest at the beginning of the trading day increasing continuously while remaining stable at the end of the trading day, and (iv) displays the expected relations with standard determinants of liquidity (trading volume, price, and volatility). Chapter 6.3.3 has already confirmed that trading volume and volatility display standard intraday patterns. It can be stated that liquidity patterns are not distinct for Xetra, but are fairly consistent with results reported from other exchanges.

Based on the choice of method described in Chapter 4.3.3, informed trading is determined through the price impact. The calculation methodology implemented takes the order information derived from the Trades table and combines it with the separate BBs and BAs from the BBA table. The calculation approach is new to the empirical literature for the Xetra open limit order book, as it does not require the extensive effort of rebuilding the order book. It presents an approach that requires less information as well as less computation effort.

The results of the price impact analysis confirm that informed trading (v) is significant in the anonymous electronic trading system Xetra, (vi) is higher for smaller firms, and (viii) shows a distinct intraday pattern being highest at the beginning of the trading day and lowest at its end. The relation of informed trading and order size (vii), i.e. the notion that medium sized orders should yield a higher price impact, is only partly supported. However, in step three of the research approach the use of order sizes of informed traders will be further analyzed. Again, it can be concluded that results for Xetra do not differ notably from the ones of other exchanges.

Finally, the correlation analysis supports the main theoretical notion of limit order books: Liquidity and informed trading are inversely related, i.e. an increase in informed trading leads to a decrease in liquidity.

Combining the descriptive market statistics presented in Chapter 6.3 with the results of the first step it is concluded that trading of the DAX instruments in Xetra is fairly comparable to other electronic limit order markets. Results are in line with other electronic limit order books, e.g. Euronext[287], the Swedish Stock Exchange[288], and SEHK[289]. Part of the results even hold

---

[287] See Beltran/Durée/Giot (2004), Biais/Hillion/Spatt (1995), Handa/Schwartz/Tiwari (2003) and, Pagano/ Padilla (2005).

[288] See Hollifield/Miller/Sandas (2004) and, Sandas (2001).

[289] See Ahn/Bae/Chan (2001), Brockman/Chung (1998), (1999), (2000) and (2002), and Chan (2005).

for other market structures, e.g. specialist markets such as NYSE and market maker structures as can be found for NASDAQ.[290]

As a consequence, the outcome of step three - the analysis of informed liquidity supply and demand behavior - should generally not be attributed to any peculiarities of the DAX instruments or the Xetra trading system. This gives a strong indication that results can be transferred to other markets.

---

[290] See Barclay/Warner (1993), Bessembinder (1999) and (2003a), Bessembinder/Kaufman (1997), Boehmer (2005), Chakravarty (2001), Chung/Van Ness/Van Ness (1999) and (2004), Handa/ Schwartz (1996b), Hasbrouck (1991a) and (1991b), Heidle/Huang (2002), Huang/Stoll (1996a) and (1996b), Lee/Mucklow/ Ready (1993), McInish/Wood (1992), Stoll (2000), and Van Ness/Van Ness/Warr (2005).

8 Trader Classification

This chapter describes the second step of the empirical analysis, the trader classification into informed, partly informed, and uninformed traders following a stepwise approach based on their trading volume and results of the price impact calculation (see Exhibit 8-1).

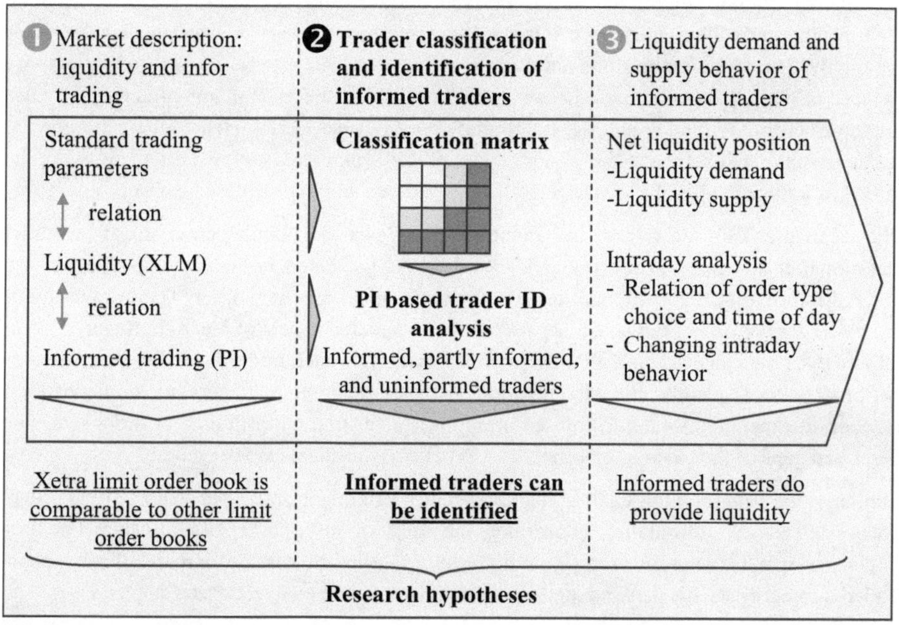

Exhibit 8-1: Research approach step 2

As informed traders do anything to camouflage themselves when trading, the main challenge is to identify and classify traders according to their level of information.

Earlier empirical studies on the behavior of informed traders have based their classification and subsequent analyses on assumptions:[291] Usually institutional market participants are classified as informed traders while retail flow is deemed uninformed. The rationale behind this assumption is that institutional traders have on the one hand better access to information while on the other hand they are able to process the available information more efficiently.

A drawback of such a simple classification is that it assumes that institutional investors only trade for informational reasons, while they might also have liquidity reasons to trade.[292] These obstacles are then overcome by further assumptions, i.e. distinguishing the size of orders or trades.[293] The implementation of assumptions is usually necessary due to the lack of suitable

---

[291] See Anand/Chakravarty/Martell (2005), p. 290. They analyze NYSE data based on a so-called account type indicator that allows determining if the particular order was entered by an individual trader or by a member firm.

[292] The different motives for trading that allow a classification of traders into informed and uninformed traders are presented in Chapter 4.2.

[293] See Anand/Chakravarty/Martell (2005), p. 293.

detailed data, i.e. data on the level of the individual trader. As a consequence, results can only be interpreted with respect to the underlying assumptions.

In contrast, traders are defined as (un)informed in the set-up of experimental studies which aim at reproducing electronic limit order books. The set-up determines who receives what information prior to and/or during the defined trading time. As a result, it is possible to identify the individual trader as informed or uninformed and to analyze his behavior separately. However, models are not able to reflect fully all aspects of the trading activity because of the reduced number of traders and thus reduced interaction among them, the rules implemented in the model, and the timeframe chosen in the model. Hence, the experimental set-up is able to overcome the shortcoming of the empirical analyses in identifying the informed traders but has the weaknesses of any modeled and thus artificial market.[294]

The available data described in Chapter 6.2 allows the implementation of a trader classification procedure at the trader ID level.[295] As presented in the previous chapter, the level of information can be determined for each individual executed order. The availability of the trader ID per order allows the extraction of all executed orders of a certain trader. This in turn enables the calculation of the level of information of each trader based on the results of his orders. Consequently, the identification and classification of traders according to their level of information does not follow assumptions such as trading institution or order size. The described gaps of the existing empirical and experimental studies are overcome.

Similarly, the data set allows extracting all executed originator orders per trader. These orders do not reveal any information concerning the level of information of the trader but they directly permit the determination of the liquidity providing behavior of a trader. Thus, once a trader is categorized, his demand and supply behavior can be analyzed (see Chapter 9).

8.1 Classification Procedure

The classification procedure is implemented in two consecutive steps: During step 1, trader IDs are classified in terms of their relative importance based on trading volume (aggressor and total trading volume), resulting in a 4x4 classification matrix. This matrix allows the identification of trader IDs that are determined as relevant in terms of trading activity for the subsequent analysis and reduces the number of trader IDs by 48%. In step 2, the price impact is calculated for the remaining trader IDs. It forms the basis for the identification of uninformed, partly informed, and informed traders according to their relative level of price impact. The relevant criteria include the distribution of traders in a percentile analysis as well as taking into account the average, minimum, and maximum price impact in the DAX instruments.

---

[294] See Bloomfield/O'Hara/Saar (2005), pp. 171-177.

[295] The Trades table also provides the member ID (MBR_ID) for each executed order. As most member firms provide a variety of services to different customers through different trader IDs, a distinction of the level of information on the member ID level would mix different types of businesses (e.g. proprietary and agent business, retail and wholesale clients) as well as different trading motives (liquidity- or information-driven).

8.1.1 Step 1: Volume Based Classification Matrix

As price impact calculation is only practicable for aggressor orders, the classification based on trading volume starts with the aggressor side and is then repeated for the total volume, i.e. the sum of aggressor and originator volume.

Based on the aggressor orders (see Chapter 6.2.2), 2,377 trader IDs were identified that entered at least one market or marketable limit order. These trader IDs were sorted in descending order based on the trading volume per trader ID and then split into four classes with a similar number of trader IDs (CLASS_ID), i.e. 594 trader IDs for classes 1, 2, and 3 and 595 for class 4. As a consequence, class 1 includes the most active trader IDs and class 4 the least active trader IDs. The classification follows the importance of traders in terms of aggressor volume, as the objective is to identify those trader IDs that are comparably active traders on the aggressor side and show at the same time superior execution results, which are analyzed during the second step of the analysis.

As presented in Exhibit 8-2, the trader IDs that form class 1 are responsible for 90.3% of aggressor trading volume, class 2 adds an additional 7.7%, and class 3 and 4 are responsible for the remaining 2%. The order distribution is similar. Classes 1 and 2 are responsible for 97.8% of aggressor orders and classes 3 and 4 for the remaining 2.3%.

The trader ID with the largest volume (approx. 25.8 bn €) is responsible for 11.4% of the aggressor trading volume. 25 trader IDs have an aggressor trading volume larger than 1.0 bn € and a further 387 trader IDs traded more than 100 m €. The last (smallest) trader ID in class 1 still entered marketable or market orders, amounting to 56.4 m €. Thus, trading volume is highly concentrated among trader IDs.[296]

CLASS_ID	Number of trader IDs	Aggressor trading volume	Volume % share	Aggressor orders	Orders % share
1	594	205,095,058,875	90.3%	3,683,023	90.5%
2	594	17,418,041,769	7.7%	296,057	7.3%
3	594	4,145,183,197	1.8%	79,524	2.0%
4	595	538,762,738	0.2%	11,919	0.3%
Total	**2,377**	**227,197,046,579**	**100%**	**4,070,523**	**100%**

Exhibit 8-2: Classification based on aggressor trading volume

The procedure is repeated for total trading volume (CLASS_ID_2), where 2,413 trader IDs are identified and classified accordingly. That means 36 trader IDs, i.e. the difference to the identified 2,377 aggressor trader IDs, did not enter any aggressive order but only originator orders and are signed as not classified (NC).

296 In class 2 aggressor trading volume ranges from 13.6 to 56.4 m €, in class 3 from 2.6 to 13.5 m €, and in class 4 from <100 € to 2.5 m €.

Exhibit 8-3 presents the results for total trading volume (CLASS_ID_2). The distribution among classes is comparable to the analysis of the aggressor volume. The concentration of trading volumes in class 1 is slightly reduced, as trader IDs that form class 1 are responsible for 88.6% while class 2 increased its share to 9.1%. Classes 3 and 4 are responsible for the remaining 2.4%. The total order distribution shows an even stronger similarity to the aggressor order distribution: Classes 1 and 2 are responsible for 97.6% of aggressor orders and classes 3 and 4 for the remaining 2.4%.

CLASS_ID_2	Number of trader IDs	Total trading volume	Volume % share	Total orders	Orders % share
1	594	402,435,471,717	88.6%	7,273,640	89.8%
2	594	41,340,282,293	9.1%	631,754	7.8%
3	594	9,431,500,373	2.1%	168,365	2.1%
4	631	1,186,838,774	0.3%	24,037	0.3%
Total	**2,413**	**454,394,093,158**	**100%**	**8,097,796**	**100%**

Exhibit 8-3: Classification based on total trading volume

The trader ID with the largest volume (approx. 28.3 bn €) is responsible for 6.2% of the total trading volume. This trader ID is also classified as largest based on aggressor trading volume and thus only responsible for 2.5 bn € originator trading volume.[297] 72 trader IDs have a total trading volume larger than 1.0 bn €. The remaining trader IDs where CLASS_ID_2 = 1 traded more than 132.9 m €.[298]

Exhibit 8-4 presents the joint results for the two classification parameters per trader ID from the aggressor perspective. Out of the 594 trader IDs that were assigned to class 1 from the aggressor perspective (CLASS_ID), 532 trader IDs are classified similarly from the total trading volume perspective, while 62 trader IDs belong to class 2.

Thus, the distribution of total trading volume among the initial classes (CLASS_ID) changes only slightly. Class 1 has a reduced percentage share of 87.1%, which is reflected in an increase in class 2 and 3. However, classes 1 and 2 are still responsible for 97.1% of the total trading volume and classes 3 and 4 for 2.9% only.

297 The trader ID is not yet classified as providing informed or uninformed order flow, but at this point it is obvious that less than 10% of his trading volume is of liquidity providing nature.

298 In class 2 total trading volume ranges from 31.1 to 132.1 m €, in class 3 from 5.7 to 31.1 m €, and in class 4 from <100 € to 5.69 m €.

CLASS_ID	CLASS_ID_2	Number of trader IDs	Aggressor trading volume	Total trading volume	Volume % share
1	1	532	200,622,829,203	388,715,876,512	85.5%
	2	62	4,472,229,672	6,955,186,889	1.5%
Sub-sum		**594**	**205,095,058,875**	**395,671,063,402**	**87.1%**
2	1	57	2,179,549,847	12,906,724,098	2.8%
	2	462	14,010,252,711	30,686,802,507	6.8%
	3	75	1,228,239,211	1,924,291,869	0.4%
Sub-sum		**594**	**17,418,041,769**	**45,517,818,474**	**10.0%**
3	1	5	45,550,677	812,871,107	0.2%
	2	63	630,058,583	3,277,662,196	0.7%
	3	465	3,266,752,971	6,979,363,006	1.5%
	4	61	202,820,966	274,625,770	0.1%
Sub-sum		**594**	**4,145,183,197**	**11,344,522,080**	**2.5%**
4	2	7	11,541,462	420,630,701	0.1%
	3	53	93,387,530	496,323,701	0.1%
	4	535	433,833,746	906,892,793	0.2%
Sub-sum		**595**	**538,762,738**	**1,823,847,194**	**0.4%**
NC	3	2		31,521,797	0.0%
	4	34		5,320,211	0.0%
Sub-sum		**36**		**36,842,008**	**0.0%**
Total		**2,413**	**227,197,046,579**	**454,394,093,158**	**100.0%**

Exhibit 8-4: Classification based on aggressor and total trading volume

The final result of this procedure is a 4x4 classification matrix that reflects all traders that could be classified in accordance with both dimensions (2,377 trader IDs). It is implemented as a first filter in identifying the trader IDs, which are important in terms of trading activity. As can be seen in the diagonal of Exhibit 8-5, more than 80% of trader IDs (1,994) are grouped in the same class from both perspectives, while some combinations do not exist. Economic intuition excludes, for example, any combination of class 1 for aggressor trading volume and class 4 for total trading volume: Even if the smallest trader in class 1 based on aggressor trading volume with 56.4 m € did not execute any originator volume, he would still at least belong to class 2 from the total trading volume perspective, as this class includes trader IDs with a total trading volume larger than 31.1 m € (see Footnote 298).

To select comparably active traders, two rules are implemented: (i) All trader IDs that belong to class 4, either from the aggressor and/or total trading volume perspective, are classified as not relevant and (ii) all trader IDs that belong in both dimensions to class 3 are also classified as not relevant.

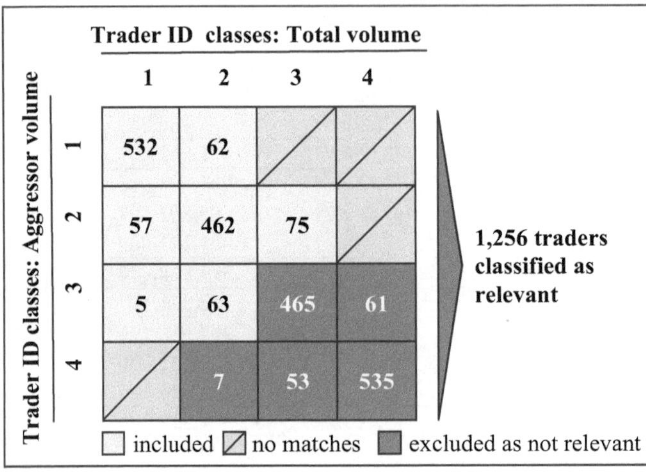

Exhibit 8-5: Trader ID classification matrix

This reduces the set of trader IDs to 1,256 (52% of 2,413 trader IDs). The remaining 1,157 trader IDs (including 36 trader IDs that entered limit orders only) are excluded from the further analyses based on their comparably low trading activity: These trader IDs account for only 1.8% of aggressor trading volume and 2% of total trading volume: Consequently, any results on trading behavior for these trader IDs cannot be representative for trading behavior of other trader IDs.[299]

8.1.2 Step 2: Price Impact Analysis

As explained in Chapter 7.2.1, the PI cannot be computed for all orders due to missing data in the BBA table. As a consequence, one further trader ID is excluded. This trader ID belonged to class 3 based on aggressor volume (CLASS_ID) and class 2 based on total trading volume (CLASS_ID_2), reducing the analyzed trader IDs to 1,255.[300]

For these trader IDs, the PI is calculated for each executed order and then further aggregated to determine the average PI per trader ID.[301] Results for the relevant trader IDs show that the average price impact per trader ID ranges from -13.8 bp to 38.2 bp, with a mean of 5.23 bp. The trader ID with the largest price impact realizes an average price impact that is almost eight times as high as the mean across all trader IDs. The distribution is positively skewed

---

299 Nevertheless, the PI is calculated and results support their exclusion from the analysis; see Footnotes 302 and 303.

300 In addition, the PI for the trader IDs that were identified as not relevant is computed. Out of the 1,121 trader IDs, six did not allow calculation. That means for 7 out of 2,377 aggressor trader IDs (0.3%), calculation of price impact is technically not possible.

301 The results are not calculated similar to the averages in Chapters 6.3 and 7.2, i.e. first as daily results and then aggregated as average for the complete time period. Instead, the objective is to identify trader IDs that generally show superior performance across all their executed orders and not trader IDs that are able to realize a positive price impact on more than half of the trading days. However, the results do not differ significantly when initially calculating the average per trader ID for each trading day and then calculating a further average.

with a median of 4.85 bp. Kolmogorov-Smirnov test results indicate that the price impact of trader IDs is not normally distributed (z-statistic = 2.56 significant at the 0.001 level).[302]

Exhibit 8-6 shows the distribution of the average price impact per trader ID clustered in intervals of 1 bp. The PI reflects the level of information of each trader ID. Thus all trader IDs that were not able to realize a positive PI can be directly classified as uninformed. The PI analysis identifies 61 trader IDs with an average negative or zero PI, i.e. approx. 5% of the 1,255 trader IDs.[303] These trader IDs account for 1% of the aggressor trading volume. For those trader IDs with a PI larger than zero (1,194), at least some level of information is given. It has to be decided how these trader IDs can be grouped, i.e. what PI level determines if a trader ID is classified as partially informed or as informed. The PI distribution is reflected in the results for the different percentiles. It shows that 25% of trader IDs realize a PI smaller than 2.68 bp while 25% of trader IDs realize a PI larger than 7.18 bp (see Exhibit 8-6).[304]

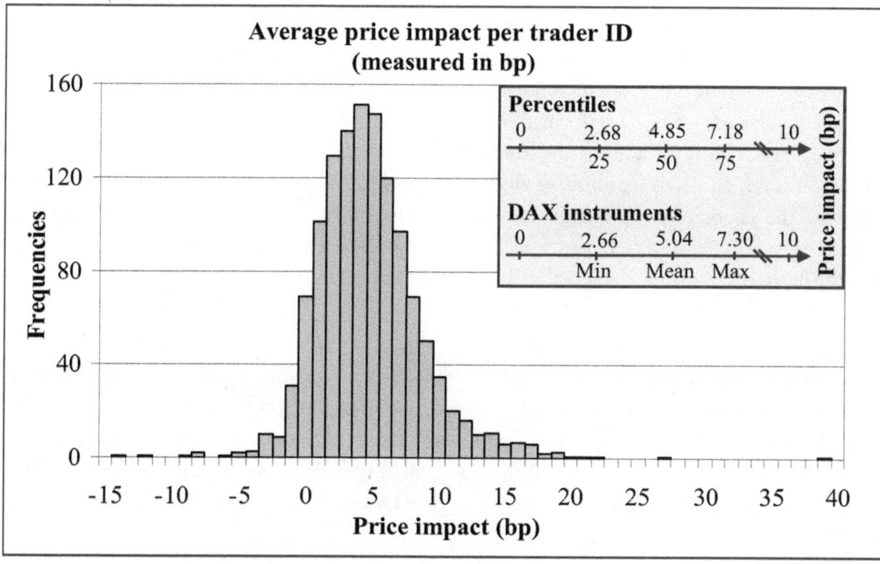

Exhibit 8-6: Trader ID distribution based on average price impact

---

302 When computing the price impact for all trader IDs (2,370), the range increases to 248 bp (-101.9 bp to 146.1 bp). This shows that the reduction in trader IDs based on trading volume (step 1) helped reducing outliers - 18 trader IDs that realized a price impact larger than 38.2 bp and 47 trader IDs that realized a price impact smaller than -13.8 bp were excluded in step 1.

303 In comparison, 328 of the 1,121 trader IDs that were identified as not relevant have a negative or zero PI, i.e. 29.3%. Thus, the ratio of uninformed traders is notably higher for less active traders. This could indicate a positive relation between trading activity (volume) and the expertise of the trader ID. The trader ID can also reflect the expertise of institutions that do not have the status of a trading member but rout their order flow. However, as the trading strategies behind each trader ID are not visible, this cannot be further investigated, as there is no data available on the customers of the trading members.

304 Only 5% of the trader IDs have a PI smaller than 0.06 bp or larger than 12.3 bp. Comparing these results to the given range from -13.8 to 38.2 bp reveals that some trader IDs realize unusually low or high price impacts.

The objective when classifying trader IDs is not to divide the observations into groups of equal size, i.e. determining upfront that one third is uninformed while a further third is partially informed and the remaining trader IDs are informed. Instead, the objective is to identify lower and upper boundaries for these categories that have an economic meaning.

As existing theory assumes that uninformed traders provide liquidity while informed traders take liquidity, increasing the size of the category of informed traders increases the risk of including uninformed traders that could dilute the results for the informed traders in the sense of overestimating the liquidity providing behavior of informed traders. As a consequence, the objective is to identify those trader IDs that have been able to realize an unusually high PI compared to (i) the other trader IDs and (ii) the realizable PI in the DAX instruments.

As shown, the mean PI of the DAX instruments is 5.04 bp (Exhibit 7-10) with a minimum and maximum price impact of 2.66 and 7.30 bp, respectively. The PI results for the individual instruments are implemented as a benchmark to the PI results for the trader IDs. The fact that the minimum and maximum results are close to the results for the 25th and the 75th percentile provides the rationale for implementing these percentiles as lower and upper boundaries for the trader ID classification. Uninformed traders are defined as trader IDs belonging to the 25th percentile, partially informed to the trader IDs from the 25th to the 75th percentile, and informed traders as the remaining with the 75th percentile as lower boundary. This allows combining the economic argumentation with the possibility of choosing trader categories of comparable sizes: Uninformed and informed trader categories include 314 trader IDs each while the partially informed category includes 627 trader IDs.[305]

8.2 Synopsis

The presented classification procedure followed a stepwise approach. It covered all trader IDs that executed at least one order during the time frame of the analysis. As described in Exhibit 8-7, 2,413 active trader IDs were identified in the data set. These trader IDs were classified in accordance to their trading activity following two dimensions, aggressor and total trading volume. 36 of these trader IDs only entered limit orders, i.e. remained as 'not classified' from the aggressor view.

Based on their relative importance as described through a 4x4 matrix, 48% (1,121) of the trader IDs were classified as not relevant for the analysis and excluded for the second step of the procedure. During the second step of the analysis, the remaining 1,255 trader IDs that did allow calculation of the price impact were classified based on their level of information. The final classification followed the results from the percentile analysis, classifying all trader IDs that belong to the 25th percentile as uninformed (314), the trader IDs between 25th and 75th percentiles as partially informed (627), and the trader IDs that are between 75th and 100th percentiles as informed (314).

---

305 In addition, a k-mean cluster analysis varying number of clusters from three to six clusters is implemented. The cluster results do not provide a superior grouping of trader IDs along the arguments presented above. Cluster results are presented in Appendix 6.

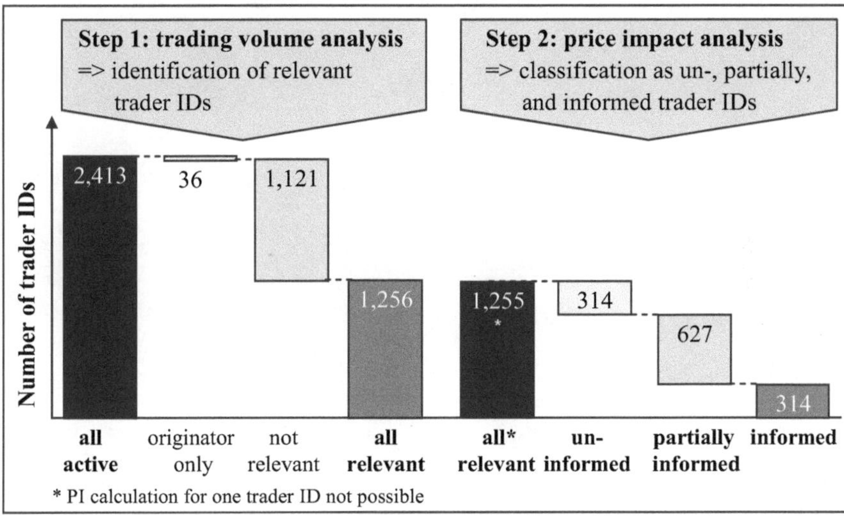

Exhibit 8-7: Synopsis of trader ID classification

This chapter provides a substantial contribution to the existing literature. So far, the identification of informed traders has not been possible at the trader level. Assumptions concerning institutions, account type, and order sizes had to be implemented to overcome the lack of suitable data. The unique data set of this study that incorporates the trader ID at the transaction and order level allows implementing a classification procedure that relies on a commonly accepted measure of informed trading. Key to the identification of informed traders is the choice of the suitable measurement method (see Chapter 4.3): The price impact as a measure for informed trading can be calculated for each executed aggressor order individually. At the same time, the trader ID enables the identification of all orders per trader ID. The level of information of the individual trader ID is calculated as the average price impact of all executed aggressor orders of a trader. This absolute figure (average price impact in bp) is then compared to the distribution across all trader IDs and the level of informed trading of the respective market (DAX instruments), allowing the determination of whether a trader shows a comparably larger level of information and can be classified as informed trader.

Once the trader ID is classified as informed, partially informed, or uninformed, a new field reflecting this classification is implemented for each trader ID in the complete data set.[306] As a consequence, each executed aggressor and originator order carries a flag by what type of trader ID it was entered. This allows the analysis of liquidity supply (originator) and demand (aggressor) behavior for the identified groups of trader IDs. The analyses in the next chapter are based on the implementation of this flag on the order level.

---

[306] The new data field INFO_TR_ID provides the following values: 0 = uninformed, 1 = informed, 2 = partially informed, and 3 = not relevant.

9 Liquidity Demand and Supply Behavior of Informed Traders

Based upon the trader categorization defined in the preceding chapter, this chapter aims at describing and analyzing the liquidity demand (aggressor) and supply (originator) behavior of the different trader categories. The behavior of informed traders will be compared to the behavior of the other trader categories and results for all trader IDs.[307] This chapter covers the last part of the empirical analysis as presented in Exhibit 9-1.

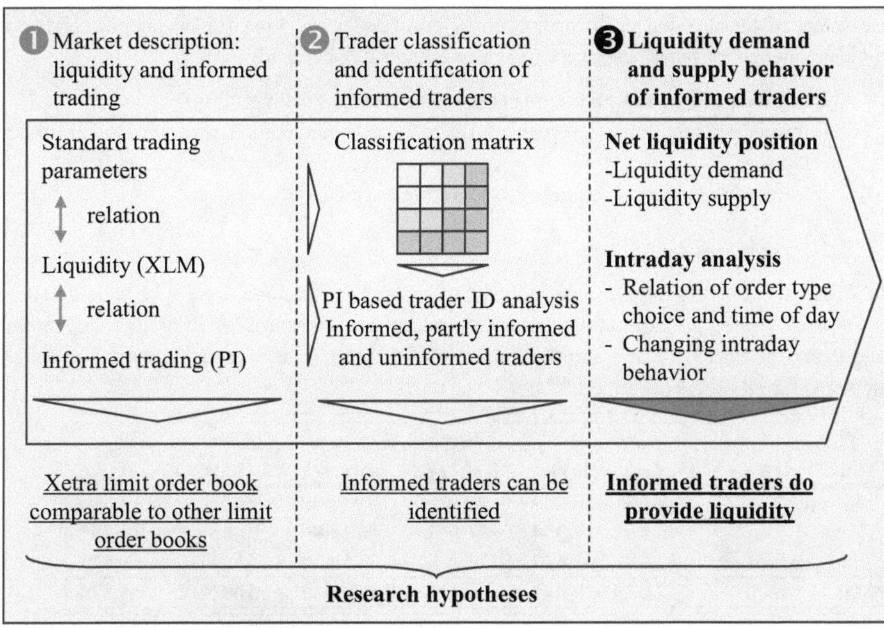

Exhibit 9-1: Research approach part 3

Within this chapter, hypotheses sets (c), (d), and (e) are tested (see Chapter 6.4.2): First, liquidity demand and supply behavior in terms of volume and orders are analyzed (Chapters 9.1 and 9.2). For the aggressor side, the effective spread and price impact are compared, while for the originator side the order aggressiveness and the average duration of executed orders in the order book are investigated. Results are further detailed to analyze the role of order size. The analyses transform into a separate description of liquidity supply and demand behavior.

Second, the net role i.e. whether a trader ID generally demands more liquidity than he provides or vice versa is determined for each trader category (Chapter 9.3).

Third, an intraday analysis, splitting the trading day into a morning and afternoon trading session is conducted for trading volume, average order size, as well as spread measures. This analysis forms the basis for testing the hypothesis on the relation of order type choice and time of day as well as concerning changing intraday behavior across the trader categories

[307] The results are comparable to those based on instruments presented in Chapters 6.3 and 7.2.

(Chapter 9.4). Finally, the results are summarized to describe the behavior and role of informed traders.

9.1 Liquidity Demand

In this chapter, the different trader categories are analyzed based on their aggressor (liquidity demand) behavior. Descriptive statistics include the distribution of trading volume, number of orders, and average order size, the results for price impact and effective spread, as well as an assessment of the use and performance of different order sizes per trader category. Results provide evidence for hypotheses set (c): Informed liquidity demand:

(x) Informed traders prefer medium size market orders (stealth trading).

(xi) Informed traders' market orders perform better than market orders of other trader categories.

(xii) Informed traders are discretionary market order traders.

9.1.1 Descriptive Statistics

The distributions of trading volume, number of orders, and average order size (calculated as the ratio of trading volume and number of orders) are presented in Exhibit 9-2. Trading volume and number of orders are from the reduced data set, as spread measures cannot be calculated for all orders described.[308]

Trader category	Aggressor trading volume	Volume % share	Aggressor orders	Orders % share	Avg. order size
Uninformed	28,405,460,440	13.1%	895,609	23.3%	31,716
Informed	**46,901,017,954**	**21.6%**	**522,686**	**13.6%**	**89,731**
Partially informed	137,881,101,617	63.5%	2,355,624	61.2%	58,533
Total	**217,035,928,849**	**100%**	**3,850,029**	**100%**	**56,373**

Exhibit 9-2: Aggressor trading volume and orders per trader category[309]

The total aggressor trading volume is generated by approx. 3.85 m orders with an average order size of approx. 56,400 €. The figures show that the trader category for informed traders is responsible for 21.6% of aggressor trading volume and only 13.6% of orders, which is reflected in their average order size of approx. 89,700 €. In contrast, uninformed traders generate 13.1% of trading volume (23.3% of orders) and show a relatively small average order size of approx. 31,700 €. Partially informed traders cause 63.5% of the trading volume (61.2% orders) and reveal an average order size (approx. 58,500 €) comparable to the average order size across all orders.

---

308 Appendix 7 provides a comparison of the volume and order distribution for both data sets: The volume distribution is almost identical before and after cleansing. What differs slightly is the distribution in number of orders, where the smaller order size classes (SIZE_ID = 1, 2, 3) show a stronger reduction in number of orders leading to an increased average order size of approx. 56,400 €, compared to approx. 55,800 € for the initial data set. The distribution along trader categories is not affected.

309 The trader IDs which were classified as not relevant in Chapter 8.1.1 account for 1.8% of aggressor trading volume (2.0% orders) and are included in the total figures presented in Exhibit 9-2.

The comparably large average order size of informed traders supports the notion that order size carries information, as informed traders implement larger orders more often. A pair-wise Mann-Whitney U-test[310] demonstrates that differences between the trader category for informed traders and the two other groups are statistically significant: Informed traders reveal a significantly higher average order size when compared to uninformed traders (z-value of -14.6) as well as partially informed traders (z-value of-10.8) both at the 0.001 level.[311]

To underpin this hypothesis, an order size analysis is conducted. Exhibit 9-3 displays the distribution of trading volume and orders across order size classes for the different trader categories as well as the distribution across all orders. Across all orders, 67.1% of aggressor orders are smaller than 50,000 € (SIZE_ID = 1, 2), a further 29.7% were classified as medium size orders (SIZE_ID = 3, 4), while only 3.2% of all aggressor orders are larger than 250,000 € (SIZE_ID = 5, 6). Small orders generate 21.7% of corresponding volume, medium and large orders 53.9% and 24.4%, respectively.[312]

Informed traders show a differing distribution: Only 50.4% of their orders are classified as small orders, while 43.0% belong to the medium size range and as much as 6.5% of their orders are categorized as large orders. This is mirrored in the volume distribution, where small orders account for 14.5% of trading volume and medium and large orders for 49.8% and 35.3%, respectively.[313]

Uninformed traders display the reverse behavior, with 83.2% of their orders categorized as small orders and only 15.4% and 1.4% categorized as medium and large orders, respectively. The volume distribution again reflects the order size distribution with 33.9%, 47.3%, and 18.9% for small, medium, and large orders. It can be concluded that uninformed traders prefer small order sizes and as a consequence small orders do not signal information. The order and volume distributions of partially informed traders come close to the average order distribution, which is a consequence of the fact that this trader category is responsible for 63.5% of the total trading volume.

---

310 In contrast to the statistical tests conducted in Chapters 6 and 7, which implemented pair-wise tests of dependent samples, in this chapter pair-wise tests for independent samples are conducted. This is due to the fact that with the trader categorization in Chapter 8, different test groups are identified and allow testing upon their behavior.

311 As presented in Chapter 8.2, the trader categories include a different number of trader IDs: for the informed and uninformed category N = 314, while for the category of partially informed N = 627. A comparison of these trader categories is based upon the averages computed for the individual trader IDs implementing tests for independent samples.

312 See the results presented in Chapter 6.3.2 and explanations given in Footnote 308.

313 Informed traders have a share of 21.6% of the total aggressor volume which varies across size classes: 14.4% volume share for small orders, 20.1% for medium size orders, and 31.3% for large orders. This is in line with Barclay/Warner (1993), p. 288, who conclude that informed traders will mainly use larger order sizes.

Trader category	SIZE_ID	Aggressor trading volume	Volume % share	Aggressor orders	Orders % share
Uninformed	1	5,103,470,202	18.0%	618,620	69.1%
	2	4,518,175,866	15.9%	126,371	14.1%
	3	6,228,102,951	21.9%	89,597	10.0%
	4	7,206,799,620	25.4%	48,536	5.4%
	5	3,317,426,420	11.7%	9,857	1.1%
	6	2,031,485,381	7.2%	2,628	0.3%
Total		28,405,460,440	100%	895,609	100%
Informed	**1**	**1,964,410,698**	**4.2%**	**131,966**	**25.2%**
	2	**4,826,096,362**	**10.3%**	**131,863**	**25.2%**
	3	**9,283,668,194**	**19.8%**	**129,810**	**24.8%**
	4	**14,258,419,136**	**30.4%**	**94,935**	**18.2%**
	5	**8,461,644,619**	**18.0%**	**24,583**	**4.7%**
	6	**8,106,778,946**	**17.3%**	**9,529**	**1.8%**
Total		**46,901,017,954**	**100%**	**522,686**	**100%**
Partially informed	1	11,383,228,667	8.3%	1,015,387	43.1%
	2	18,461,948,259	13.4%	506,087	21.5%
	3	32,255,921,851	23.4%	458,100	19.4%
	4	45,637,188,307	33.1%	303,522	12.9%
	5	19,443,589,129	14.1%	58,566	2.5%
	6	10,699,225,404	7.8%	13,962	0.6%
Total		137,881,101,617	100%	2,355,624	100%
All orders	**1**	**18,843,509,778**	**8.7%**	**1,805,881**	**46.9%**
	2	**28,311,127,864**	**13.0%**	**778,265**	**20.2%**
	3	**48,623,836,051**	**22.4%**	**689,617**	**17.9%**
	4	**68,316,269,943**	**31.5%**	**455,054**	**11.8%**
	5	**31,771,578,898**	**14.6%**	**94,650**	**2.5%**
	6	**21,169,606,315**	**9.8%**	**26,562**	**0.7%**
Total		**217,035,928,849**	**100%**	**3,850,029**	**100%**

Exhibit 9-3: Distribution of aggressor trading volume and orders across order size classes

Informed trader IDs implement both medium and large orders more often compared to the average order distribution. To test whether informed traders reveal a significantly larger share in medium and large order sizes, a Mann-Whitney U-test is conducted. It compares the order distribution across size classes based upon the percentage share of orders (last column in Exhibit 9-3) for the combined size classes of small, medium, and larger orders. Informed traders reveal a significantly smaller percentage share of orders in small order sizes and both a significantly larger share in medium and large orders when compared to the results for uninformed and partially informed traders (all results are significant at the 0.001 level, with z-values ranging from -5.1 to -14.5).

Thus, results partially support hypothesis (x) Informed traders prefer medium size market orders (stealth trading). Informed traders disclose a significantly larger average order size of approx. 89,700 € when compared to the other trader categories. In addition, medium size orders have a significantly higher share in their order size distribution. However, this is equally true for large orders. The results indicate that order size is an indicator but not a unique identifier for informed orders as informed traders use all order sizes, preferring medium and large orders. Consequently, the results of studies that rely upon order size as an identifier for informed trading have to be interpreted with care.

9.1.2 Spread Measures as Performance Criteria

Exhibit 9-4 provides the average effective spread and price impact for the identified trader categories. In line with Chapter 8.1.2, results are computed as averages across all transactions of each trader ID and then aggregated to reflect averages per trader category.[314] As price impact was the underlying criterion in classifying the trader IDs, it is a direct implication that informed traders have the highest average price impact of 10.3 bp, followed by partially informed traders with 4.9 bp and uninformed traders with only 0.7 bp.[315]

Trader category	Effective spread	Price impact	PI/ES	Avg. order size
Uninformed	5.837	0.673	12%	31,716
Informed	**6.556**	**10.338**	**158%**	**89,731**
Partially informed	5.517	4.864	88%	58,533
Average	**5.751**	**4.613**	**80%**	**56,373**

Exhibit 9-4: Spread measures and average order size per trader category

At the same time, informed traders realize the largest average effective spread of 6.56 bp, while partially informed traders show the lowest with 5.52 bp, followed by 5.84 bp for uninformed traders. Mann-Whitney U-test results support this finding, as the effective spread of informed traders is significantly larger compared to the partially informed traders as well as uninformed traders at the 0.001 level (z-statistics of -9.4 and -5.9, respectively).

The comparably low effective spread of partially informed traders demonstrates that they are able to minimize their ex-post liquidity costs through monitoring the order book, i.e. they enter their orders when the liquidity in the order book is high, consequently reducing their effective spread. As presented in Chapter 7.1.1, order size and ex-ante liquidity costs (XLM) are positively related, i.e. the liquidity costs increase with increasing order size. This result was further supported in Chapter 7.2.4, where the positive relation of ex-post liquidity costs

---

[314] The averages for both spread measures differ in comparison to the results presented in Chapter 7.2.2, with lower results for the instrument based spread measures: 5.75 bp compared to 5.87 bp (effective spread) and 4.61 bp compared to 5.04 bp (price impact). The difference stems from the different views taken on the data. In Chapter 7.2.2, the spread measures are computed as daily averages per instrument, while in this chapter results are calculated as averages across all transactions for each trader ID, further aggregated as averages per trader category. For both calculations, the weighting is based on orders and not on volume, as the volume effect is already reflected in the spread measures themselves through implementing the average executing price (P_t) per order in the calculation.

[315] Mann-Whitney U-test results find a significantly larger price impact of informed traders at the 0.001 level compared to uninformed traders (z-statistic of -21.7) and partially informed traders (z-statistic of -25.4).

(effective spread) and order size is documented. Thus, effective spread should be interpreted in the context of average order size.

The finding that partially informed traders are discretionary traders is underpinned when comparing their results to uninformed traders. Uninformed traders generate a significantly larger effective spread (z-statistic of -3.02 significant at the 0.01 level), while their average order size of approx. 31,700 € is significantly smaller at the 0.001 level (z-statistic of -10.78). Uninformed traders do not execute their orders depending on the liquidity in the order book.

There are several possible reasons for this outcome: (i) they do not have discretion over the timing of order execution, (ii) they do not have the data and/or the skills to monitor the order book to minimize liquidity costs, or (iii) both.[316]

In contrast, the significantly higher effective spread of informed traders comes together with a significantly larger average order size of approx. 89,700 € (see Chapter 9.1.1). The data does not allow the exclusion of the fact that informed traders are also discretionary traders who realize lower effective spreads, as the average order size of informed traders is 1.5 times as high as that of the partially informed traders, while the effective spread is only 1.2 times as high. The order size analysis below provides further insight into this hypothesis.

In addition, the relation of price impact to effective spread shows that informed traders realize double the ratio (158%) of the average across all trader IDs (80%), partially informed traders are slightly higher than average (88%), while uninformed traders realize only a third of the average (12%). Mann-Whitney U-test results show significantly larger results for informed traders at the 0.001 level (z-statistics range from -19.4 to -21.7). The described results support hypothesis (xi) that informed traders' market orders generally perform better as measured through larger price impact and a significantly larger ratio of price impact to effective spread.

Whether informed traders also act as discretionary traders realizing opportunities, preferably when the liquidity in the order book is high, is further investigated by taking order size into account. The discussion of the performance of medium size orders in Chapter 7.2.4 revealed that the hypothesis of medium size orders showing the best performance measured is only partially supported by the data: Both effective spread and price impact increase with order size, while the price impact to effective spread ratio increased from small to medium size orders but remained stable between medium and large orders; thus, medium and large orders have a comparable relative performance.[317]

---

[316] As the data does not allow the identification of whether the order flow behind the trader ID is able to monitor the order book, this remains an open question. Gomber/Schweickert/Theissen (2005), p. 18, find that large orders are timed. As the average order size of trader IDs that are categorized as uninformed is rather small, it can be assumed that mostly retail order flow belongs to this trader category. Retail investors do not have direct access to the trading system and usually do not have access to order book information via vendors (which are quite costly). As a consequence, there is no possibility to monitor the order book.

[317] A further distinction by instrument classes (GROUP_ID) showed that the hypothesis was fully supported for the ten most liquid instruments, but not for the remaining instruments.

Exhibit 9-5 displays the results for effective spread, price impact, and the price impact to effective spread ratio per trader category and across all orders. Results are computed as averages across all transactions that belong to a size class per trader ID and are then aggregated to reflect averages per order size class for each trader category.

	Uninformed			**Informed**		
SIZE_ID	**Effective spread**	**Price impact**	**PI/ES**	**Effective spread**	**Price impact**	**PI/ES**
1	5.669	0.561	10%	**5.982**	**10.034**	**168%**
2	5.675	1.138	20%	**6.170**	**10.307**	**167%**
3	5.758	1.271	22%	**6.196**	**9.882**	**159%**
4	6.071	1.485	24%	**6.649**	**10.964**	**165%**
5	7.691	3.266	42%	**7.569**	**11.850**	**157%**
6	10.380	3.273	32%	**8.962**	**15.571**	**174%**
Average	5.837	0.673	12%	**6.556**	**10.338**	**158%**

	Partially Informed			**All Traders**		
SIZE_ID	**Effective spread**	**Price impact**	**PI/ES**	**Effective spread**	**Price impact**	**PI/ES**
1	5.243	4.983	95%	5.714	4.374	77%
2	5.334	4.625	87%	5.781	4.611	80%
3	5.363	4.674	87%	5.895	4.687	80%
4	5.703	5.337	94%	6.319	5.908	94%
5	6.530	6.203	95%	7.488	6.697	89%
6	8.143	7.661	94%	8.898	8.779	99%
Average	5.517	4.864	88%	5.751	4.613	80%

Exhibit 9-5: Order size dependent on effective spread and price impact per trader category

Independent of the order size class, informed traders reveal that their average effective spread is larger than the average effective spread across all orders and increases continuously. Mann-Whitney U-test results find significantly larger effective spreads for informed traders for size classes one to four compared to uninformed traders (z-statistics range from -3.9 to -7.8) and for all size classes when compared to partially informed traders (z-statistics range from -3.4 to -4.2) at the 0.001 level.

Consequently, it cannot be concluded that informed traders act as discretionary traders and hypothesis (xii) is rejected when tested based upon results for effective spreads. However, effective spreads only measure the ability of a trader category to manage implicit transaction costs; it does not provide any information on the profitability of the trading strategies. This is given by the price impact and price impact to effective spread ratio.

Informed traders disclose a larger average price impact compared to the other trader categories increasing continuously except for SIZE_ID = 3 with the lowest price impact of 9.9 bp. The fact that the average price impact for SIZE_ID = 3 is smallest is unique to informed traders. A possible explanation is that orders of this size (medium size) are expected to be informed and this information is already priced. However, in the open limit order book traders who post limit orders do not have the choice to discriminate other traders as their orders are automatically executed upon arrival of a market order. They do not know the size of the order upfront or the identity of the trader, thus price discrimination is not possible. Accordingly, there is no obvious explanation. Instead, this phenomenon would have to be analyzed with additional data sets spanning either different time horizons or other instruments to capture if it is peculiar to this data set or generally true.

The average price impact of informed traders is significantly larger across all order sizes compared to uninformed traders as well as partially informed traders (z-statistics range from -5.7 and -18.3) at the 0.001 level. This is also reflected in the comparably larger price impact to effective spread ratio. The ratio is significantly larger across all order size classes compared to the other trader categories (z-statistics range from -4.7 to -17.6) at the 0.001 level. That means informed traders' orders reveal a better performance across all order size classes; i.e. their orders generally perform better. These results provide evidence independent of order size for hypotheses (xi) that informed traders' market orders generally perform better as measured through larger price impact and a significantly larger ratio of price impact to effective spread.

The price impact to effective spread ratio is approx. 167.5% for small order sizes, approx. 161.5% (159% for SIZE_ID = 3 and 165% for SIZE_ID = 4) for medium size orders, and approx. 161.7% for large orders. Results do not reveal a continuously increasing pattern and medium as well as large orders reveal a comparable ratio (no significant differences are found). Small orders are relatively more profitable than medium size orders.

As presented in Chapter 9.1.1, informed traders prefer medium and large orders, implying that order size can signal information. However, open electronic limit order books do not allow discriminating incoming market orders as these orders are automatically executed against limit orders standing in the book. In addition, the stealth trading hypothesis - hypothesis (x) - is only partly supported, as all orders of informed traders independent of their size perform better compared to the other trader categories - average price impact as well as the ratio of price impact and effective spread are significantly larger across all order size classes. Besides, medium and large order sizes reveal a comparable ratio of price impact and effective spread (approx. 162%), which is lower than for smaller orders (approx. 167.5%). The better performance of small orders is an indication that informed traders take advantage of opportunities arising in the order book, i.e. mispriced small orders. As uninformed traders prefer small order sizes for the aggressor side, it has to be analyzed for the liquidity supply side if this trader category provides opportunities with small orders in the order book, which could explain the superior performance of small aggressor orders of informed and partially informed traders.

For uninformed traders, both effective spread and price impact increase with increasing order size. They show a comparably low price impact to effective spread ratio, ranging from 10% to 42% increasing until SIZE_ID = 5 but decreasing for SIZE_ID = 6, when price impact remains stable but the effective spread increases further.

Partially informed traders' orders' effective spread increases continuously across size classes. While the price impact increases from size class two to six, it is higher for SIZE_ID = 1 in comparison to two and three. Consequently the results for the ratio are driven by the results for price impact. Partially informed traders realize the highest ratio of approx. 95% for SIZE_ID = 1, while the next two size classes realize a ratio of 87%. This ratio increases again to 94-95% for the remaining size classes.

While partially informed traders are defined as discretionary traders as they manage to realize lower implicit transaction costs (lower effective spreads) through monitoring of the order book, informed traders monitor the order book to realize profitable trading opportunities, which is reflected in the significantly larger price impact to effective spread ratio. As they trade upon their informational advantage, they can accept realizing larger effective spreads which are overcompensated by the realized price impacts. They trade when they can realize profits, i.e. they trade with discretion but for other reasons than the partially informed traders. In summary, hypothesis (xii) stating that informed traders are discretionary traders, is supported.

9.2 Liquidity Supply

Complementing the previous chapter, the different trader categories are analyzed based on their liquidity supply (originator) behavior. Descriptive statistics cover the distributions of trading volume, orders, and average order size per trader category. In addition, the use and performance of different limit order sizes are examined. In a second step, limit orders are further analyzed depending on their order aggressiveness at order entry as well as their average duration until execution in the order book.

To determine the order aggressiveness of a limit order, the limit order price of each order at its first execution is compared to the BBA at order entry. As explained in Chapter 6.2.3, the BBA table can have at times missing or invalid results: The data set is reduced to 3,957,173 orders as valid BBs and BAs could not be computed for 70,100 orders. The remaining orders still reflect 98.4% of the initial originator trading volume (98.3% of initial originator orders). This chapter investigates hypotheses set (d): Informed liquidity supply:

(xiii) Informed traders use limit orders as part of their trading strategies.

(xiv) Informed traders prefer medium size limit orders (stealth trading).

(xv) Informed traders reveal stronger limit order aggressiveness.

9.2.1 Descriptive Statistics

Exhibit 9-6 displays the originator trading volume, number of orders and average order size per trader category. Similar to the aggressor analysis trading volume and number of orders are taken from the reduced data set. The total originator trading volume is generated by approx. 3.96 m orders with an average order size of approx. 56,500 €.[318]

---

[318] Appendix 8 provides a comparison of the volume and order distribution for both data sets: Both volume and order distributions are almost identical before and after BBA_ID calculation. This is also reflected in the comparable average execution size of approx. 56,400 € for the initial data set compared to approx. 56,500 € for the reduced data set. Similar to the aggressor side, the distribution along trader categories is not affected by the cleansing of the data set.

Trader category	Originator trading volume	Volume % share	Originator orders	Orders % share	Avg. order size
Uninformed	40,781,252,546	18.2%	919,762	23.2%	44,339
Informed	**41,144,517,670**	**18.4%**	**277,653**	**7.0%**	**148,187**
Partially informed	136,860,459,844	61.2%	2,681,318	67.8%	51,042
Total	**223,626,184,640**	**100.0%**	**3,957,173**	**100.0%**	**56,512**

Exhibit 9-6: Originator trading volume and orders per trader category[319]

It shows that informed traders provide 18.4% of the total originator trading volume with only 7% of the orders. This yields an average order size of approx. 148,200 €, which deviates significantly from the other trader categories and is almost triple the average execution size of approx. 56,500 €. Results of a pair-wise Mann-Whitney U-test support this observation, as informed traders display a significantly higher average order size compared to uninformed traders (z-value of -12.5) and partially informed traders (z-value of -9.1) for both at the 0.001 level.

This suggests that order size carries information also for the liquidity providing side. The positive relation of order size and information was initially found for the liquidity demand side only where specialist markets were analyzed concerning the order size of incoming market orders. This was in line with the general assumption of the information driven models that informed traders only implement market orders. As a consequence, in these models, liquidity providing limit orders and their order size could not comprise information. For an open limit order book, Cao/Hansch/Wang (2004) find evidence that limit orders provide informational content even beyond the BBA.[320] Their results point out that limit orders do provide information, i.e. that informed traders also implement limit orders as part of their trading strategies, supporting the fact that the order size of limit orders could comprise information.

When comparing the average order sizes for the aggressor and originator side, it is apparent that the average order size of informed traders is significantly larger for liquidity providing limit orders (approx. 148,200 €) than for liquidity demanding aggressor orders (approx. 89,700 €).[321] In addition, compared to the other trader categories, informed traders implement larger orders both for the aggressor and originator side, as demonstrated by the Mann-Whitney U-test results.

Several fundamentals provide an explanation: (i) the different attributes of market and limit orders which are immediacy and price risk versus predetermined prices and execution risk, (ii) the discretionary trading behavior of informed traders, and (iii) the superior information level of informed traders. The higher average order size for originator orders compared to the aggressor order size can be attributed to the different order types (i). The fact that both

---

319 The trader IDs that were classified as not relevant in Chapter 8.1.1 account for 2.2 % of originator trading volume (2.0% orders) and are included in the total figures presented in Exhibit 9-6.

320 See Cao/Hansch/Wang (2004), p. 23.

321 Paired Wilcoxon signed-ranks tests for informed traders demonstrate that the average originator size is significantly larger than the average aggressor order size (z-statistic = -3.89, significant at the 0.001 level).

(originator and aggressor) average order sizes are larger compared to the averages across all orders can be explained through their discretion when trading (ii) and the superior information of informed traders (iii): Their superior information reduces price risk while their discretion reduces execution risk, allowing them in both cases to implement larger orders at lower risk. Central to this explanation is that informed traders closely monitor the order book.

Uninformed traders provide 18.2% of trading volume (23.2% of orders), leading to a relatively small average execution size of approx. 44,300 €. Similar to the informed traders, their average order size is also significantly larger for originator orders compared to their average aggressor order size.[322]

Similar to their results for the aggressor side, partially informed traders are responsible for the major part of the total trading volume or liquidity provided, as reflected in their volume share of 61.2% (67.8% of orders). In contrast to the other traders, their average order size for aggressor orders (approx. 58,500 €) is significantly larger than for originator orders (approx. 51,000 €).[323] This could be due to the fact that although they have some discretion over their orders, their trading is often liquidity motivated, meaning that they have to execute in a defined timeframe and execution risk is valued higher than price risk.

The above findings support hypothesis (xiii) that informed traders do provide liquidity by implementing limit orders as part of their trading strategies. In addition, their average order size indicates that informed traders prefer medium order sizes as assumed with hypothesis (xiv). This is further investigated based on order size distribution for the different trader categories. Exhibit 9-7 presents originator trading volume and orders across order size classes. It shows that across all orders approx. 70.1% of originator orders are defined as small (SIZE_ID = 1 and 2), a further 26.5% are labeled medium (SIZE_ID = 3 and 4), while 3.4% of orders are large (SIZE_ID = 5 and 6).[324]

As already pointed out, informed traders have a significantly larger average order size This is a consequence of a differing order size distribution: Only 39.1% of their orders are classified as small orders, while 45.8% of their orders belong to the medium size range and 15.1% belong to the large size categories. This is reflected in the volume distribution where small orders only account for 6.4% of their trading volume and medium and large orders account for 35.5% and 58%, respectively. Mann-Whitney U-test results support the above findings as the percentage share of small orders is significantly smaller while the percentage shares of medium and large orders are significantly larger compared to uninformed and partially informed traders (z-values ranging from -3.2 to -11.8 at the 0.001 level). These results support hypothesis (xiv) Informed traders prefer medium size limit orders (stealth trading). However, they do not only show a preference for medium size orders but also for large orders, which is in line with the results found for the aggressor side.

---

322 Paired Wilcoxon signed ranks tests for uninformed traders support the finding that the average originator size is larger than the average aggressor order size (z-statistic = -9.08, significant at the 0.001 level).

323 Paired Wilcoxon signed ranks tests for partially informed traders show that the average aggressor order size is significantly larger than the average originator order size (z-statistic = -7.61, significant at the 0.001 level).

324 See also the results presented in Chapter 6.3.2.

Trader category	SIZE_ID	Originator trading volume	Volume % share	Originator orders	Orders % share
Uninformed	1	5,843,848,815	14.3%	524,873	57.1%
	2	6,186,021,522	15.2%	172,893	18.8%
	3	8,902,404,667	21.8%	128,385	14.0%
	4	11,070,380,180	27.1%	74,032	8.0%
	5	5,051,919,081	12.4%	15,099	1.6%
	6	3,726,678,280	9.1%	4,480	0.5%
Total		40,781,252,546	100%	919,762	100%
Informed	**1**	**736,106,226**	**1.8%**	**57,176**	**20.6%**
	2	**1,905,473,459**	**4.6%**	**51,461**	**18.5%**
	3	**4,511,948,374**	**11.0%**	**62,680**	**22.6%**
	4	**10,109,094,469**	**24.6%**	**64,519**	**23.2%**
	5	**9,137,870,388**	**22.2%**	**26,019**	**9.4%**
	6	**14,744,024,754**	**35.8%**	**15,798**	**5.7%**
Total		**41,144,517,670**	**100%**	**277,653**	**100%**
Partially informed	1	16,133,894,736	11.8%	1,392,840	51.9%
	2	18,743,065,274	13.7%	522,860	19.5%
	3	31,899,221,426	23.3%	454,595	17.0%
	4	35,548,771,140	26.0%	239,959	8.9%
	5	17,301,551,908	12.6%	51,255	1.9%
	6	17,233,955,360	12.6%	19,809	0.7%
Total		136,860,459,844	100%	2,681,318	100%
All orders	**1**	**23,111,719,733**	**10.3%**	**2,007,917**	**50.7%**
	2	**27,513,727,265**	**12.3%**	**766,326**	**19.4%**
	3	**46,288,624,468**	**20.7%**	**659,474**	**16.7%**
	4	**58,188,952,309**	**26.0%**	**388,158**	**9.8%**
	5	**32,192,021,685**	**14.4%**	**94,456**	**2.4%**
	6	**36,331,139,179**	**16.2%**	**40,842**	**1.0%**
Total		**223,626,184,640**	**100%**	**3,957,173**	**100%**

Exhibit 9-7: Distribution of originator trading volume and orders across order size classes

Similar to the findings for the aggressor order size distribution, uninformed traders show the reverse behavior compared to informed traders, with 75.9% of their orders classified as small and only 22.0% and 2.1% categorized as medium and large orders, respectively. As stated in Chapter 9.1.2, informed traders demonstrate a superior performance for small aggressor orders, which can be explained through picking off mispriced small limit orders standing in the order book. This is supported, as uninformed traders implement a large portion of their originator orders as small orders.

Partially informed traders show an order and volume distribution that comes close to the total distribution, which is again a consequence of the fact that this trader category is responsible for 61.2% of the total trading volume (67.8% of orders).

9.2.2 Limit Order Aggressiveness

The level of aggressiveness of executed orders can be distinguished as follows: (1) high for market orders or marketable limit orders, (2) medium for orders with a limit price at or better than the current BBA, and (3) low for orders with a limit price behind the current BBA. Per definition, all orders that belong to level (1) are aggressor orders, while limit orders that are categorized as level (2) or (3) are originator orders.[325]

Originator orders are limit orders that are not immediately executed and remain in the limit order book as a source of liquidity supply. When entering a limit order, the trader has to choose the aggressiveness of the order, either setting a limit price at or better than the current BB or BA (2) or behind the current BB or BA (3). With the limit set, the trader ensures the price at which the order is executed. This is due to the discriminatory pricing rule during continuous trading, where limit orders standing in the order book do not get price improvement but are executed at the specified limit.[326]

The aggressiveness of the limit price chosen is relevant for its execution probability. Orders that have an aggressive limit increase their short term execution probability compared to orders that are entered within the book. The latter assume that the market will turn towards them or expect to be hit by a larger order that matches into the order book and executes orders at more than one limit.

For all executed originator orders, the BB or BA prevailing at order entry is determined similar to the procedure for the aggressor orders. For each buy (sell) order the execution timestamp is determined from the Trades table. Then the respective BB (BA) that was valid at order entry is determined with the following rule (including milliseconds):[327]

REGIONAL_TIMESTAMP > START_TIME and ≤ END_TIME

A new data field BBA_ID, which reflects the level of aggressiveness, is introduced: it takes on the value 0 for orders entered behind the BBA, i.e. for buy orders with a limit smaller than the BB and for sell orders with a limit larger than the BA. It yields the value 1 for orders entered at or better than the BBA, i.e. for buy orders with a limit larger than or equal to the BB and for sell orders with a limit smaller than or equal to the BA.

---

325 In this analysis, only orders that are executed are part of the data set. Thus orders that enter the order book but do not execute either being deleted before execution or remaining in the order book are not included. Strictly speaking, limit orders that enter the order book and are not executed do not provide liquidity, as at their price limit there is no liquidity demand. In addition, Hasbrouck/Saar (2002), p. 21ff. and Hasbrouck/Saar (2004), p. 4 have identified so-called fleeting orders, which are limit orders that are cancelled within an extremely brief time, e.g. two seconds after their submission. They find that these limit orders are close substitutes to market orders that demand immediacy.

326 See Chapter 2.3 for details on the market model.

327 As a crosscheck, the respective BA (BB) is also identified. This is done to ensure that the limit price of the buy (sell) order does not lead to a crossed order book, which would have led to an immediate execution of the order. In that case, the order is excluded from the sample, as the BBA Table obviously has a missing value for that order.

Exhibit 9-8 provides the originator trading volume, corresponding orders, and average order size per trader category following the classification of aggressiveness. The results show that there is no major difference in order aggressiveness between the different trader categories. Across all trader IDs, approx. 76.1% of orders are entered at or better than the current BBA, while only 23.9% are entered deeper into the order book. Results for trading volume are comparable with 72.5% entered at or better than the current BBA and 27.5% behind the quote. Results for the different trader groups divert slightly from this number.

Trader category	BBA_ID	Originator trading volume	Originator orders	Avg. order size	Volume % share	Orders % share
Uninformed	0	11,583,517,791	242,587	47,750	28.3%	26.4%
	1	29,197,734,755	677,175	43,117	71.4%	73.6%
Informed	**0**	**11,220,994,492**	**63,952**	**175,460**	**27.3%**	**23.0%**
	1	**29,923,523,178**	**213,701**	**140,025**	**72.7%**	**77.0%**
Partially informed	0	37,037,527,799	614,458	60,277	27.1%	22.9%
	1	99,822,932,045	2,066,860	48,297	72.9%	77.1%
All orders	**0**	**61,592,993,763**	**945,888**	**65,117**	**27.5%**	**23.9%**
	1	**162,033,190,877**	**3,011,285**	**53,809**	**72.5%**	**76.1%**
Total or average		**223,626,184,640**	**3,957,173**	**56,512**		

BBA_ID: 0 = behind the BBA and 1 = at or better than the BBA

Exhibit 9-8: Order aggressiveness per trader category

Across all trader categories, the major portion of orders and corresponding volume is entered at or better than the current BBA. As a consequence, it cannot be directly assumed that limit order aggressiveness is a differentiation criterion between trader types. When implementing Mann-Whitney U-tests comparing the percentage share of orders and trading volumes entered at or better than the BBA (BBA_ID = 1), significant differences are found at the 0.01 level: Informed traders implement a significantly higher share of their orders and corresponding trading volume at or better than the BBA when compared to uninformed and partially informed traders (z-values ranging from -2.9 to -5.3). Thus, hypothesis (xv) that informed traders show stronger limit order aggressiveness than other trader categories is supported by the data.

It should be noted, however, that the data set only comprises executed orders. That means all orders that enter the order book and are not executed because either being deleted before a possible execution or remaining in the order book during the end of the analysis time frame are not part of the analysis. The number of unexecuted limit orders is found to be large in Xetra.[328] As informed traders closely monitor the order book and actively time their trades, it can be derived that they actively enter and cancel limit orders when they are not executed.

[328] Kempf/Mayston (2005), p. 8f. analyze the order book as well as the order flow for the DAX instruments in Xetra during 2 January to 31 March 2004. They find that only ~25% of limit orders entered are also executed. For the limit orders that did not execute, they do not provide any information concerning their aggressiveness or the time they remained in the order book before they were cancelled.

However, with the available data it cannot be analyzed if limit orders that did not execute and were cancelled would alter the presented pattern in terms of aggressiveness.

Analyzing the average order size for the two aggressiveness levels across the different trader categories, it can be seen that the average order size is significantly smaller for orders entered at or better than the BBA (BBA_ID = 1) than for orders entered behind the BBA. Wilcoxon signed ranks tests support the outcome for all trader categories separately (z-statistics range from -8.12 to -18.01 significant at the 0.001 level). The conclusion is that from the perspective of the liquidity demander traders are willing to provide liquidity for larger quantities, only at less favorable prices.

9.2.3 Limit Order Execution Duration

The average duration of a limit order in the order book before its execution is calculated as the difference between the order entry timestamp and the corresponding execution timestamp. If orders are executed more than once (partial execution), the first execution timestamp is chosen, as this was the first time when the market reached the execution price determined by the limit of the order. As presented in Chapter 6.2.2, all analyses are based on the Trades table, which only includes executed orders. Orders that enter the limit order book but remain unexecuted are not included in the sample. Exhibit 9-9 provides the average duration (in seconds and minutes) for the different trader categories as well as across all orders depending on order aggressiveness (BBA_ID).

Trader category	BBA_ID	Avg. duration in seconds/minutes		Originator orders	Originator trading volume
Uninformed	0	1620.4	27.0	242,587	11,583,517,791
	1	158.6	2.6	677,175	29,197,734,755
Total or average		544.2	9.1	919,762	40,781,252,546
Informed	**0**	**1281.5**	**21.4**	**63,952**	**11,220,994,492**
	1	**138.6**	**2.3**	**213,701**	**29,923,523,178**
Total or average		**401.8**	**6.7**	**277,653**	**41,144,517,670**
Partially informed	0	1210.1	20.2	614,458	37,037,527,799
	1	128.4	2.1	2,066,860	99,822,932,045
Total or average		376.3	6.3	2,681,318	136,860,459,844
All orders	**0**	**1339.4**	**22.0**	**945,888**	**61,592,993,763**
	1	**136.5**	**2.3**	**3,011,285**	**162,033,190,877**
Total or average		**424.1**	**7.1**	**3,957,173**	**223,626,184,640**

BBA_ID: 0 = behind the BBA and 1 = at or better than the BBA

Exhibit 9-9: Average execution duration per trader category

Across all orders, the average duration for an order between its entry and its execution is 7.1 minutes. This can be further differentiated as orders that are entered at or better than the BBA are executed on average after 2.3 minutes, while orders that are entered behind the BB or BA remain on average for 22.0 minutes in the order book until they are executed by an incoming market order. This result is straightforward, as orders entered at or better than the BBA are priced more aggressively, which should increase their likelihood of execution. For orders which are entered with a limit price behind the BBA, all orders which stand in front of them in the order book need to execute first, which in return reduces the likelihood of immediate execution of these orders. The longer duration of orders entered behind the BBA in comparison to orders entered at or better than the BBA is significant at the 0.001 level across all trader categories (z-statistics range from -15.2 to -21.6). Generally, the execution of limit orders depends on the possibility that a counterparty market order enters the order book, if further orders with a better limit are entered, and on the direction of the price development in that instrument.

Partially informed traders show shorter average durations compared to the results for all orders. Compared to the results for informed traders, time to execution is more favorable for orders of partially informed traders - approx. 10 seconds for orders at or better than the BBA and 71 seconds for orders behind the quote. However, Mann-Whitney U-test results do not reveal any significant differences (p-values of 0.83 for orders behind the BBA and 0.26 for orders at or better than the BBA).

As presented in Chapter 9.1.2, both trader categories monitor the order book. As they actively handle their orders, it can be assumed that if their orders do not execute they are potentially deleted. If they still have trading needs (partially informed traders trading for liquidity reasons), they either enter a new limit order at a better price limit or if they require timely execution choose to enter a market order.[329] The consequence of active order handling and monitoring of the order book is that for these traders, the time of all their orders either executed or again deleted from the order book will be shorter. Similar to the analysis concerning the aggressiveness of orders, this cannot be further investigated, as the data set only covers executed orders.

Uninformed traders show longer execution durations compared to the two other trader categories with 2.6 minutes for orders at or better than the BBA and 27 minutes for orders behind the BBA. However, the results are only significantly larger at the 0.05 level for orders entered at or better than the BBA (z-statistic of -1.96) when compared to the results of partially informed traders as well as for orders entered behind the BBA (z-statistic of -1.96) when compared to the results for informed traders.

It should be noted that a shorter time to execution is not per se a quality criterion, as time to execution does not entail any information concerning the pricing of the limit order. A short time to execution can mean both an order priced at the current market price that is executed by liquidity demand or a mispriced order that is picked off by a better informed trader.

---

329 Harris (1990), pp. 6-9 distinguishes two types of liquidity providers - passive traders that try to capture the spread and precomitted traders that try to lower their execution costs but switch to a liquidity demanding strategy if they are not executed.

9.3 Net Role of Trader Categories

The results for the different trader categories have been presented separately for the liquidity demand and supply side based on the reduced data sets. In this chapter, the general role of each trader category is further analyzed looking at the net position, i.e. comparing their trading volume demanded and supplied. To allow a direct comparison of aggressor and originator trading volume, the complete data set is implemented. This is necessary as the aggressor data set was reduced by 4.5% of the trading volume (see Chapter 7.2.1) when determining the spread measures while the originator data set was reduced by 1.6% of trading volume only when computing the order aggressiveness (see Chapter 9.2).[330] This chapter analyzes hypothesis (xvi) as part of hypotheses set (e).

Exhibit 9-10 displays the results for aggressor and originator trading volume, the percentage share of aggressor volume, and z-statistics for paired Wilcoxon signed rank tests, including direction of the results, i.e. if the z-statistic is relevant for aggressor trading volume being larger than the originator volume (>) or vice versa (<).

Trader category	Aggressor trading volume	Originator trading volume	Aggressor volume % share	z-statistic
Uninformed	29,834,501,655	41,917,967,277	41.6%	-3.77 < ***
Informed	**48,981,723,891**	**41,889,400,437**	**53.9%**	**2.23 < ***
Partially informed	144,366,772,083	138,322,861,335	51.1%	-4.49 > ***
Total or average	**227,197,046,579**	**227,197,046,579**	**50.0%**	

*** = significant at the 0.001 level, ** = 0.01 level, * 0.05 level

Exhibit 9-10: Distribution of aggressor and originator trading volume per trader category[331]

Informed traders have a higher share in aggressor than in originator trading volume, classifying this trader category as net liquidity demander (53.9%), which is in line with results presented in the previous chapters where informed traders provide approx. 18.4% of the trading volume while they demand approx. 21.6%. As the difference between aggressor and originator trading volume for this trader category is quite large, it is an unexpected outcome that z-statistics reveal a significant difference at the 0.05 level, where the aggressor volume is smaller than the originator volume as indicated by '<' in the table: 163 trader IDs out of 314 trader IDs classified as informed traders had a larger originator volume.

This seems conflictive as the percentage share of aggressor volume and the absolute figures indicate that more volume is demanded than supplied. When analyzing the data at the individual trader ID level, the explanation is straightforward: The large absolute difference can be explained by one particular trader ID which is responsible for 11.2% (10.7 bn €) of the

---

330 All statistics and tests are also computed for the reduced data sets yielding qualitatively identical results. However, for the case where the aggressor volume is larger than the originator volume the differences are less pronounced while for the case where the originator volume is larger the differences become stronger. This is a direct consequence of the cleansing differences.

331 Totals include the volume of the trader IDs which were classified as not relevant in Chapter 8.1.1. Results for the reduced data sets are similar and presented in Appendix 9.

total trading volume of all trader IDs categorized as being informed and has an aggressor share of 97.8%; i.e. only 2.2% of his total trading volume is originator trading volume. The difference of 10.25 bn € between aggressor and originator trading volume of this individual trader ID is more than the absolute difference for the entire trader category (7.09 bn € = 48.98 bn € - 41.89 bn €).[332] As a consequence, when comparing the absolute results, informed traders as a category are net liquidity demanders. However, when analyzing the individual trader IDs of the informed traders, more than half of the trader IDs are net liquidity providers. Hypothesis (xvi), that informed traders are net liquidity providers, is not rejected at a significance level of 0.05, which is rather low considering the number of cases (N = 314). Still, the data proves that at least half of the informed traders are net liquidity providers.

The statistics for uninformed traders reveal that only 41.6% of their total trading volume is assigned to aggressive liquidity demanding orders. The difference is highly significant at the 0.001 level, where 180 out of 314 trader IDs have a higher originator trading volume. In this case, absolute differences and results of individual trader IDs are consistent: Uninformed traders are net liquidity providers.

The absolute difference between aggressor and originator trading volume of partially informed traders (6.04 bn €) is slightly smaller than the volume difference of informed traders. However, this trader category shows that aggressor volume is significantly larger at the 0.001 level, with 348 out of 627 trader IDs generating a higher aggressor than originator trading volume. Again, absolute differences and individual results are consistent. Thus, partially informed traders are net liquidity demanders.

Summarizing, when comparing the absolute net positions (the difference between aggressor and originator trading volume) for the different trader categories, only uninformed traders are net liquidity providers while the two other trader categories are net liquidity demanders. However, when implementing significance tests at the trader ID level, the initial findings are only supported for uninformed and partially informed traders. For informed traders, the large net difference is explained through the trading behavior of one trader ID while more than half of the trader IDs are net liquidity providers. Test statistics support hypothesis (xvi) that informed traders are net liquidity providers.

---

332 This trader ID is responsible for a total trading volume of 10.7 bn €, which is 4.7% of the total trading volume across all trader IDs. It is ranked third in terms of total trading volume. The first and second ranked trader IDs are responsible for 28.3 bn € and 12.2 bn €, respectively.

9.4 Intraday Results

In the last part of the trader category analyses, the relation of order type choice and time of day is examined. Similar to the intraday analyses performed in Chapters 6.3.3 and 7.2.5, the trading day is split into a morning and an afternoon trading session, implementing the intraday auction as the natural break of the trading day. As a consequence, the two sessions differ in their length and data of the afternoon trading session is adjusted to reflect the longer duration.[333] The structure of this chapter follows hypothesis (xvii): Informed traders show a net role change during the trading day:

(a) Informed traders prefer market orders earlier in the trading day.

(b) Informed traders prefer limit orders later in the trading day.

(c) Informed traders switch from a net liquidity demander to a net liquidity provider role.

As a sideline, the intraday performance of market orders per trader category is analyzed.

9.4.1 Market Order Results

As described in Chapter 6.3.3, the intraday distribution of trading volume follows a U-shaped pattern, with the highest trading volume after 4:00 pm. A comparison of morning and afternoon trading volume based on the DAX instruments reveals that the trading volume is significantly higher during the afternoon trading session.[334]

Exhibit 9-11 provides the adjusted aggressor trading volume for the morning and afternoon trading session. In addition, z-statistics, which compare results for the two parameters for the trading sessions, are reported, including the direction of results, i.e. if the trading volume or average size is larger in the morning than in the afternoon trading session (>) or vice versa (<).[335] The total figures disclose that during the morning session 47% of the trading volume are traded with an average order size of approx. 55,400 €. During the afternoon 53% of the volume is traded at an average size of approx. 56,200 €. However, the disparity between the two trading sessions in general is not found for all trader categories.[336]

---

[333] The trading volumes and the number of orders of the afternoon trading session are multiplied with $0.\overline{88}$ (= 4/4.5).

[334] The results presented compare the aggressor trading volume for morning and adjusted afternoon trading session. Separate results for the originator trading volume were not presented, as these would have been identical as the originator side is the trade counterparty.

[335] Totals include the volume of trader IDs which were classified as not relevant in Chapter 8.1.1. Results for the reduced data set are presented in Appendix 10. The results for number of orders during the two trading sessions are not reported as they can be derived from the results for trading volume and average order size: If the average order size is higher during a trading session, this can be either through increased trading volume with stable number of orders or through stable trading volume with fewer orders. Z-statistics did not disclose any significant differences for number of orders between the two trading sessions across all trader categories.

[336] The significance of intraday differences in trading volume is demonstrated in Chapter 6.3.3.

Trader category	Trading session	Adjusted aggressor trading volume	Trading session % share	z-statistics	Avg. order size	z-statistics
Uninformed	morning	13,395,033,916	47.8%	-0.72	29,489	-0.10
	afternoon	14,612,860,213	52.2%	ns	34,164	ns
Informed	**morning**	**22,831,562,040**	**49.6%**	**-0.61**	**90,051**	**-2.07**
	afternoon	**23,244,588,312**	**50.4%**	**ns**	**88,459**	*** (>)**
Partially informed	morning	61,913,839,638	45.8%	-2.84	58,370	-0.96
	afternoon	73,291,495,507	54.2%	** (<)	57,025	ns
Total or average	**morning**	**100,159,733,796**	**47.0%**		**55,380**	
	afternoon	**112,922,055,807**	**53.0%**		**56,163**	

** significant at the 0.01 level, * = 0.05 level, ns = not significant

Exhibit 9-11: Intraday distribution of aggressor trading volume per trader category[337]

Informed traders do not show a significant difference in trading volume for the morning and afternoon trading session, which is consistent with the almost comparable absolute results for the two trading sessions. This is a first indication from the aggressor side that informed traders do not have a particular preference for the time of the day. Thus sub-hypothesis (a) has to be rejected. Their average order size is slightly higher during the morning trading session, although significant only at the 0.05 level.

Uninformed traders show a stronger absolute difference with a higher trading volume in the afternoon trading session. This difference is insignificant, as almost half of the trader IDs trade stronger during the morning trading session. Although the average order size is larger during the afternoon trading session, test results again yield insignificant differences: Uninformed traders do not demonstrate a preference for implementing aggressor orders depending on the time of the day.

Partially informed traders show consistent results between absolute trading volumes and test statistics. These trader IDs implement significantly larger trading volumes during the afternoon trading session. As the number of orders implemented increases accordingly, the average order size does not vary significantly. Partially informed traders reveal a time of day preference, increasing the number of market orders they trade within the afternoon.[338] An explanation could be that these traders trade at least partially for liquidity reasons and have to fulfill their trading needs until the end of the trading day. As the time till trading ends becomes shorter, they trade with market orders. If this assumption is true, these traders would also trade a stable or decreasing share of limit orders in the second half of the trading day, which will be evaluated in the next chapter.

In a second step, the performance of market orders per trader category is analyzed. Initially, the reverse J-shaped intraday distributions of effective spread and price impact are analyzed in Chapter 7.2.5. A comparison of morning and afternoon trading session reveals that both

337 Totals include the volume of trader IDs, which were classified as not relevant in Chapter 8.1.1.

338 If the reduced data set is implemented, no significant results are found for partially informed traders; see Appendix 10.

spread measures are significantly higher during the morning trading session based on the results for the DAX instruments. Exhibit 9-12 provides the results for spread measures for the two trading sessions across the trader categories, including the results for pair-wise Wilcoxon signed ranks tests.

Trader category	Spread measures	Morning session	Afternoon session	Difference	z-statistic
Uninformed	Effective spread	6.153	5.316	0.836	-12.17 ***
	Price impact	1.126	1.276	-0.150	-1.16 ns
Informed	**Effective spread**	**6.833**	**5.999**	**0.833**	**-11.82** ***
	Price impact	**10.923**	**8.963**	**1.960**	**-5.40** ***
Partially informed	Effective spread	5.806	5.150	0.656	-16.15 ***
	Price impact	5.349	4.320	1.029	-6.77 ***
*** = significant at 0.001 level, ** = 0.01 level, ns = not significant					

Exhibit 9-12: Intraday differences of spread measures per trader category

Across all trader categories, the effective spread is significantly higher during the morning trading session at the 0.001 level. For informed and partially informed traders, the price impact is also significantly higher during the morning trading session while uninformed traders demonstrate a comparably low figure for both trading sessions.

In line with the results presented in Chapter 9.1.2, informed traders reveal a significantly larger effective spread, price impact, and price impact to effective spread ratio compared to partially informed as well as uninformed traders during both the morning and the afternoon trading session; i.e. results found are independent of the time of day.[339]

Overall the results for the DAX instruments documented in Chapter 7.2.5 are further underpinned. The finding that informed traders realize larger effective spreads while their orders perform better measured by price impact and price impact to effective spread ratio (see Exhibit 9-4) is still valid when analyzing the two trading intervals separately. Thus, their superior trading results are independent on the time of the day.

9.4.2 Limit Order Results

When analyzing the originator trading volume from an intraday perspective, the following calculation procedure has to be taken into account: In Chapter 6.2.2, the transfer from trade data to order data is described. This transfer is necessary as orders can be partially executed during the course of the trading day.[340] Trades which belong to one order are allotted

[339] Mann-Whitney U-tests provide a significantly larger average effective spread at least at the 0.01 level (z-statistics range from -2.6 to -5.5), a significantly larger average price impact (z-statistics range from -15.9 and -19.7), and a significantly larger price impact to effective spread ratio (z-statistics range from -13.4 to -19.0) at the 0.001 level for both trading sessions.

[340] As presented in Exhibit 9-8, 27.5% of the executed originator volume initially enters the order book behind the BB or BA. In addition, these orders are significantly larger than orders entered at or better than the BB or BA. These orders wait in the order book and expect to be hit by incoming large orders or when prices move into their direction, e.g. due to intraday volatility. The fee and pricing schedule of Deutsche Boerse AG is order based. As a consequence, partial executions are not separately priced and traders can implement strategies that lead to partial executions without incurring higher transaction fees.

implementing the ORDER_NO as unique identifier. For these orders, the trading volume of the different trades is accumulated and the average execution price is calculated. As a consequence, a new order based data set is generated.

In this data set, only one execution timestamp is kept, which is the timestamp reflecting the first (partial) execution of the order. The accumulated volume of partially executed orders is thus assigned to their first execution. For orders that are executed during both trading sessions, the volume is assigned to the morning trading session. As a consequence, the order volume assigned to the morning trading session is overestimated. However, when comparing the total trading volume of the originator side (100.75 bn €, Exhibit 9-13) to the aggressor trading volume (100.16 bn €, Exhibit 9-11), this difference (approx. 0.58%) is rather small and should not dilute the results. The fact that trading volume is accumulated per originator order does not play a role in the calculation of the average order size, as the number of orders allotted to a trading session also depends on the timestamp of first execution.

Exhibit 9-13 displays the adjusted originator trading volume, corresponding average order sizes, and z-statistics, including direction of the results for the two parameters, i.e. if results are larger for the morning trading session (>) or vice versa (<).[341]

Trader category	Trading session	Adjusted originator trading volume	Trading session % share	z-statistics	Avg. order size	z-statistics
Uninformed	morning	18,065,014,509	46.2%	-2.13	44,093	-1.00
	afternoon	21,068,172,823	53.8%	* (<)	42,534	ns
Informed	**morning**	**19,665,356,332**	**49.9%**	**-0.56**	**150,461**	**-2.45**
	afternoon	**19,754,705,871**	**50.1%**	**ns**	**147,879**	*** (<)**
Partially informed	morning	60,431,242,883	46.6%	-0.73	52,507	-2.41
	afternoon	69,236,994,179	53.4%	ns	50,386	* (<)
Total or average	**morning**	**100,749,604,292**	**47.3%**		**58,106**	
	afternoon	**112,397,726,477**	**52.7%**		**55,136**	

* significant at the 0.05 level, ns = not significant

Exhibit 9-13: Intraday distribution of originator trading volume per trader category[342]

Informed traders do not show a preference for trading with limit orders in either of the trading sessions, as reflected in the small absolute difference of trading volume for the two trading sessions and the results of the z-statistics of -0.56. The average order size is a little higher during the morning trading session. Z-statistics reveal the opposite (<), as more traders implement a larger average order size in the afternoon compared to the morning trading session. However, as more orders are implemented in the afternoon, the average order size

341 Totals include the volume of trader IDs which were classified as not relevant in Chapter 8.1.1. Similar to the previous chapter, the data for number of orders and corresponding z-statistics are not presented. Results are insignificant for informed and partially informed trader categories. However, for the uninformed trader IDs, the number of orders is significantly higher during the afternoon trading session (z-statistic = -3.15, significant at 0.01 level).

342 Appendix 11 provides the results for the reduced data set. Totals include the volume of trader IDs, which were classified as not relevant in Chapter 8.1.1.

across all orders decreases. Sub-hypothesis (b) that informed traders prefer limit orders later in the trading day is not supported by the data; informed traders do not reveal a relation between the time of the day and entry of limit orders. This is in line with the results presented for market orders.

Uninformed traders reveal the largest relative difference between morning and afternoon trading volume, where 53.8% of originator trading volume is traded later in the trading day. Z-statistics support this observation as results are significantly smaller for the morning trading session at the 0.05 level; 192 out of 314 trader IDs have a larger trading volume during the second half of the trading day. Thus, uninformed traders show at least some preference for trading with limit orders in the afternoon trading session. The results presented for market orders did not support a relation between the time of the day and their order choice. The fact that the average order size is insignificantly smaller during the afternoon trading session is a result of the number of orders increasing stronger than the trading volume. Although the absolute difference between the two trading sessions of the originator trading volume for partially informed traders is relatively large, z-statistics show that trader IDs do not systematically trade more in the afternoon trading session. As the trading volume is larger in the afternoon, it can be concluded that those traders that are more active in the afternoon do trade relatively more compared to the trader IDs that trade during the morning trading session. This is supported by the results for average order size. Although the average order size across all orders is smaller in the afternoon trading session, z-statistics show the opposite, as more traders implement larger average orders in the afternoon than in the morning trading session. In contrast to the relation found between the time of the day and market order trading for this trader category, the statistics do not support a relation between the time of the day and limit order trading for partially informed traders.

9.4.3 Proportions of Market Orders and Limit Orders

In Chapter 9.3, the net role of the different trader categories is analyzed, concluding that uninformed traders are net liquidity providers and partially informed traders are net liquidity demanders. While informed traders are from an absolute perspective net liquidity demanders, test statistics reveal that more than half of the trader IDs are on the liquidity providing side. This relation is further evaluated concerning the possibility of a role change during the trading day.

First, the total trading volume, i.e. the sum of aggressor and originator trading volume, is analyzed to understand if a trader category demonstrates a general preference for the morning or afternoon trading session. Second, the net trading volume calculated as the difference between originator and aggressor trading volume is investigated to reveal if the net role of the trader categories depends on the time of the day.

Exhibit 9-14 displays the total trading volume per trader category, the relative share for the two trading sessions, as well as z-statistics for differences in the two trading sessions, including direction of results, i.e. morning trading volume is larger than afternoon trading (>) or vice versa (<).

Trader category	Trading session	Adjusted total trading volume	Trading session % share	z-statistics
Uninformed	morning	31,460,048,425	46.8%	-1.41
	afternoon	35,681,033,036	53.2%	ns
Informed	**morning**	**42,496,918,371**	**49.7%**	**-0.76**
	afternoon	**42,999,294,183**	**50.3%**	**ns**
Partially informed	morning	122,345,082,522	46.2%	-1.97
	afternoon	142,528,489,686	53.8%	* (<)
Total	**morning**	**200,909,338,088**	**47.1%**	
	afternoon	**225,319,782,284**	**52.9%**	

* = significant at the 0.05 level, ns = not significant

Exhibit 9-14: Intraday total trading volume per trader category[343]

Informed traders do not show significant intraday differences; i.e. their overall trading volume does not depend on the time of the day, which confirms the earlier findings for the originator and aggressor trading volume.

The same holds true for uninformed traders, although the relative share of the afternoon trading session is larger (53.2% compared to 46.8%). For the aggressor trading volume, no significant differences are found (see Exhibit 9-11), while for the originator volume the afternoon trading volume is significantly higher at the 0.05 level (see Exhibit 9-13).In contrast, total trading volume is significantly larger during the afternoon trading session at the 0.05 level for partially informed traders. These trader IDs show a significantly higher aggressor trading volume during the afternoon trading session, while no significant differences are found for the originator side (see Exhibit 9-13).

It can be concluded that the total trading volume does not depend on the time of the trading day for informed and uninformed traders, while partially informed traders trade significantly more during the second half of the trading day.

Exhibit 9-15 provides the net trading volume calculated as the difference between originator and aggressor trading volume, the percentage share of aggressor volume, as well as z-statistics and corresponding direction for the different trader categories.

---

343 Totals include the volume of trader IDs, which were classified as not relevant in Chapter 8.1.1.

Trader category	Trading session	Net trading volume (originator - aggressor)	Aggressor volume % share	z-statistics
Uninformed	morning	4,669,980,593	42.6%	-0.39
	afternoon	6,455,312,610	41.0%	ns
Informed	**morning**	**-3,166,205,708**	**53.7%**	**-0.65**
	afternoon	**-3,489,882,441**	**54.1%**	**ns**
Partially informed	morning	-1,482,596,755	50.6%	-2.33
	afternoon	-4,054,501,328	51.4%	* (<)

* = significant at the 0.05 level, ns = not significant

Exhibit 9-15: Intraday net trading volume per trader category

Informed traders show a net liquidity demanding role for both trading sessions with no significant differences found. Thus, sub-hypothesis (c) that informed traders switch from a net liquidity demanding to a net liquidity providing role has to be rejected. As a consequence, hypothesis (xvii) is generally rejected, including all three sub-hypotheses.

Uninformed traders are net liquidity providers. This role does not change during the trading day. At the same time, the decrease in aggressor share is not significant. Partially informed traders show a significantly stronger net liquidity demanding role in the afternoon trading session at the 0.05 level. This corresponds to the intraday results for the aggressor volume where aggressor volume is significantly larger during the afternoon and the results for the total trading volume which is also significantly larger in the afternoon.

Summarizing, none of the trader categories demonstrates a switch in its role as liquidity provider or demander depending on the time of the day.

9.5 Synopsis

The third part of the research approach describes the liquidity supply and demand behavior of the different trader categories and tests the hypotheses sets (c), (d), and (e), defined for informed traders (see Chapter 6.4.2).

First, informed traders' liquidity demand behavior is analyzed: Informed traders are responsible for more than 20% of the total aggressor trading volume. Their average order size is significantly larger compared to the other trader categories (uninformed and partially informed traders). This is reflected in a significantly differing order size distribution, i.e. medium and large orders are preferred. In addition, their market orders perform significantly better than the other trader categories in terms of price impact and price impact to effective spread ratio, due to their discretionary behavior and superior information (hypotheses (xi) and (xii)). However the stealth trading hypothesis is only partly supported, as all their orders independent of order size reveal a superior performance compared to the orders of the other trader categories. Instead, small orders perform even better than medium and large orders based on their price impact to effective spread ratio (hypothesis (x)). This indicates that informed traders are ready to pick off mispriced small orders standing in the order book.

Second, informed traders' liquidity supply behavior is investigated: Informed traders also implement limit orders as part of their trading strategies and provide liquidity (hypothesis (xiii)). They are responsible for almost 20% of the originator volume with an average order size of nearly € 150,000, which is significantly larger compared to the average order size of the other trader categories. The order size distribution shows similar to the aggressor side that both medium and large orders are preferred, only partially supporting the stealth trading hypothesis (hypothesis (xiv)). Compared to the aggressor side, their average originator order size is significantly larger and almost triple the average originator order size across all orders. The implementation of larger limit order sizes is attributed to the different characteristics of order types, discretionary trading behavior, and the superior information level of informed traders. In addition, informed traders reveal a significantly stronger limit order aggressiveness (hypothesis (xv)).

Third, the net role of informed traders is discussed: Comparing the volume shares for originator and aggressor trading volume, informed traders take on the role of liquidity demanders. This is rejected when analyzing the trader ID level, where more than half of the trader IDs provide more liquidity than they demand (hypothesis (xvi)). This result provides evidence for the experimental finding from Bloomfield/O'Hara/Saar (2005) that informed traders enter even more limit than market orders. As a consequence, the data not only supports that informed traders take on the role of liquidity providers but that some of them even provide more liquidity than they actually demand from the other traders.

Fourth, when analyzing the intraday behavior, informed traders do not show any preference for the time of the day, either for implementing market orders or limit orders. As a consequence, their net role does not change during the trading day; hypothesis (xvii) is rejected. This holds true for the other trader categories that also keep their role independent on the time of the day. In addition, the superior performance of their market orders already demonstrated in the second part is further supported as it holds independent on the time of the day.

Summarizing, with the third part of the research approach the initial question of whether informed traders provide liquidity in Xetra can be positively answered. Thus, Chapter 9 provides first evidence from an anonymous open limit order book against the general theoretical notion that informed traders are liquidity demanders only. This should change the general perception of informed traders' behavior in order-driven markets. In Chapter 4.1, it is argued based on the information paradigm that informed traders make prices more informative when trading while they redistribute wealth to the disadvantage of uninformed traders. The results from this chapter clearly indicate that informed traders fulfill an additional function: As they are least subject to adverse selection risk, they can provide liquidity at lowest risk. When they act as liquidity providers, they ensure that the order-driven market structure remains a viable and self-sustaining market.

Consequently, this chapter supports existing evidence from an experimental order book as well as empirical results for NYSE. However, in contrast to the earlier empirical results, its outcome is based on a methodological identification of informed traders and does not need to implement assumptions based upon order sizes and types of institutions. This is particularly important as results on order sizes for both market and limit orders do not support the clear predictions from the stealth trading hypothesis. Thus, analyses that depend on order size as an underlying assumption should be interpreted with respect to this caveat.[344]

---

[344] Anand/Chakravarty/Martell (2005) and Kaniel/Liu (2006) find evidence for NYSE that limit orders convey more information than market orders concluding that informed traders implement limit orders. Bloomfield/O'Hara/Saar (2005) provide evidence for an experimental limit order book.

10 Résumé

This chapter discusses whether the purpose of this study and the underlying research questions defined in Chapter 1 have been answered. It includes a résumé of the most important results of this thesis as well as a critical discussion of the transferability of results to other equity markets. Finally, further research areas are suggested.

The purpose of this study was to identify informed traders and to describe their liquidity providing behavior in an open limit order book. It followed a new branch in literature assuming that informed traders not only implement market orders but implement both market and limit orders as part of their trading strategies. Consequently, informed traders take on the role of liquidity providers.

The starting point of this thesis is a twofold research gap: First, although order-driven market structures play by now a dominant role in equities markets, the literature lacks an empirical analysis of informed traders' behavior for this market structure. Second, the existing literature on informed traders relies on assumptions and does not provide an unambiguous method to identify them. This study closes both research gaps.

A contribution to the literature is made concerning the initially phrased questions that cater three research objectives:

(i) the qualification of the Xetra open limit order book as a securities market with standard attributes,

(ii) the identification of informed traders, and

(iii) the analyses of liquidity providing behavior of informed traders.

These objectives underlie the defined research approach and are addressed consecutively. While the first objective provides the point of reference for the interpretation of results of the trader categories and concerns the transferability of results to other securities markets, the two remaining objectives close the described research gaps.

To answer the first question, the DAX instruments were analyzed, providing descriptive statistics of trading parameters and testing standard hypotheses sets for informed trading and liquidity (see Chapters 6.3 and 7). The anonymous open limit order book Xetra showed characteristics for standard trading parameters (trading volume and volatility) similar to other limit order book markets as well as other market structures either hybrid or quote-driven. In addition, liquidity patterns as well as results for informed trading are fairly consistent with results from other securities exchanges. Results support the general theoretical notion of a negative relation of liquidity and informed trading; i.e. an increase in informed trading leads to a decrease in liquidity. Thus, the initial research question was positively answered: The anonymous electronic open limit order book Xetra behaves fairly normally; i.e. the research results of this study cannot be related to any peculiarities of the Xetra trading system.

The second research objective concerned the classification and identification of informed traders. Based upon the choice of the ad hoc method (Chapter 4.3), Chapter 8 successfully categorized traders as uninformed, partially informed, or informed, based upon their trading activity and their level of information measured through price impact. As a consequence, it was possible to overcome existing deficits in the identification of informed traders providing a substantial contribution to the existing literature and for future research.

The third question directly transformed into the purpose of this study, which was to provide evidence for informed traders' liquidity providing behavior in open limit order books. The separate analysis of the liquidity demand and supply behavior revealed that informed traders use both liquidity demanding market orders and liquidity providing limit orders. Generally, they implement significantly larger orders when compared to the other trader categories, while the average order size for limit orders is significantly larger than for market orders.

The stealth trading hypothesis, which assumes that informed traders prefer medium size orders and that these orders reveal a superior performance is not unambiguously supported. In fact, all their orders independent of order size disclose a significantly better performance, while small orders outperform medium and large orders when analyzing the price impact to effective spread ratio. This raises concerns against order size as an identification criterion as implemented in earlier empirical studies.

When analyzing informed traders' net role (difference between liquidity supplied and liquidity demanded), it is found that from an absolute perspective this trader category demands more liquidity than it supplies, indicating a net liquidity demander role. In contrast, when analyzing the individual trader IDs, it is found that more than half of the trader IDs provide more liquidity than they demand. Consequently, informed traders form a heterogeneous group of traders. However, the majority is net liquidity provider.

Summarizing, the empirical results support existing research that informed traders do provide liquidity also in open limit order books (order-driven market structures). The remaining questions are whether these results can be transferred directly to other order-driven (LSE, Euronext or SEHK) or even to hybrid market structures (NYSE) and which areas should be addressed in future research.

As described in Chapter 2.3, the market model comprehends the principles of order matching and price determination, and defines market participants, order types, trading models, and transparency regimes. The trading model reflects the market structure as order-driven, hybrid or quote-driven and is directly related to the principles of order matching and price determination as well as to market participants. As basic order types (market and limit orders) are common among securities exchanges, the main differentiation between securities exchanges lies in the trading model and transparency regimes. Accordingly, the transferability of the study's research results can be discussed for securities markets that rely upon the same trading mechanism (order-driven market structures) or that implement a differing trading mechanism (hybrid market structures). In this discussion, quote-driven market structures are excluded, as in these markets only market makers can post quotes. Thus, uninformed and informed traders are not able to provide liquidity through limit orders.

When evaluating the transferability of results to other securities exchanges in the context of this study it has to be determined which element of the market model is particularly relevant for informed traders. Informed traders do anything to disguise themselves to profit from their information, which is reflected in the fact that informed trading is much more pronounced in anonymous environments. Consequently, anonymity is a prerequisite for informed traders' willingness to trade, which is determined through the transparency regime.

The Xetra limit order book foresees full pre-trade and post-trade transparency, i.e. immediate distribution of all order book information (price limits, corresponding number of shares, and number of orders behind the limit) and transactions (transaction price and corresponding volumes) taking place. However, pre-trade anonymity is granted as the order book information does not include the trading member or the trader ID. In addition, Xetra foresees a central counterparty function which ensures post-trade anonymity. That means even after a trade has taken place, the details of the trade will not include any information on the participating parties. In this environment, informed traders can be confident that when implementing either a market order or a limit order, they will not directly reveal any information upfront (while standing in the limit order book) or after the completion of the trade.

Concerning pre-trade anonymity, recent research predicts that limit order anonymity increases liquidity, i.e. in an anonymous set-up more traders are willing to provide liquidity. The argument is that with non-anonymous limit orders, the incentive to acquire information diminishes as other traders can free-ride on the information of informed traders.[345] Concerning post-trade anonymity, results indicate that the introduction of anonymity results in increased liquidity, i.e. more traders are willing to provide liquidity following the same argument.[346] Then, informed liquidity demand and supply is expected to be much lower in a non-anonymous environment as other traders could identify the informed traders in the order book or as their counterparties and free-ride on their information. Consequently, the results for informed traders' liquidity supply and demand behavior should be transferable only to other anonymous market structures, taking into account that for informed liquidity supply both pre-trade and post-trade anonymity are decisive.

The order-driven equity markets of LSE and Euronext both rely upon a similar market model as the Xetra trading system, i.e. they offer continuous trading with a matching algorithm that follows price-time priority and foresees pre-trade anonymity by concealing member information in the order book, and provide post-trade anonymity for highly liquid instruments through central counterparty functions. Consequently, results should be transferable to these markets.

In contrast, the SEHK reveals broker IDs for the orders in the limit order book (pre-trade non-anonymity).[347] Even though this market structure is comparable to the Xetra trading system in terms of trading and matching rules, it cannot be assumed that results are directly transferable. In this market it would be expected that informed traders do not provide liquidity to that extent, as they would then share their information with the other traders. However, an empirical analysis of the SEHK would have to evaluate this hypothesis.

---

345 See Comerton-Forde/Frino/Mollica (2005), p. 534f., Foucault/Moinas/Theissen (2004), p. 38f., and Perotti/ Rindi (2006), p. 100.

346 See Hachmeister/Schiereck (2006), p. 10f.

347 See Ahn/Bae/Chan (2001), p. 771f. In addition to the SEHK, the KSE also reveals broker identities, see Comerton-Forde/Frino/Mollica (2005), p. 530.

Initial empirical results for informed liquidity provision were documented for the NYSE, which provides a hybrid market structure where both the specialist and limit order traders compete in liquidity provision. At first sight, this indicates that the market structure is not decisive for informed liquidity provision. However, during the analysis period, the specialist only participated in less than 10% of the transactions, which means limit orders of traders play a much stronger role.[348] Trading thus resembles the order-driven structure for most transactions. Both pre- and post-trade anonymity are fulfilled, with one exception: The specialist does have the technical possibility to look up the trading member behind an order but has to look into a separate screen. However, as trading members can reveal different trading motives, this is at best an indicator for the level of information. In addition, as the other trading participants do not have access to this information, the level of anonymity is large enough for informed traders to trade in that market and provide liquidity. Taking the above argumentation into account, it cannot be concluded with certainty that market structure does not play a role.

In line with the above discussion, results should be transferable to other equity markets, depending on their market design (transparency regime and possibly market structure). However, new questions arise from the results and should be addressed in future research.

First, the role of market structure needs to be further evaluated, providing additional evidence for hybrid markets. In continental Europe, both the Xetra trading system as well as Euronext foresee a market model with designated liquidity providers for less liquid instruments, reflecting a hybrid market structure based upon an order-driven market structure. These market models are implemented for instruments that require additional liquidity and could serve as the basis for an analysis of the relevance of market structure in the context of informed traders' liquidity providing behavior.

Second, the results presented in Chapter 9 indicate that informed traders form a heterogeneous group of traders where more than half of them are net liquidity providers while the rest take on the role of net liquidity demanders. A more detailed analysis is needed that clusters traders identified as informed according to their trading behavior. This yields the potential to better understand whether different types of informed traders exist and which types of trading motives and strategies result in informed liquidity provision. Understanding this trader category is crucial, as they could be the liquidity providers of last resort in volatile markets, as in contrast to uninformed traders they do not face adverse selection risk.

This thesis yields new insights into the trading behavior of informed traders. It provides evidence that in contrast to standard theoretical notion, informed traders do implement limit orders, with the majority taking on the role of net liquidity providers changing the general perception of informed traders' role in securities trading. Thus, future research on the evolution of liquidity should incorporate this finding either when deriving new theoretical models or when interpreting empirical results.

---

[348] Anand/Chakravarty/Martell (2005), p. 308 report that specialist participation was 9.9% in 1991 and 15% during 2001 and 2002. See also Kaniel/Liu (2006), p. 1883.

Appendix

Appendix 1: RATE_PRICE_TYPE_ID – field values and description

RATE_PRICE_TYPE		
ID	**Category**	**Name**
1	Trade	Previous day
2	Trade	Opening
3	Trade	Variable
4	Trade	Fixing
5	Trade	First and last rate (Opening and Closing)
6	Trade	Closing
7	Pre-trade	Indicative bid rate (information sources BOS system)
8	Pre-trade	Indicative asked rate (information sources BOS system)
9	Pre-trade	Estimated rate "bid"(information sources BOS system)
10	Pre-trade	Estimated rate "ask" (information sources BOS system)
11	Pre-trade	Assignment quota
12	Trade	Settlement price
13	Trade	Potential opening price (information source Eurex only)
14	Trade	Adjusted open interest quantity (Eurex only)
15	Pre-trade	Bid rate (information source DEVISE only)
16	Pre-trade	Ask rate (information source DEVISE only)
17	Pre-trade	Bid and ask rate (information source DEVISE only)
18	Trade	Official middle rate (information source DEVISE only)
19	Trade	End of price entry BOS system
20	BestBidAsk	Volatility interruption best bid
21	BestBidAsk	Volatility interruption best ask
22	Trade	Volatility interruption trade
23	BestBidAsk	Volatility interruption indicative price
24	Trade	OTC trade
25	BestBidAsk	Opening auction best bid
26	BestBidAsk	Opening auction best ask
27	Trade	Opening auction trade
28	BestBidAsk	Opening auction indicative price
29	BestBidAsk	Continuous trading best bid
30	BestBidAsk	Continuous trading best ask
31	Trade	Continuous trading trade
32	BestBidAsk	Intraday auction best bid
33	BestBidAsk	Intraday auction best ask
34	Trade	Intraday auction trade
35	BestBidAsk	Intraday auction indicative price
36	BestBidAsk	Closing auction best bid
37	BestBidAsk	Closing auction best ask
38	Trade	Closing auction trade

Appendix 2: Largest executed aggressor order per trading day per instrument

	Largest executed aggressor order per trading day		
Instrument	**maximum**	**minimum**	**average**
ADIDAS-SALOMON AG O.N.	2,316,936	221,938	814,641
ALLIANZ AG VNA O.N.	8,275,751	1,042,000	2,431,893
ALTANA AG O.N.	1,660,768	137,267	472,607
BASF AG O.N.	2,340,169	431,400	1,001,530
BAY.HYPO-VEREINSBK.O.N.	1,900,202	265,486	797,993
BAY.MOTOREN WERKE AG ST	2,491,703	433,402	895,881
BAYER AG O.N.	1,519,915	307,867	730,653
COMMERZBANK AG O.N.	2,883,847	340,619	1,045,615
CONTINENTAL AG O.N.	2,311,068	291,195	703,363
DAIMLERCHRYSLER AG NA O.N.	5,110,400	730,031	1,502,432
DEUTSCHE BANK AG NA O.N.	3,900,000	800,172	1,728,913
DEUTSCHE BOERSE NA O.N.	2,031,147	215,808	710,356
DEUTSCHE POST AG NA O.N.	2,618,067	363,767	873,923
DT.TELEKOM AG NA	7,916,650	1,311,390	3,165,467
E.ON AG O.N.	4,101,497	699,111	1,539,422
FRESEN.MED.CARE AG O.N.	2,126,002	136,196	485,516
HENKEL KGAA VZO O.N.	1,787,496	101,433	441,602
INFINEON TECH.AG NA O.N.	3,180,860	357,300	916,151
LINDE AG O.N.	3,117,443	185,546	457,058
LUFTHANSA AG VNA O.N.	1,813,815	279,736	668,888
MAN AG ST O.N.	2,966,198	197,100	537,512
METRO AG ST O.N.	1,081,184	202,950	532,795
MUENCH.RUECKVERS.VNA O.N.	4,439,296	531,375	1,502,844
RWE AG ST O.N.	3,074,591	483,439	1,380,230
SAP AG O.N.	4,718,253	561,439	1,284,396
SCHERING AG O.N.	2,554,035	261,250	644,540
SIEMENS AG NA	12,309,725	704,992	1,783,706
THYSSENKRUPP AG O.N.	2,191,282	316,200	780,518
TUI AG NA	1,170,603	276,667	605,172
VOLKSWAGEN AG ST O.N.	4,998,793	421,813	1,338,527
All instruments	**12,309,725**	**101,433**	**1,059,138**

Appendix 3: Largest executed originator order per trading day per instrument

	Largest executed originator order per trading day		
Instrument	**maximum**	**minimum**	**average**
ADIDAS-SALOMON AG O.N.	3,213,925	283,100	1,262,544
ALLIANZ AG VNA O.N.	9,575,964	1,462,847	3,775,742
ALTANA AG O.N.	4,359,551	179,000	787,964
BASF AG O.N.	5,840,000	619,800	2,061,658
BAY.HYPO-VEREINSBK.O.N.	4,607,144	338,000	1,440,007
BAY.MOTOREN WERKE AG ST	4,669,516	540,035	1,422,816
BAYER AG O.N.	3,297,245	485,773	1,387,506
COMMERZBANK AG O.N.	4,455,451	381,347	1,569,381
CONTINENTAL AG O.N.	3,162,500	344,200	1,168,785
DAIMLERCHRYSLER AG NA O.N.	7,587,702	1,070,000	2,227,932
DEUTSCHE BANK AG NA O.N.	7,655,568	1,160,204	3,274,123
DEUTSCHE BOERSE NA O.N.	3,904,505	149,800	1,283,415
DEUTSCHE POST AG NA O.N.	4,989,441	371,835	1,294,372
DT.TELEKOM AG NA	9,297,581	1,283,682	3,149,643
E.ON AG O.N.	7,399,416	1,014,082	2,635,816
FRESEN.MED.CARE AG O.N.	3,004,000	151,700	728,719
HENKEL KGAA VZO O.N.	2,954,000	116,025	661,216
INFINEON TECH.AG NA O.N.	3,236,159	500,500	1,067,736
LINDE AG O.N.	3,702,156	154,750	753,060
LUFTHANSA AG VNA O.N.	1,603,169	279,300	813,407
MAN AG ST O.N.	2,110,745	391,600	955,126
METRO AG ST O.N.	1,612,702	248,280	782,984
MUENCH.RUECKVERS.VNA O.N.	5,527,500	809,522	2,703,309
RWE AG ST O.N.	5,032,197	981,989	2,045,012
SAP AG O.N.	6,352,595	642,369	1,936,531
SCHERING AG O.N.	2,172,151	263,218	876,402
SIEMENS AG NA	7,127,763	920,419	2,460,279
THYSSENKRUPP AG O.N.	3,400,000	422,529	993,894
TUI AG NA	3,436,000	288,347	842,454
VOLKSWAGEN AG ST O.N.	4,766,943	699,605	1,877,885
All instruments	**9,575,964**	**116,025**	**1,607,991**

Appendix 4: Wilcoxon signed-ranks test for intraday results of LP and XLM(V)

Panel A: LP

SLICE_ID start time	9.00 am z-statistics	10.00 am z-statistics	11.00 am z-statistics	12.00 am z-statistics	1.00 pm z-statistics	2.00 pm z-statistics	3.00 pm z-statistics	4.00 pm z-statistics
9.00 am								
10.00 am	-4.78 ***							
11.00 am	-4.78 ***	-4.78 ***						
12.00 am	-4.78 ***	-4.78 ***	-4.37 ***					
1.00 pm	-4.78 ***	-4.76 ***	-2.09 *	-3.32 ***				
2.00 pm	-4.78 ***	-4.76 ***	-2.62 **	-1.59 ns	-1.72 ns			
3.00 pm	-4.78 ***	-4.78 ***	-4.66 ***	-3.47 ***	-4.52 ***	-4.52 ***		
4.00 pm	-4.78 ***	-4.78 ***	-4.10 ***	-0.61 ns	-3.14 ***	-1.92 ns	-4.39 ***	
5.00 pm	-4.78 ***	-4.78 ***	-3.71 ***	-0.79 ns	-2.97 **	-2.31 *	-3.12 **	-1.20 ns

Panel B: XLM(50)

SLICE_ID start time	9.00 am z-statistics	10.00 am z-statistics	11.00 am z-statistics	12.00 am z-statistics	1.00 pm z-statistics	2.00 pm z-statistics	3.00 pm z-statistics	4.00 pm z-statistics
9.00 am								
10.00 am	-4.78 ***							
11.00 am	-4.78 ***	-4.78 ***						
12.00 am	-4.78 ***	-4.78 ***	-4.17 ***					
1.00 pm	-4.78 ***	-4.76 ***	-0.90 ns	-3.82 ***				
2.00 pm	-4.78 ***	-4.76 ***	-2.27 *	-1.22 ns	-2.58 *			
3.00 pm	-4.78 ***	-4.78 ***	-4.56 ***	-3.69 ***	-4.66 ***	-4.64 ***		
4.00 pm	-4.78 ***	-4.78 ***	-3.10 **	-0.28 ns	-3.65 ***	-1.92 ns	-4.72 ***	
5.00 pm	-4.78 ***	-4.78 ***	-3.59 ***	-1.08 ns	-3.40 ***	-2.07 *	-3.49 ***	-0.48 ns

*** = 0.001, ** = 0.01, * = 0.05, ns = not significant

Appendix 4 (continued):

Panel C: XLM(250)

SLICE_ID start time	9.00 am z-statistics	10.00 am z-statistics	11.00 am z-statistics	12.00 am z-statistics	1.00 pm z-statistics	2.00 pm z-statistics	3.00 pm z-statistics	4.00 pm z-statistics
9.00 am								
10.00 am	-4.78 ***							
11.00 am	-4.78 ***	-4.78 ***						
12.00 am	-4.78 ***	-4.78 ***	-3.30 ***					
1.00 pm	-4.78 ***	-4.76 ***	-0.73 ns	-2.66 **				
2.00 pm	-4.78 ***	-4.76 ***	-1.74 ns	-0.22 ns	-3.12 **			
3.00 pm	-4.78 ***	-4.78 ***	-4.25 ***	-3.75 ***	-4.66 ***	-4.66 ***		
4.00 pm	-4.78 ***	-4.78 ***	-2.60 **	-1.59 ns	-3.47 ***	-1.96 *	-4.47 ***	
5.00 pm	-4.78 ***	-4.78 ***	-3.67 ***	-2.31 *	-3.49 ***	-2.46 *	-2.25 *	-0.46 ns

Panel D: XLM(500)

SLICE_ID start time	9.00 am z-statistics	10.00 am z-statistics	11.00 am z-statistics	12.00 am z-statistics	1.00 pm z-statistics	2.00 pm z-statistics	3.00 pm z-statistics	4.00 pm z-statistics
9.00 am								
10.00 am	-4.78 ***							
11.00 am	-4.78 ***	-4.78 ***						
12.00 am	-4.78 ***	-4.78 ***	-2.31 *					
1.00 pm	-4.78 ***	-4.74 ***	-1.04 ns	-2.34 *				
2.00 pm	-4.78 ***	-4.76 ***	-0.73 ns	-0.67 ns	-2.29 *			
3.00 pm	-4.78 ***	-4.78 ***	-3.80 ***	-3.59 ***	-4.29 ***	-4.52 ***		
4.00 pm	-4.78 ***	-4.78 ***	-2.15 *	-1.66 ns	-2.85 **	-1.92 ns	-4.15 ***	
5.00 pm	-4.78 ***	-4.78 ***	-3.75 ***	-2.93 **	-3.36 ***	-2.87 **	-1.16 ns	-1.29 ns

*** = 0.001, ** = 0.01, * = 0.05, ns = not significant

Appendix 5: Wilcoxon signed-ranks test for intraday results of ES and PI

Panel A: Effective spread

SLICE_ID start time	9.00 am z-statistics	10.00 am z-statistics	11.00 am z-statistics	12.00 am z-statistics	1.00 pm z-statistics	2.00 pm z-statistics	3.00 pm z-statistics	4.00 pm z-statistics
9.00 am								
10.00 am	-4.78 ***							
11.00 am	-4.78 ***	-4.45 ***						
12.00 am	-4.78 ***	-4.76 ***	-3.91 ***					
1.00 pm	-4.78 ***	-4.62 ***	-2.83 **	-1.49 ns				
2.00 pm	-4.78 ***	-4.47 ***	-1.40 ns	-2.36 *	-0.86 ns			
3.00 pm	-4.78 ***	-4.70 ***	-4.03 ***	-1.88 ns	-3.12 **	-3.63 ***		
4.00 pm	-4.78 ***	-4.78 ***	-4.76 ***	-2.17 *	-2.90 **	-4.25 ***	-0.29 ns	
5.00 pm	-4.72 ***	-4.72 ***	-4.78 ***	-4.74 ***	-4.72 ***	-4.78 ***	-4.29 ***	-3.82 ***

Panel B: Price impact

SLICE_ID start time	9.00 am z-statistics	10.00 am z-statistics	11.00 am z-statistics	12.00 am z-statistics	1.00 pm z-statistics	2.00 pm z-statistics	3.00 pm z-statistics	4.00 pm z-statistics
9.00 am								
10.00 am	-3.90 ***							
11.00 am	-4.60 ***	-4.68 ***						
12.00 am	-4.47 ***	-4.49 ***	-0.50 ns					
1.00 pm	-4.19 ***	-3.65 ***	-0.11 ns	-0.65 ns				
2.00 pm	-4.12 ***	-3.30 ***	-1.94 ns	-1.29 ns	-1.02 ns			
3.00 pm	-3.86 ***	-2.95 **	-2.21 *	-1.76 ns	-1.92 ns	-0.42 ns		
4.00 pm	-4.15 ***	-2.40 *	-3.10 **	-2.89 **	-2.66 **	-2.11 *	-1.80 ns	
5.00 pm	-4.43 ***	-4.29 ***	-1.31 ns	-1.66 ns	-1.35 ns	-2.77 **	-2.97 **	-4.19 ***

*** = 0.001, ** = 0.01, * = 0.05, ns = not significant

Appendix 6: K-mean cluster results for selected trader IDs

Average price impact per trader ID measured in bp									
Cluster	**Number of cases**	**Cluster center**	**Min**	**Max**	**Cluster**	**Number of cases**	**Cluster center**	**Min**	**Max**
Panel A: three clusters					**Panel B: four clusters**				
1	129	13.2	9.9	38.2	1	63	15.8	12.3	38.2
2	605	6.4	4.2	9.8	2	311	8.6	6.7	12.1
3	521	1.9	-13.8	4.1	3	531	4.8	2.9	6.7
					4	350	1.0	-13.8	2.9
Panel C: five clusters					**Panel D: six clusters**				
1	2	32.9	27.6	38.2	1	2	32.9	27.6	38.2
2	78	14.5	11.4	22.9	2	72	14.7	11.6	22.9
3	323	8.2	6.4	11.3	3	305	8.4	6.7	11.5
4	537	4.6	2.7	6.4	4	491	4.9	3.3	6.6
5	315	0.9	-13.8	2.7	5	355	1.6	-1.0	3.2
					6	30	-3.7	-13.8	-1.1

Appendix 7: Comparison of initial and reduced aggressor data set

Panel A: Initial aggressor dataset

SIZE_ID	Aggressor trading volume	Aggressor orders	Volume % share	Orders % share
1	20,174,960,624	1,924,389	8.9%	47.3%
2	29,881,270,101	821,940	13.2%	20.2%
3	51,050,347,313	724,524	22.5%	17.8%
4	71,095,748,092	473,755	31.3%	11.6%
5	32,989,471,116	98,292	14.5%	2.4%
6	22,005,249,334	27,623	9.7%	0.7%
Total	**227,197,046,579**	**4,070,523**	**100%**	**100%**

Panel B: Reduced aggressor dataset (after price impact calculation)

SIZE_ID	Aggressor trading volume	Aggressor orders	Volume % share	Orders % share
1	18,843,509,778	1,805,881	8.7%	46.9%
2	28,311,127,864	778,265	13.0%	20.2%
3	48,623,836,051	689,617	22.4%	17.9%
4	68,316,269,943	455,054	31.5%	11.8%
5	31,771,578,898	94,650	14.6%	2.5%
6	21,169,606,315	26,562	9.8%	0.7%
Total	**217,035,928,849**	**3,850,029**	**100%**	**100%**

Panel C: Difference between panel A and B

SIZE_ID	Aggressor trading volume	Aggressor orders	Volume % difference	Orders % difference
1	1,331,450,846	118,508	6.60%	6.16%
2	1,570,142,236	43,675	5.25%	5.31%
3	2,426,511,261	34,907	4.75%	4.82%
4	2,779,478,149	18,701	3.91%	3.95%
5	1,217,892,218	3,642	3.69%	3.71%
6	835,643,019	1,061	3.80%	3.84%
Total	**10,161,117,730**	**220,494**	**4.5%**	**5.4%**

Appendix 8: Comparison of initial and reduced originator data set

Panel A: Initial originator dataset

SIZE_ID	Originator trading volume	Originator orders	Volume % share	Orders % share
1	23,458,179,487	2,055,351	10.33%	51.04%
2	27,797,072,558	774,135	12.23%	19.22%
3	46,764,617,576	666,154	20.58%	16.54%
4	58,998,734,491	393,465	25.97%	9.77%
5	32,804,942,082	96,212	14.44%	2.39%
6	37,373,500,385	41,956	16.45%	1.04%
Total	**227,197,046,579**	**4,027,273**	**100.00%**	**100.00%**

Panel B: Reduced originator dataset (after price impact calculation)

SIZE_ID	Originator trading volume	Originator orders	Volume % share	Orders % share
1	23,111,719,733	2,007,917	10.33%	50.74%
2	27,513,727,265	766,326	12.30%	19.37%
3	46,288,624,468	659,474	20.70%	16.67%
4	58,188,952,309	388,158	26.02%	9.81%
5	32,192,021,685	94,456	14.40%	2.39%
6	36,331,139,179	40,842	16.25%	1.03%
Total	**223,626,184,640**	**3,957,173**	**100.00%**	**100.00%**

Panel C: Difference between panel A and B

SIZE_ID	Originator trading volume	Originator orders	Volume % difference	Orders % difference
1	346,459,753	47,434	1.48%	2.31%
2	283,345,293	7,809	1.02%	1.01%
3	475,993,107	6,680	1.02%	1.00%
4	809,782,183	5,307	1.37%	1.35%
5	612,920,397	1,756	1.87%	1.83%
6	1,042,361,206	1,114	2.79%	2.66%
Total	**3,570,861,939**	**70,100**	**1.57%**	**1.74%**

Appendix 9: Distribution of aggressor and originator trading volume per trader category for reduced data set[349]

Trader category	Aggressor trading volume	Originator trading volume	Aggressor volume % share	z-statistic
Uninformed	28,405,460,440	40,781,252,546	41.1%	-9.08 < ***
Informed	**46,901,017,954**	**41,144,517,670**	**53.3%**	**-3.09 <** **
Partially informed	137,881,101,617	136,860,459,844	50.2%	-5.46 > ***
Total or average	**217,035,928,849**	**223,626,184,640**	**49.3%**	

*** = significant at the 0.001 level, ** = 0.01 level

[349] The trader IDs, which were classified as not relevant in Chapter 8.1.1 account for 1.8% (2.2%) of aggressor (originator) trading volume, and are included in the total figures.

Appendix 10: Intraday distribution of aggressor trading volume per trader category for reduced data set[350]

Trader category	Trading session	Adjusted aggressor trading volume	Trading session % share	z-statistics	Avg. order size	z-statistics
Uninformed	morning	13,031,139,595	48.8%	-1.83	29,514	-0.52
	afternoon	13,666,062,973	51.2%	ns	33,858	ns
Informed	**morning**	**22,303,426,719**	**50.5%**	**-1.13**	**90,670**	**-2.40**
	afternoon	**21,864,525,542**	**49.5%**	**ns**	**88,896**	* (>)
Partially informed	morning	60,146,258,440	46.5%	-0.33	59,437	-0.70
	afternoon	69,097,638,379	53.5%	ns	57,852	ns
Total or average	**morning**	**97,454,153,975**	**47.8%**		**56,057**	
	afternoon	**106,294,911,000**	**52.2%**		**56,632**	

* significant at the 0.05 level, ns = not significant

[350] Totals include the volume of trader IDs, which were classified as not relevant in Chapter 8.1.1.

Appendix 11: Intraday distribution of originator trading volume per trader category for reduced data set[351]

Trader category	Trading session	Adjusted originator trading volume	Trading session % share	z-statistics	Avg. order size	z-statistics
Uninformed	morning	17,310,960,696	45.3%	-0.75	45,881	-0.16
	afternoon	20,862,481,644	54.7%	ns	43,266	ns
Informed	**morning**	**19,665,356,332**	**50.1%**	**-1.39**	**153,398**	**-2.95**
	afternoon	**19,596,025,125**	**49.9%**	**ns**	**147,506**	** (<)
Partially informed	morning	60,431,242,883	46.7%	-1.83	52,996	-3.07
	afternoon	68,897,328,343	53.3%	ns	50,298	** (<)
Total or average	**morning**	**98,147,903,389**	**46.8%**		**58,234**	
	afternoon	**111,536,250,000**	**53.2%**		**55,234**	

** significant at the 0.01 level, * = 0.05 level, ns = not significant

[351] Totals include the volume of trader IDs, which were classified as not relevant in Chapter 8.1.1.

Bibliography

Admati, Anat/ Pfleiderer, Paul (1988): A Theory of Intraday Patterns: Volume and Price Variability, in: Review of Financial Studies, Vol. 1, pp. 3 – 40.

Admati, Anat/ Pfleiderer, Paul (1991): Sunshine Trading and Financial Market Equilibrium, in: Review of Financial Studies, Vol. 4, pp. 443 – 481.

Ahn, Hee-Joon/ Bae, Kee-Hong/ Chan, Kalok (2001): Limit Orders, Depth, and Volatility: Evidence from the Stock Exchange of Hong Kong, in: Journal of Finance, Vol. 56, pp. 767 – 788.

Aitken, Michael/ Comerton-Forde, Carole (2003): How Should Liquidity be Measured?, in: Pacific-Basin Finance Journal, Vol. 11, pp. 45 – 59.

Amihud, Yakov (2002): Illiquidity and Stock Returns: Cross-Section and Time-Series Effects, in: Journal of Financial Markets, Vol. 5, pp. 31 – 56.

Amihud, Yakov/ Mendelson, Haim (1980): Dealership Market: Market-Making with Inventory, in: Journal of Financial Economics, Vol. 8, pp. 31 – 53.

Amihud, Yakov/ Mendelson, Haim (1986): Asset Pricing and the Bid-Ask Spread, in: Journal of Financial Economics, Vol. 17, pp. 223 – 249.

Amihud, Yakov/ Mendelson, Haim/ Lauterbach, Beni (1997): Market Microstructure and Securities Values: Evidence from the Tel Aviv Stock Exchange, in: Journal of Financial Economics, Vol. 45, pp. 365 – 390.

Anand, Amber/ Chakravarty, Sugato/ Martell, Terrence (2005): Empirical Evidence on the Evolution of Liquidity: Choice of Market versus Limit Orders by Informed and Uninformed Traders, in: Journal of Financial Markets, Vol. 8, pp. 288 – 308.

Bae, Kee-Hong/ Jang, Hasung/ Park, Kyung Suh (2003): Traders' Choice between Limit and Market Orders: Evidence from NYSE Stocks, in: Journal of Financial Markets, Vol. 6, pp. 517 – 538.

Bagheot, Walter (1971): The only Game in Town, in: Financial Analysts Journal, Vol. 7, No. 2, pp. 12 – 14.

Barclay, Michael J./ Hendershott, Terrence/ McCormick, Timothy D. (2003): Competition among Trading Venues: Information and Trading on Electronic Communication Networks, in: Journal of Finance, Vol. 58, pp. 2637 – 2666.

Barclay, Michael J./ Warner, Jerold B. (1993): Stealth Trading and Volatility: Which Trades Move Prices?, in: Journal of Financial Economics, Vol. 34, pp. 281 – 305.

Behr, Matina L. (2000): Insiderhandel und Optionspreisspannen, Wiesbaden.

Beltran, Helena/ Durré, Alain/ Giot, Pierre (2004): How Does Liquidity React to Stress Periods in a Limit Order Market, Working Papers Research Series, No. 49, available at National Bank of Belgium: http://www.nbb.be/doc/oc/repec/reswpp/ WP49.pdf.

Beltran, Helena/ Giot, Pierre/ Grammig, Joachim (2005): Commonalities in the Order Book, January 2005, Working Paper, available at SSRN: http://ssrn.com/ abstract=884363.

Benston, George J./ Hagerman, Robert L. (1974): Determinants of Bid-Ask Spreads in the Over-the-Counter Market, in: Journal of Financial Economics, Vol. 1, pp. 353 – 364.

Bernhardt, Dan/ Miao, Jianjun (2004): Informed Trading when Information Becomes Stale, in: Journal of Finance, Vol. 59, pp. 339 – 390.

Bernstein, Peter L. (1987): Liquidity, Stock Markets and Market Makers, in: Financial Management, Vol. 16, Issue 2, pp. 54 – 62.

Bessembinder, Hendrik (1999): Trade Execution Costs on NASDAQ and the NYSE: A Post-Reform Comparison, in: Journal of Financial and Quantitative Analysis, Vol. 34, pp. 387 – 407.

Bessembinder, Hendrik (2003a): Quote-Based Competition and Trade Execution Costs in NYSE-Listed Stocks, in: Journal of Financial Economics, Vol. 70, pp. 385 – 422.

Bessembinder, Hendrik (2003b): Issues in Assessing Trade Execution Costs, in: Journal of Financial Markets, Vol. 6, pp. 233 – 257.

Bessembinder, Hendrik/ Kaufman, Herbert M. (1997): A Comparison of Trade Execution Costs for NYSE and NASDAQ-listed stocks, in: Journal of Financial and Quantitative Analysis, Vol. 32, pp. 287 – 310.

Biais, Bruno/ Glosten, Larry/ Spatt, Chester (2005): Market Microstructure: A Survey of Microfoundations, Empirical Results, and Policy Implications, in: Journal of Financial Markets, Vol. 8, pp. 217 – 264.

Biais, Bruno/ Hillion, Pierre/ Spatt, Chester (1995): An Empirical Analysis of the Limit Order Book and the Order Flow in the Paris Bourse, in: Journal of Finance, Vol. 50, pp. 1655 – 1689.

Bikker, Jacob A./ Spierdijk, Laura/ van der Sluis, Pieter Jelle (2004): The Implementation Shortfall of Institutional Equity Trades, March 2004, Working Paper, available at SSRN: http://ssrn.com/abstract=567087.

Black, Fischer (1986): Noise, in: Journal of Finance, Vol. 41, pp. 529 – 543.

Bloomfield, Robert J./ O'Hara, Maureen/ Saar, Gideon (2005): The "Make or Take" Decision in an Electronic Market: Evidence on the Evolution of Liquidity, in: Journal of Financial Economics, Vol. 75, pp. 165 – 199.

Boehmer, Ekkehart (2005): Dimensions of Execution Quality: Recent Evidence for U.S. Equity Markets, in: Journal of Financial Economics, Vol. 78, pp. 553 – 582.

Boehmer, Ekkehart/ Grammig, Joachim/ Theissen, Erik (2007): Estimating the Probability of Informed Trading - Does Trade Misclassification Matter?, in: Journal of Financial Markets, Vol. 10, pp. 26-47.

Book, Thomas (2001): Elektronischer Börsenhandel und globale Märkte: Eine ökonomische Analyse der Veränderungen an Terminbörsen, Wiesbaden.

Booth, Geoffrey/ Iversen, Peter/ Sarkar, Sali/ Schmidt, Hartmut/ Young, Allen (1995): Market Structure and Bid-Ask Spreads: IBIS vs. NASDAQ, in: European Journal of Finance, Vol. 5, pp. 51 – 71.

Brockman, Paul/ Chung, Dennis Y. (1998): Inter- and Intraday Liquidity Patterns on the Stock Exchange of Hong Kong, in: Journal of International Financial Markets, Institutions and Money, Vol. 8, pp. 279 – 300.

Brockman, Paul/ Chung, Dennis Y. (1999): Bid-Ask Spread Components in an Order-Driven Environment, in: Journal of Financial Research, Vol. 22, pp. 227 – 246.

Brockman, Paul/ Chung, Dennis Y. (2000): Informed and Uninformed Trading in an Electronic Order-Driven Environment, in: Financial Review, Vol. 35, pp. 125 – 146.

Brockman, Paul/ Chung, Dennis Y. (2002): Commonality in Liquidity: Evidence from an Order-Driven Market, in: Journal of Financial Research, Vol. 25, pp. 521 – 539.

Brown, Stephen/ Hillegeist, Stephen A. (2006): How Disclosure Quality Affects the Long-Run Level of Information Asymmetry, January 2006, Working Paper, available at SSRN: http://ssrn.com/abstract=297371, Review of Accounting Studies, forthcoming.

Brunner, Antje (1996): Meßkonzepte zur Liquidität auf Wertpapiermärkten, Beiträge zur Theorie der Finanzmärkte, Institut für Kapitalmarktforschung, Nr. 13, Frankfurt/ Main.

Campbell, John Y./ Lo, Andrew W./ MacKinlay, A. Craig (1997): The Econometrics of Financial Markets, Princeton.

Cao, Charles/ Hansch, Oliver/ Wang, Xiaoxin (2004): The Informational Content of an Open Limit Order Book, March 2004, Working Paper, available at SSRN: http://ssrn.com/abstract= 565324.

CESR (2005): CESR's Technical Advice on Possible Implementing Measures of the Directive 2004/ 39/ EC on Markets in Financial Instruments, CESR/ 05-290b, available at CESR: http://www.cesr-eu.org/index.php?docid=3263.

Chakravarty, Sugato (2001): Stealth-Trading: Which Traders' Trades Move Stock Prices?, in: Journal of Financial Economics, Vol. 61, pp. 289 – 307.

Chakravarty, Sugato/ Holden, Craig W. (1995): An Integrated Model of Market and Limit Orders, in: Journal of Financial Intermediation, Vol. 4, pp. 213 – 241.

Chan, Yue-cheong (2005): Price Movement Effects on the State of the Electronic Limit Order Book, in: Financial Review, Vol. 40, pp. 195 – 221.

Chordia, Tarun/ Roll, Richard/ Subrahmanyam, Avandidhar (2000): Commonality in Liquidity, in: Journal of Financial Economics, Vol. 56, pp. 3 – 28.

Chordia, Tarun/ Roll, Richard/ Subrahmanyam, Avandidhar (2001): Market Liquidity and Trading Activity, in: Journal of Finance, Vol. 56, pp. 501 – 530.

Chordia, Tarun/ Roll, Richard/ Subrahmanyam, Avandidhar (2002): Order Imbalance, Liquidity, and Market Returns, in: Journal of Financial Economics, Vol. 65, pp. 111 – 130.

Chordia, Tarun/ Sarkar, Asani/ Subrahmanyam, Avandidhar (2005a): An Empirical Analysis of Stock and Bond Market Liquidity, in: Review of Financial Studies, Vol. 18, pp. 85 – 129.

Chordia, Tarun/ Sarkar, Asani/ Subrahmanyam, Avandidhar (2005b): The Joint Dynamics of Liquidity, Returns, and Volatility across Small and Large Firms, Staff Report No. 207, available at Federal Reserve Bank New York: http://www.ny.frb.org/research/staff_reports/sr207.html.

Chung, Kee H./ Charoenwong, Charlie (1998): Insider Trading and the Bid-Ask Spread, in: Financial Review, Vol. 33, pp. 1 – 20.

Chung, Kee H./ Li, Mingsheng (2003): Adverse-Selection Costs and the Probability of Information-Based Trading, in: Financial Review, Vol. 38, pp. 257 – 272.

Chung, Kee H./ Li, Mingsheng/ McInish, Thomas H. (2005): Probability of Information Based Trades, Price Impact, and Trade Autocorrelation, in: Journal of Banking and Finance, Vol. 29, pp. 1645 – 1669.

Chung, Kee H./ Van Ness, Bonnie F./ Van Ness, Robert A. (1999): Limit Orders and the Bid-Ask Spread, in: Journal of Financial Economics, Vol. 53, pp. 255 – 287.

Chung, Kee H./ Van Ness, Bonnie F./ Van Ness, Robert A. (2004): Specialists, Limit-Order Traders, and the Components of the Bid-Ask Spread, in: Financial Review, Vol. 39, pp. 255 – 270.

Chung, Kee H./ Van Ness, Robert A. (2001): Order Handling Rules, Tick Size, and the Intraday Patterns of Bid-Ask Spreads for NASDAQ Stocks, in: Journal of Financial Markets, Vol. 4, pp. 143 – 161.

Clarke, Jonathan/ Shastri, Kuldeep (2000): On Information Asymmetry Metrics, November 2000, Working Paper, available at SSRN: http://ssrn.com/abstract =251938.

Clayton, Matthew J./ Jorgensen, Bjorn N./ Kavajecz, Kenneth A. (2006): On the Presence and Market-Structure of Exchanges around the World, in: Journal of Financial Markets, Vol. 9, pp. 27 – 48.

Cohen, Kalman J./ Maier, Steven F./ Schwartz, Robert A./ Whitcomb, David K. (1981): Transaction Costs, Order Placement Strategy, and Existence of the Bid-Ask Spread, in: Journal of Political Economy, Vol. 89, pp. 287 – 305.

Cohen, Kalman J./ Maier, Steven F./ Schwartz, Robert A./ Whitcomb, David K. (1986): The Microstructure of Securities Markets, New Jersey.

Comerton-Forde, Carole/ Frino, Alex/ Mollica, Vito (2005): The Impact of Limit Order Anonymity on Liquidity: Evidence from Paris, Tokyo and Korea, March 2005, in: Journal of Economics and Business, Vol. 57, pp. 528 – 540.

Cooper, S. Kerry/ Groth, John C./ Avera, William E. (1985): Liquidity, Exchange Listing, and Common Stock Performance, in: Journal of Economics and Business, Vol. 37, pp. 19 – 33.

Copeland, Thomas E./ Galai, Dan (1983): Information Effects and the Bid-Ask Spread, in: Journal of Finance, Vol. 38, pp. 1457 – 1469.

Coppejans, Mark/ Domowitz, Ian/ Madhavan, Ananth (2004): Resilience in an Automated Auction, December 2004, Working Paper, available at ITG Inc.: http://www.itg.com/ news_events/papers/automated_auction.pdf.

Coughenour, Jay F./ Shastri, Kuldeep (1999): Symposium on Market Microstructure: A Review of Empirical Research, in: Financial Review, Vol. 34, pp. 1 – 28.

Daníelsson, Jon/ Payne, Richard (2001): Measuring and Explaining Liquidity on an Electronic Limit Order Book: Evidence from Reuters D2000-2, January 2001, Working Paper, available at SSRN: http://ssrn.com/ abstract=276541.

Degryse, Hans/ de Jong, Frank/ Ravenswaaij, Maarten/ Wuyts, Gunther (2005): Aggressive Orders and the Resilience of a Limit Order Market, in: Review of Finance, Vol. 9, pp. 201 – 242.

Demsetz, Harold (1968): The Cost of Transacting, in: Quarterly Journal of Economics, Vol. 82, pp. 33 – 53.

Dennis, Patrick J./ Weston, James P. (2001): Who's Informed? An Analysis of Stock Ownership and Informed Trading, June 2001, Working Paper, available at SSRN: http://ssrn.com/abstract=267350.

Deutsches Aktieninstitut (2005): DAI-Factbook, October 2005, available at DAI: http://www.dai.de/ internet/dai/dai-2-0.nsf/dai_statistiken.htm.

Deutsche Boerse AG (2002): Calculating the Exchange Liquidity Measure (XLM), Unpublished Document, pp. 1 – 3.

Deutsche Boerse AG (2003): Europe's Premier Listing Platform: Standards, Transparency, Liquidity, available at http://deutsche-boerse.com/dbag/dispatch/en/binary/gdb_content_pool/imported_files/public_files/10_downloads/33_going_being_public/40_stock_market_segmentation/sm_rcm_broschuere.pdf.

Deutsche Boerse AG (2004a): Functional Description, Xetra Release 7.1, available only to Xetra and Floor members at http://deutsche-boerse.com/dbag/dispatch/de/kir/gdb_navigation/trading_members/80_Members_only.

Deutsche Boerse AG (2004b): Market Model Equities, Xetra Release 7.1, available at http://deutsche-boerse.com/dbag/dispatch/en/binary/gdb_content_pool/imported_files/public_files/10_downloads/31_trading_member/10_Products_and_Functionalities/20_Stocks/50_Xetra_Market_Model/Marktmodell_Aktien_R7.pdf.

Deutsche Boerse AG (2006a): Fact Book 2005, Version January 2006, available at http://www3.deutsche-boerse.com/INTERNET/IP/ip_stats.nsf/(KIR+Factbook+Kassamarkt)/2D61B831AD36E547C12571770059CAA9/$FILE/Factbook_2005_d.pdf?OpenElement.

Deutsche Boerse AG (2006b): Guide to the Equity Indices of Deutsche Boerse, Version 6.0, available at http://deutsche-boerse.com/dbag/dispatch/en/binary/gdb_content_pool/imported_files/public_files/10_downloads/50_informations_services/30_Indices_Index_Licensing/21_guidelines/10_share_indices/equity_indices_guide.pdf.

Deutsche Boerse AG (2006c): Cash Market Monthly Statistics for December 2005, available at http://www3.deutsche-boerse.com/INTERNET/IP/ip_stats.nsf/(KIR+Monatsstatistik+Kassamarkt)/B5F0980A4960EFA0C12570EC005009FF/$FILE/fwb_monthly.pdf?OpenElement.

Deutsche Boerse AG (2006d): Entry Standard: Tailor-Made Capital Market Access for Small and Mid-Caps, April 2006, available at http://deutsche-boerse.com/dbag/dispatch/en/binary/gdb_content_pool/imported_files/public_files/10_downloads/33_going_being_public/50_others/entry_standard_broschuere_06.9.pdf.

De Winne, Rudy/ Majois, Christophe (2004): A Comparison of Alternative Spread Decomposition Models on Euronext Brussels, June 2004, Working Paper, available at SSRN: http://ssrn.com/abstract=421240.

Domowitz, Ian (1992): Automating the Price Discovery Process: Some International Comparisons and Regulatory Implications, in: Journal of Financial Services Research, Vol. 6, pp. 305 – 326.

Domowitz, Ian (1993): A Taxonomy of Automated Trading Systems, in: Journal of International Money and Finance, Vol. 12, pp. 607 – 631.

Domowitz, Ian (2001): Liquidity, Transaction Costs, and Reintermediation in Electronic Markets, in: Journal of Financial Services Research, Vol. 22, pp. 141 – 157.

Domowitz, Ian/ Glen, Jack/ Madhavan, Ananth (2001): Liquidity, Volatility, and Equity Trading Costs across Countries and over Time, in: International Finance, Vol. 4, pp. 221 – 255.

Domowitz, Ian/ Hansch, Oliver/ Wang, Xiaoxin (2002): Liquidity Commonality and Return Co-Movement, in: Journal of Financial Markets, Vol. 8, pp. 351 – 376.

Easley, David/ Engle, Robert F./ O'Hara, Maureen/ Wu, Liuren (2001): Time-Varying Arrival Rates of Informed and Uninformed Trades, December 2001, Working Paper, available at SSRN: http://ssrn.com/abstract=294870.

Easley, David/ Hvidkjaer, Soeren/ O'Hara, Maureen (2002): Is Information Risk a Determinant of Asset Returns?, in: Journal of Finance, Vol. 57, pp. 2185 – 2221.

Easley, David/ Hvidkjaer, Soeren/ O'Hara, Maureen (2004): Factoring Information Into Returns, August 2004, Working Paper, available at SSRN: http://ssrn.com/ abstract=556079.

Easley, David/ Kiefer, Nicholas M./ O'Hara Maureen (1996): Cream-Skimming or Profit-Sharing? The Curious Role of Purchased Order Flow, in: Journal of Finance, Vol. 51, p. 811 – 833.

Easley, David/ Kiefer, Nicholas M./ O'Hara Maureen (1997a): One Day in the Life of a Very Common Stock, in: Review of Financial Studies, Vol. 10, pp. 805 – 835.

Easley, David/ Kiefer, Nicholas M./ O'Hara Maureen (1997b): The Information Content of the Trading Process, in: Journal of Empirical Finance, Vol. 4, pp. 159 – 186.

Easley, David/ Kiefer, Nicholas M./ O'Hara, Maureen/ Paperman, Joseph B. (1996): Liquidity, Information and Infrequently Traded Stocks, in: Journal of Finance, Vol. 51, pp. 1405 – 1436.

Easley, David/ O'Hara Maureen (1987): Price, Trade Size and Information in Securities Markets, in: Journal of Financial Economics, Vol. 19, pp. 69 – 90.

Easley, David/ O'Hara, Maureen/ Paperman, Joseph (1998): Financial Analysts and Information Based Trading, in: Journal of Financial Markets, Vol. 1, pp. 175 – 201.

Engle, Robert F./ Lange, Joe (1997): Measuring, Forecasting and Explaining Time Varying Liquidity in the Stock Market, November 1997, Working Paper, available at SSRN: http://ssrn.com/abstract=58278.

Fama, Eugene F. (1970): Efficient Capital Markets: A Review of Theory and Empirical Work, in: Journal of Finance, Vol. 25, pp. 383 – 417.

Fernandez, Frank A. (1999): Liquidity Risk: New Approaches to Measurement and Monitoring, Securities Industry Association (SIA) Working Paper, available at http://www.sia.com/research/html/liquidity_risk.html.

Foster, F. Douglas/ Viswanathan, S. (1994): Strategic Trading with Asymmetrically Informed Traders and Long-Lived Information, in: Journal of Financial and Quantitative Analysis, Vol. 29, pp. 499 – 518.

Foucault, Thierry (1999): Order Flow Composition and Trading Costs in a Dynamic Limit Order Market, in: Journal of Financial Markets, Vol. 2, pp. 99 – 134.

Foucault, Thierry/ Kadan, Ohad/ Kandel, Eugene (2005): Limit Order Book as a Market for Liquidity, in: Review of Financial Studies, Vol. 18, pp. 1171 – 1217.

Foucault, Thierry/ Moinas, Sophie/ Theissen, Erik (2004): Does Anonymity Matter in Electronic Limit Order Markets?, May 2004, Working Paper, available at SSRN: http://ssrn.com/abstract=424962, Review of Financial Studies, forthcoming.

Freihube, Thorsten/ Theissen, Erik (2001): An Index is an Index is an Index?, in: Schmalenbach Business Review, Vol. 53, pp. 295 – 320.

Frey, Stefan/ Grammig, Joachim (2006): Liquidity Supply and Adverse Selection in a Pure Limit Order Book Market, in: Empirical Economics, Vol. 30, pp. 1007 - 1033.

Garbade, Kenneth D. (1982): Securities Markets, New York.

George, Thomas J./ Kaul, Gautam/ Nimalendran, M. (1991): Estimation of the Bid-Ask Spread and Its Components: A New Approach, in: Review of Financial Studies, Vol. 4, pp. 623 – 656.

Giot, Pierre/ Grammig, Joachim (2006): How Large is Liquidity Risk in an Automated Auction Market?, in: Empirical Economics, Vol. 30, pp. 867 – 887.

Glosten, Lawrence R. (1994): Is the Electronic Open Limit Order Book Inevitable, in: Journal of Finance, Vol. 49, pp. 1127 – 1161.

Glosten, Lawrence R./ Harris, Lawrence E. (1988): Estimating the Components of the Bid/Ask Spread, in: Journal of Financial Economics, Vol. 21, pp. 123 – 142.

Glosten, Lawrence R./ Milgrom, Paul R. (1985): Bid, Ask and Transactions Prices in a Specialist Market with Heterogeneously Informed Traders, in: Journal of Financial Economics, Vol. 14, pp. 71 – 100.

Goldstein, Michael A./ Kavajecz, Kenneth A. (2000): Eighths, Sixteenths, and Market Depth: Changes in Tick Size and Liquidity Provision on the NYSE, in: Journal of Financial Economics, Vol. 56, pp. 125 – 149.

Goldstein, Michael A./ Van Ness, Bonnie F./ Van Ness, Robert A. (2006): The Intraday Probability of Informed Trading on the NYSE, in: Advances in Quantitative Analysis of Finance and Accounting, Vol. 3, chapter 7, pp. 139 – 158.

Gomber, Peter/ Schweickert, Uwe (2002a): Der Market Impact: Liquiditätsmaß im elektronischen Wertpapierhandel, in: Die Bank, Vol. 7, pp. 485 – 489.

Gomber, Peter/ Schweickert, Uwe (2002b): Market Quality in Electronic Order Book Trading: Most Active versus Most Liquid Xetra Instruments, Unpublished Working Paper, Deutsche Boerse AG, Xetra Research.

Gomber, Peter/ Schweickert, Uwe/ Theissen, Erik (2005): Zooming in on Liquidity, February 2005, Working Paper, available at SSRN: http://ssrn.com/abstract= 559406.

Grammig, Joachim/ Heinen, Andréas/ Rengifo, Erick (2004): Trading Activity and Liquidity Supply in a Pure Limit Order Book Market. An Empirical Analysis Using a Multivariate Count Data Model, August 2004, Working Paper, available at SSRN: http://ssrn.com/abstract=676567.

Grammig, Joachim/ Schiereck, Dirk/ Theissen, Erik (2000): Informationsbasierter Aktienhandel über IBIS, in: zfbf, Vol. 52, pp. 619 – 642.

Grammig, Joachim/ Schiereck, Dirk/ Theissen, Erik (2001): Knowing Me, Knowing You: Trader Anonymity and Informed Trading in Parallel Markets, in: Journal of Financial Markets, Vol. 4, pp. 385 – 412.

Griese, Knut/ Kempf, Alexander (2006): Liquiditätsdynamik am deutschen Aktienmarkt, in: Die Betriebswirtschaft, Vol. 66, pp. 402 – 417.

Grossman, Sanford J./ Miller, Merton H. (1988): Liquidity and Market Structure, in: Journal of Finance, Vol. 43, pp. 617 – 633.

Hachmeister, Alexandra/ Schiereck, Dirk (2006): The Impact of Post-Trade Anonymity on Liquidity and Informed Trading: Evidence from the Introduction of the Xetra Central Counterparty (CCP), May 2006, Unpublished Working Paper, European Business School.

Handa, Puneet/ Schwartz, Robert A. (1996a): How Best to Supply Liquidity to a Securities Market, in: Journal of Portfolio Management, Vol. 22, Issue 2, pp. 44 – 51.

Handa, Puneet / Schwartz, Robert A. (1996b): Limit Order Trading, in: Journal of Finance, Vol. 51, pp. 1835 – 1861.

Handa, Puneet/ Schwartz, Robert A./ Tiwari, Ashish (1998): The Ecology of an Order-Driven Market, in: Journal of Portfolio Management, Vol. 24, Issue 2, pp. 47 – 55.

Handa, Puneet/ Schwartz, Robert A./ Tiwari, Ashish (2003): Quote Setting and Price Formation in an Order-Driven Market, in: Journal of Financial Markets, Vol. 6, pp. 461 – 489.

Handa, Puneet/ Schwartz, Robert A./ Tiwari, Ashish (2004): The Economic Value of a Trading Floor: Evidence from the American Stock Exchange, in: Journal of Business, Vol. 77, pp. 331 – 355.

Hanousek, Jan/ Podpiera, Richard (2002): Information-Driven Trading at the Prague Stock Exchange: Evidence from Intra-Day Data, in: Economics of Transition, Vol. 10, pp. 743 – 755.

Harris, Lawrence E. (1990): Liquidity, Trading Rules, and Electronic Trading Systems, New York University Salomon Centre, Monograph series in Finance and Economics, Monograph 1990-4.

Harris, Lawrence E. (1998): Optimal Dynamic Order Submission Strategies in Some Stylized Trading Problems, in: Financial Markets, Institutions & Instruments, Vol. 7, No. 2, pp. 1 – 76.

Harris, Lawrence E. (2003): Trading and Exchanges: Market Microstructure for Practitioners, New York.

Harris, Lawrence E./ Panchapagesan, Venkatesh (2005): The Information Content of the Limit Order Book: Evidence from NYSE Specialist Trading Decisions, in: Journal of Financial Markets, Vol. 8, pp. 25 – 67.

Hasbrouck, Joel (1988): Trades, Quotes, Inventories, and Information, in: Journal of Financial Economics, Vol. 22, pp. 229 – 252.

Hasbrouck, Joel (1990): Security Markets, Information, and Liquidity, in: Finanzmarkt und Portfolio Management, Vol. 4, pp. 230 – 242.

Hasbrouck, Joel (1991a): Measuring the Information Content of Stock Trades, in: Journal of Finance, Vol. 46, pp. 179 – 207.

Hasbrouck, Joel (1991b): The Summary Informativeness of Stock Trades: An Econometric Analysis, in: Review of Financial Studies, Vol. 4, pp. 571 – 595.

Hasbrouck, Joel (1993): Assessing the Quality of a Security Market: A new Approach to Transaction-Cost Measurement, in: Review of Financial Studies, Vol. 6, pp. 191 – 212.

Hasbrouck, Joel (1995): One Security, Many Markets: Determining the Contributions to Price Discovery, in: Journal of Finance, Vol. 50, pp. 1175 – 1199.

Hasbrouck, Joel/ Saar, Gideon (2002): Limit Orders and Volatility in a Hybrid Market: The Island ECN, July 2002, Working Paper, available at SSRN: http://ssrn.com/abstract=310940.

Hasbrouck, Joel/ Saar, Gideon (2004): Technology and Liquidity Provision: The Blurring of Traditional Definitions, November 2004, Working Paper, available at Rice University: http://www.ruf.rice.edu/~jgsfss/HS4.pdf.

Hasbrouck, Joel/ Schwartz, Robert A. (1988): Liquidity and Execution Costs in Equity Markets, in: Journal of Portfolio Management, Vol. 14, Issue 3, pp. 10 – 16.

Hasbrouck, Joel/ Seppi, Duane J. (2001): Common Factors in Prices, Order Flows and Liquidity, in: Journal of Financial Economics, Vol. 59, pp. 383 – 411.

Hautsch, Nikolaus/ Pohlmeier, Winfried (2002): Econometric Analysis of Financial Transaction Data: Pitfalls and Opportunities, in: Allgemeines Statistisches Archiv/ Journal of the German Statistical Society, Vol. 86, p. 5 – 30.

Heidle, Hans G./ Huang, Roger D. (2002): Information-Based Trading in Dealer and Auction Markets: An Analysis of Exchange Listings, in: Journal of Financial and Quantitative Analysis, Vol. 37, pp. 391 – 424.

Holden, Craig W./ Subrahmanyam, Avandidhar (1992): Long-Lived Private Information and Imperfect Competition, in: Journal of Finance, Vol. 57, pp. 247 – 270.

Hollifield, Burton/ Miller, Robert A./ Sandas, Patrik (2004): Empirical Analysis of Limit Order Markets, in: Review of Economic Studies, Vol. 71, pp. 1027 – 1063.

Huang, Roger D./ Stoll, Hans R. (1996a): Dealer versus Auction Markets: A Paired Comparison of Execution Costs on NASDAQ and the NYSE, in: Journal of Financial Economics, Vol. 41, pp. 313 – 357.

Huang, Roger D./ Stoll, Hans R. (1996b): Competitive Trading of NYSE Listed Stocks: Measurement and Interpretation of Trading Costs, in: Financial Markets, Institutions and Instruments, Vol. 5, No. 2, pp. 1 – 55.

Huang, Roger D./ Stoll, Hans R. (1997): The Components of the Bid-Ask Spread: A General Approach, in: Review of Financial Studies, Vol. 10, pp. 995 – 1034.

Huberman, Gur/ Halka, Dominika (2001): Systematic Liquidity, in: Journal of Financial Research, Vol. 24, pp. 161 – 178.

Irvine, Paul/ Benston, George/ Kandel, Eugene (2000): Liquidity Beyond the Inside Spread: Measuring and Using Information in the Limit Order Book, May 2000, Working Paper, available at SSRN: http://ssrn.com/abstract=229959.

Iversen, Peter (1994): Geld-Brief-Spannen deutscher Standardwerte, Wiesbaden.

Jacoby, Gady/ Fowler, David J./ Gottesman, Aron A. (2000): The Capital Asset Pricing Model and the Liquidity Effect: A Theoretical Approach, in: Journal of Financial Markets, Vol. 3, pp. 69 – 81.

Jain, Pankaj K. (2003): Institutional Design and Liquidity at Stock Exchanges around the World, December 2003, Working Paper, available at SSRN: http://ssrn.com/abstract=869253.

Jain, Pankaj K./ Jiang, Christine X./ McInish, Thomas H./ Taechapiroontong, Nareerat (2003): Informed Trading in Parallel Auction and Dealer Markets: An Analysis on the London Stock Exchange, July 2003, Working Paper, available at SSRN: http://ssrn.com/abstract=487982.

Jones, Charles M./ Lipson, Marc L. (2001): Sixteenths: Direct Evidence on Institutional Execution Costs, in: Journal of Financial Economics, Vol. 59, pp. 253 – 278.

Kaniel, Ron/ Liu, Hong (2006): So What Orders Do Informed Traders Use?, in: Journal of Business, Vol. 79, pp. 1867 – 1913.

Kempf, Alexander (1999): Wertpapierliquidität und Wertpapierpreise, Wiesbaden.

Kempf, Alexander/ Mayston, Daniel L. (2005): Commonalities in Liquidity in Pure Order-Driven Markets, February 2005, Working Paper, available at SSRN: http://ssrn.com/abstract=676964.

Kindermann, Sebastian (2005): Liquiditäts- und Effizienzmessung im Aktienhandel, Dimensionen des Preisbildungsprozesses auf einem kontinuierlichen elektronischen Anlegerauktionsmarkt, Wiesbaden.

Kumar, Santosh (2003): Liquidity: Persistence and Forecast in Open Electronic Limit Order Book Market, July 2003, Working Paper, available at SSRN: http://ssrn.com/abstract=451841.

Kyle, Albert S. (1985): Continuous Auctions and Insider Trading, in: Econometrica, Vol. 53, pp. 1315 – 1335.

Lee, Charles M./ Mucklow, Belinda/ Ready, Mark J. (1993): Spreads, Depths and the Impact of Earnings Information: an Intraday Analysis, in: Review of Financial Studies, Vol. 6, pp. 345 – 374.

Lee, Charles M./ Ready, Mark J. (1991): Inferring Trade Direction from Intraday Data, in: Journal of Finance, Vol. 46, pp. 733 – 746.

Lei, Qin/ Wu, Guojun (2005): Time-Varying Informed and Uninformed Trading Activities, in: Journal of Financial Markets, Vol. 8, pp. 153 – 181.

Lin, Ji-Chai/ Sanger, Gary C./ Booth, Geoffrey G. (1995): Trade Size and Components of the Bid-Ask Spread, in: Review of Financial Studies, Vol. 8, pp. 1153 – 1183.

London Stock Exchange (2006): Trading Services, Price List as of 1 April 2006, available at http://investaquest.londonstockexchange.com/NR/rdonlyres/9EE907C2-8BCF-4979-AE32-AA2A6B861EF4/0/TRADINGSERVICESPriceListupdatedcopy 20706JAM.pdf.

Ma, Tai/ Hsieh, M. H./ Chen, J. H. (2001): The Probability of Informed Trading and the Performance of Stock in an Order-Driven Market, January 2001, Working Paper, available at SSRN: http://ssrn.com/abstract=264765.

Madhavan, Ananth (1992): Trading Mechanisms in Securities Markets, in: Journal of Finance, Vol. 47, pp. 607 – 642.

Madhavan, Ananth (2000): Market Microstructure: A Survey, in: Journal of Financial Markets, Vol. 3, pp. 205 – 258.

Madhavan, Ananth/ Panchapagesan, Venkatesh (2002): The First Price of the Day: Auctions Are Not Practical for Trading All Securities, in: Journal of Portfolio Management, Vol. 28, Issue 2, pp. 101 – 111.

Madhavan, Ananth/ Richardson, Matthew/ Roomans, Mark (1997): Why Do Security Prices Change? A Transaction-Level Analysis of NYSE Stocks, in: Review of Financial Studies, Vol. 10, pp. 1035 – 1064.

Markowitz, Harry M. (1952): Portfolio Selection, in: Journal of Finance, Vol. 7, pp. 77 – 91.

Marsh, Terry/ Rock, Kevin (1986): Exchange Listing and Liquidity. A Comparison of the American Stock Exchange with the NASDAQ National Market System, in: American Stock Exchange Transactions Data Research Project, Report 2, New York.

McInish, Thomas H./ Van Ness, Bonnie F. (2002): An Intraday Examination of the Components of the Bid-Ask Spread, in: Financial Review, Vol. 37, pp. 507 – 524.

McInish, Thomas H./ Wood, Robert A. (1992): An Analysis of Intraday Patterns in Bid/Ask Spreads for NYSE stocks, in: Journal of Finance, Vol. 47, pp. 753 – 764.

Nyholm, Ken (2002): Estimating the Probability of Informed Trading, in: Journal of Financial Research, Vol. 25, pp. 485 – 505.

Oesterhelweg, Olaf (1998): Anlegerorientierte Handelsverfahren für den deutschen Aktienmarkt, Wiesbaden.

Oesterhelweg, Olaf/ Schiereck, Dirk (1993): Meßkonzepte für die Liquidität von Finanzmärkten, in: Die Bank, Vol. 33, pp. 390 – 397.

O'Hara, Maureen (1997): Market Microstructure Theory, Blackwell, Cambridge.

Pagano, Michael S./ Padilla, Jorge A. (2005): The Economics of Cash Trading: An Overview, A report for Euronext, May 2005, LECG (Law and Economics Consulting Group).

Parlour, Christine (1998): Price Dynamics in Limit Order Markets, in: Review of Financial Studies, Vol. 11, pp. 789 – 816.

Parlour, Christine/ Seppi, Duane J. (2003): Liquidity-Based Competition for Order Flow, in: Review of Financial Studies, Vol. 16, pp. 301 – 343.

Perold, André F. (1988): The Implementation Shortfall: Paper versus Reality, in: Journal of Portfolio Management, Vol. 14, Issue 3, pp. 4 – 9.

Perotti, Pietro/ Rindi, Barbara (2006): Market for Information and Identity Disclosure in an Experimental Open Limit Order Book, in: Economic Notes, Vol. 35, pp. 97 – 119.

Ranaldo, Angelo (2004): Order Aggressiveness in Limit Order Book Markets, in: Journal of Financial Markets, Vol. 7, pp. 53 – 74.

Rindi, Barbara (2002): Informed Traders as Liquidity Providers: Transparency, Liquidity, and Price Formation, December 2002, Working Paper, available at SSRN: http://ssrn.com/abstract=358801.

Roll, Richard (1984): A Simple Implicit Measure of the Effective Bid-Ask Spread in an Efficient Market, in: Journal of Finance, Vol. 39, pp. 1127 – 1139.

Ross, Stephen A./ Westerfield, Randolph W./ Jaffee, Jeffrey (1996): Corporate Finance, 4th ed., McGraw-Hill, New York.

Sandas, Patrik (2001): Adverse Selection and Competitive Market Making: Empirical Evidence from Limit Order Markets, in: Review of Financial Studies, Vol. 14, pp. 705 – 734.

Sharpe, William F. (1964): Capital Asset Prices: A Theory of Market Equilibrium under Conditions of Risk, in: Journal of Finance, Vol. 19, pp. 425 – 442.

Schiereck, Dirk (1995): Internationale Börsenplatzentscheidungen institutioneller Investoren, Wiesbaden.

Schiereck, Dirk (1996a): Börsenplatzentscheidungen institutioneller Investoren beim Handel deutscher Aktien, in: Zeitschrift für Betriebswirtschaft, Vol. 66, pp. 1057 – 1079.

Schiereck, Dirk (1996b): Die Ziele eines Anlegers bei der Wahl des Börsenplatzes, in: Zeitschrift für Bankrecht und Bankwirtschaft, Vol. 8, pp. 185 – 196.

Schmidt, Hartmut (1977): Vorteile und Nachteile eines integrierten Zirkulations-marktes für Wertpapiere gegenüber einem gespaltenen Effektenmarkt, Kommission der Europäischen Gemeinschaft (Herausgeber), Brüssel.

Schmidt, Hartmut/ Iversen, Peter (1991): Geld-Brief-Spannen deutscher Standardwerte in IBIS und MATIS, in: Zeitschrift für Bankrecht und Bankwirtschaft, Vol. 3, pp. 209 – 226.

Schwartz, Robert A. (1988): Equity Markets: Structure, Trading, and Performance, New York.

Schwartz, Robert A./ Whitcomb, David K. (1988): Transaction Costs and Institutional Investor Trading Strategies, New York University Salomon Center, Monograph Series in Finance and Economics, Monograph 1988-2/3.

Schwartz, Robert A./ Francioni, Reto (2004): Equity Markets in Action: The Fundamentals of Liquidity, Market Structure and Trading, New Jersey.

SEC (2001): Report on the Comparison of Order Executions across Equity Market Structures, Office of Economic Analysis, United States Securities Exchange Commission, January 2001, Report, available at SEC: http://www.sec.gov/pdf/ ordrxmkt.pdf.

Seppi, Duane J. (1997): Liquidity Provision with Limit Orders and a Strategic Specialist, in: Review of Financial Studies, Vol. 10, pp. 103 – 150.

Stoll, Hans R. (1978): The Pricing of Security Dealer Service: An Empirical Study of NASDAQ Stocks, in: Journal of Finance, Vol. 33, pp. 1153 – 1172.

Stoll, Hans R. (1989): Inferring the Components of the Bid-Ask Spread: Theory and Empirical Test, in: Journal of Finance, Vol. 44, pp. 115 – 134.

Stoll, Hans R. (2000): Friction, in: Journal of Finance, Vol. 55, pp. 1479 – 1514.

Theissen, Erik (2002): Floor versus Screen Trading: Evidence from the German Stock Market, in: Journal of Institutional and Theoretical Economics, Vol. 158, pp. 32 – 54.

Theissen, Erik (2003a): Organized Equity Markets, March 2003, CFS Working Paper No. 2003/17, available at SSRN: http://ssrn.com/abstract=427020.

Theissen, Erik (2003b): Trader Anonymity, Price Formation, and Liquidity, in: European Finance Review, Vol. 7, pp. 1 – 26.

Tinic, Seha (1972): The Economics of Liquidity Services, in: Quarterly Journal of Economics, Vol. 86, pp. 79 – 93.

Treske, Kai (1996): Komponenten der Geld-Brief-Spannen am deutschen Aktienmarkt, Wiesbaden.

Van Ness, Bonnie F./ Van Ness, Robert A./ Warr, Richard S. (2001a): How well do Adverse Selection Components Measure Adverse Selection, in: Financial Management, Vol. 30, No. 3, pp. 77 – 98.

Van Ness, Bonnie F./ Van Ness, Robert A./ Warr, Richard S. (2001b): Determinants of Adverse Selection on the NYSE and NASDAQ: A Paired Comparison, June 2001, Working Paper, available at SSRN: http://ssrn.com/abstract=274369.

Van Ness, Bonnie F./ Van Ness, Robert A./ Warr, Richard S. (2005): NASDAQ Trading and Trading Costs: 1993-2002, in: Financial Review, Vol. 40, pp. 281 – 304.

Venter, Johannes H./ de Jongh, Dawid C. J. (2004): Extending the EKOP Model to Estimate the Probability of Informed Trading, May 2004, Working Paper, available at SSRN: http://ssrn.com/abstract=547062.

Weston, James P. (2000): Competition on the NASDAQ and the Impact of Recent Market Reforms, in: Journal of Finance, Vol. 55, pp. 2565 – 2598.

Wolff, Jürgen (2003): Eine Intermarket-Analyse der Komponenten der Geld-Brief-Spanne, Am Beispiel des deutschen Aktienmarktes, Wiesbaden.

Wyss, Rico von (2004): Measuring and Predicting Liquidity in the Stock Market, Dissertation Nr. 2899, St. Gallen.

FSC
www.fsc.org
MIX
Papier | Fördert gute Waldnutzung
FSC® C083411

Kolibri 360 GmbH
Ferdinand-Jühlke-Straße 7
99095 Erfurt, Deutschland
produktsicherheit@kolibri360.de